Racer Series

Dale Jarrett

John Regruth

MBI Publishing Company

First published in 2002 by MBI Publishing Company,
380 Jackson Street, Suite 200, St. Paul, MN 55101-3885 USA

MBI Publishing Company books are also available at discounts
in bulk quantity for industrial or sales-promotional use. For
details write to Special Sales Manager at Motorbooks
International Wholesalers & Distributors, 380 Jackson Street,
Suite 200, St. Paul, MN 55101-3885 USA

Library of Congress Cataloging-in-Publication Data Available
ISBN 0-7603-1324-5

On the front cover 1: Dale Jarrett entered into one of
NASCAR's most lucrative sponsorship agreements when he
signed with United Parcel Service before the 2001 season.

On the front cover 2: Since being added to the Winston Cup
schedule in 1997, Texas Motor Speedway has been one of
Jarrett's best tracks. He ranks first or second in nearly every
statistical category in the track's brief history.

On the frontispiece: Jarrett preparing for a race at Phoenix
in 2000.

On the title page: Dale Jarrett leading the pack at the Penn
500 in 1997.

On the back cover: The cost of the horsepower generated by
Robert Yates Racing engines is a lack of fuel efficiency. In the
inaugural race at California Speedway in 1997, a late stop for
fuel dropped him from fourth to eighth.

Table of contents page: Dale Jarrett zooming past the stands at
Dover in 1998.

Acquired by Lee Klancher
Edited by Amy Glaser
Designed by Joe Fahey

Printed in China

Contents

Quick Facts about Dale Jarrett's Career

Number of races run before 1st victory	129
Most consecutive victories	2 (twice)—1997 (3/9—Atlanta, 3/23—Darlington) and 2001 (4/1—Texas, 4/8—Martinsville)
Most consecutive races without a victory (after getting first win)	55 (Race 2 of 1993 through Race 26 of 1994)
Most consecutive Top 5 finishes	7 (1999)
Most consecutive Top 10 finishes	19 (1999)
Fewest points earned in a race	37 three times (1989 at Sears Point, 1995 at Daytona, 1998 at Martinsville)
Number of times earned maximum 185 points	9 one time (1996), four times (1997), two times (1999), once (2000), once (2001)
Most wins in a season	7 (1997)
Most DNFs in a season	14 (1988)
Fewest DNFs in a season	1 twice (1997, 1999)
Largest single-race prize	$2,277,975 (2000 Daytona 500)
Smallest single-race prize	$835 (1984 Warner W. Hodgdon American 500/Rockingham)
Number of poles	14
Worst starting position	41st five times(1987–Budweiser 400/Riverside, 1987–Pepsi Firecracker 400/Daytona, 1989–DieHard 500/Talladega, 1994–Daytona 500, 1994–Goodwrench Service 500/Rockingham)
Worst finish	42 three times (1989 at Sears Point, 1995 at Daytona, 1998 at Martinsville)
Lowest position in point standings (full-time seasons only)	37th (1992, Week 1)
Lowest finish in point standings (full-time seasons only)	24th (1989)
Number of times led the most laps	20 one time (1995), twice (1996), seven times (1997), twice (1998), four times (1999), three times (2000), once (2001)
Most laps led in a single race	323 of 393 (1997 Goodwrench Service 400/Rockingham)
Highest percentage of laps led, race	82.2, 323 of 393 (1997 Goodwrench Service 400/Rockingham)
Most laps led in a season	2,083 (1997)
Least number of laps completed in a race	2 of 500 (1995 Miller 500/Dover)
Tracks where Jarrett has won	Atlanta, Bristol, Charlotte, Darlington, Daytona, Dover, Indianapolis, Martinsville, Michigan, New Hampshire, Phoenix, Pocono, Richmond, Rockingham, Talladega, Texas
Tracks where Jarrett has not won	California, Chicagoland, Homestead-Miami, Las Vegas, Kansas, North Wilkesboro*, Riverside*, Sears Point, Watkins Glen
Tracks where Jarrett has won a pole	Atlanta, Darlington, Daytona, Dover, Las Vegas, Michigan, Rockingham, Watkins Glen
Tracks where Jarrett has not won a pole	Bristol, California, Charlotte, Chicagoland, Homestead–Miami, Indianapolis, Las Vegas, Kansas, Martinsville, New Hampshire, North Wilkesboro*, Phoenix, Pocono, Richmond, Riverside*, Sears Point, Talladega, Texas
Track where Jarrett has won most often	Daytona (4)
Tracks where Jarrett won the most poles	Darlington and Daytona (3)
Most lucrative track, career	Daytona—$4,314,907
Worst-to-first: worst starting spot in an eventual victory	24 (1996 Brickyard 400/Indianapolis)
First-to-worst: worst finish after starting from the pole	40 (1998 Las Vegas 400)
Favorite starting spot in victories	2nd (four victories)
No. of times won from the pole	2
No. of times won No Bull Million	2 (1997 Winston 500/Talladega, 2000 Daytona 500)

* — Tracks no longer on Winston Cup schedule

Perseverance & Strength

Garage gossips, critics, journalists, and schemers were all talking about Dale Jarrett's future by the time the Winston Cup series went to Pocono for a second time in 1995. Even Jarrett was talking. He was exploring his options, discussing deals with prospective owners and sponsors. Perhaps he would return to funding his own operation and join a dwindling number of owner-drivers on the circuit. Perhaps a second-tier team could use a driver whose career was marked by promising but uneven performances. Whatever Jarrett's future held, it certainly did not appear to include Robert Yates Racing (RYR).

Eight months after joining RYR in November 1994, Jarrett had promptly run one of NASCAR's most coveted rides—the No. 28 Havoline Ford—into the ground. Confirming garage-area suspicions that he just didn't have the right stuff for a top-flight team, he had driven a perennial Top 5 car straight to 16th in the Winston Cup point standings by the middle of the 1995 season. At Yates Racing, according to perception, the car isn't to blame. Davey Allison and Ernie Irvan were instant winners in the No. 28. Possessing the same cars, the same team and the same crew chief, why couldn't Jarrett do the same?

With disappointment, rumors, and uncertainty racing three-wide in his mind, Jarrett buckled into a car that no one believed was his, and he saved his career. He won at Pocono that day, thanks to a pretty good car and a fuel-mileage gamble borne of a nothing-left-to-lose attitude. Though not obvious at the time, the 1995 Miller Genuine Draft 500 was

Dale Jarrett emerged from NASCAR's shadows with Robert Yates Racing. Before joining Yates, Jarrett raced for 10 different car owners while searching for a stable, competitive race team. He found it in 1996 when he took over Yates' No. 88 Ford.

the lynchpin of Jarrett's career. Before that race, his career was a mushy collection of uninspiring results and unfulfilled potential, sprinkled lightly with glimpses of promise.

After that victory, however, the pieces began to fall into place. Jarrett followed Pocono with a second-place finish at Talladega and a strong third in the Brickyard 400. Suddenly, Jarrett had momentum. Three weeks later at Bristol, Yates offered him the opportunity to stay on and pilot a second RYR car.

That offer, and Jarrett's enthusiastic acceptance, launched an unimaginable turnaround in what had been a journeyman's career. Jarrett soon surpassed all expectations. He started to contend, for wins and championships, and he evolved into one of the most powerful forces in NASCAR. When he succeeded in winning the 1999 Winston Cup title, he and Yates basked in the glow of accomplishment, each understanding the other's struggles. Jarrett's feat may not have been any more historic than other championships won through the years, but it is difficult to think of a championship with more NASCAR history tied to it. Yates began his quest 35 years before and had won just about everything he could as an engine builder, crew chief, and owner. He'd also lost just about everything with the death of Davey Allison and the near-death of Ernie Irvan within a 14-month period. It was a staggering turn of events: Jarrett, who was scorned and all but driven from the No. 28 car four years earlier, was the driver who not only rebuilt Robert Yates Racing but also delivered its first championship.

Jarrett's Journey

When he decided to pursue a career in racing, Jarrett was in a unique and characteristically disadvantaged position. The son of a two-time NASCAR champion, he enjoyed instant name recognition. Unlike Richard Petty and Bobby Allison, however, Ned Jarrett was in no position to offer anything but advice to his son. Ned retired from racing in 1966, a year after his second title. Though still loosely associated with NASCAR, he had all but deserted the garage area. He didn't have a shop filled with cars, a warehouse full of parts, or a wealth of experience under current race conditions to boost his son's endeavors. When Dale Jarrett went racing, he was on his own.

Anchored by Hickory (North Carolina) Motor Speedway, Jarrett started racing late models in 1979. When NASCAR established the Busch Grand National series in 1982, he became a charter member and a fixture on the circuit. He competed full-time in the series until 1987, finishing 6th or better in the final point standings each season (including a career-best 3rd in 1984 and 1986). When he retired from the series in 1999 (racing for the final time at Darlington, where he finished 39th) he was among the BGN's career leaders in starts (324), wins (11), poles (14), Top 5s (102), and Top 10s (172). Thanks to his devotion to the circuit, he has been described as the father of the Busch series.

In 1987, Jarrett became one of the first drivers to compete extensively in both the Busch and Winston Cup series, a double-barreled pursuit most recently and successfully undertaken by Kevin Harvick in 2001. Like Harvick, Jarrett's Winston Cup opportunity was unexpected. He was hired a month into the 1987 season to fill the vacated driver's seat of Eric Freedlander's No. 18 Chevrolet after Freedlander's team found itself in a dilemma. Its driver, Tommy Ellis, one of Jarrett's fellow Busch series regulars, quit the team in frustration at Darlington with 24 races left on the schedule. Jarrett's five solid seasons in the Busch series lent him enough credentials to be called on as a relief driver for a struggling

Dale Jarrett was the talk of NASCAR's garage area by the middle of the 1995 season, though for dubious reasons. He was under enormous pressure due to his poor performance in one of the series' best cars. He turned his season – and career – around with a timely and inspiring win at Pocono.

team. He competed in all 27 Busch series races that season, along with the remaining 24 Winston Cup events.

The 1987 season was Jarrett's first exposure to the Winston Cup series as a full-time driver. He had raced four times in NASCAR's top series in 1984 and 1986, but only on a spot basis, getting his first Cup start at Martinsville in 1984 for Emanuel Zervakis, then racing at Daytona,

Ned vs. Dale
A Comparison of Dale and Ned Jarrett's Winston Cup/Grand National Careers

Driver	Championships	Starts	Wins	Top 5s	Top 10s	Poles	Laps Led	Races Led	Money
Ned Jarrett (1953–1966)	2	352	50	185	239	35	9,468	111	$348,967
Dale Jarrett (1984–2001)	1	459	28	141	210	14	6,515	171	$33,313,332

Jarrett and his son Jason await the start of a Busch Grand National series race at Charlotte in 1998. Unlike Jason, Dale was largely on his own when he began his professional racing career. Ned Jarrett had been retired for nearly 15 years when Dale began his professional racing career and couldn't provide the kind of head start that other racing kids, such as Kyle Petty and Davey Allison, enjoyed.

Rockingham, and Bristol. Though not an ideal situation, Freedlander's ride was a golden opportunity. For the first time in his career, Jarrett competed weekly against the very best. While he couldn't overcome the rocky situation into which he was thrust, he enjoyed some success, posting Top-10 finishes at Bristol and Martinsville.

Since the unexpected invitation in 1987, Jarrett has been a regular on the Winston Cup series. Regular starts did not translate into stable rides, of course. In his first six seasons, he drove for four different teams. In one of the most unusual arrangements of his career, he jumped in and out of four different cars 15 times in 1988. That season, he drove for Cale Yarborough, but only when Yarborough wasn't driving the car himself. The Winston Cup legend ran a 10-race farewell tour, handing the steering wheel to Jarrett for the other 19 races.

When Yarborough raced, Jarrett found rides elsewhere, hopping into cars owned by Hoss Ellington, Buddy Arrington, and Ralph Ball.

In 1990, the Darlington wreck that forced Neil Bonnett out of racing for nearly four years resulted in Jarrett taking over in relief for a second time. He joined the Wood Brothers for the remainder of the 1990 season and, when Bonnett's injuries forced him to remain out of racing, he signed on for a full campaign in 1991. Jarrett called his chance to drive the storied No. 21 Ford the most important break of his career. For the first time in his professional racing career, he was part of an established team with the knowledge and resources to be competitive. Though the Wood Brothers were not the same organization that had propelled Yarborough and David Pearson to dominance, they were light years beyond the fledgling organizations

that Jarrett had competed for during his previous three seasons.

The highlight of his tenure with the Woods was his first career victory at Michigan in August 1991. In a thrilling conclusion, Jarrett and Davey Allison raced side-by-side for nearly 4 miles on the 2-mile track before Jarrett nosed ahead at the finish line. His margin of victory was less than a foot. Beating Allison, the Winston Cup series' most dominant driver in 1991, gave Jarrett a well-timed boost in the eyes of Joe Gibbs, a new car owner looking to set up and staff his new organization for the upcoming 1992 season. A native of North Carolina, Gibbs sought to supplement his successful career as coach of the NFL Washington Redskins with NASCAR ownership. Revealing early knowledge of NASCAR's family tradition, he hired brothers-in-law Jarrett and Jimmy Makar to assume his team's top posts. Gibbs signed Jarrett as driver and Makar as crew chief; Makar is married to Jarrett's sister, Patti.

The opportunity with Joe Gibbs Racing represented the second big break in Jarrett's career. Thanks to Gibbs' high profile beyond

Two of the Busch series' greatest competitors, Jarrett and Mark Martin, compare notes at Charlotte in 1995. Martin is the all-time winningest driver in Busch history, while Jarrett ranks among the all-time leaders in starts, wins, poles, Top 5s and Top 10s.

One of the earliest and biggest breaks in Jarrett's career came in 1991 when he signed to drive for new Winston Cup owner Joe Gibbs. He drove the No. 18 Interstate Batteries Chevy for three seasons beginning in 1992.

stock car racing, Jarrett had the backing of a competitive sponsorship deal. One month after Gibbs led the Redskins to a lopsided 37 to 24 victory over the Buffalo Bills in Super Bowl XXVI, he watched Jarrett run the 1992 Daytona 500, the first race in Joe Gibbs Racing history. The season proved to be a learning experience for the new team, which failed to win a race and finished a disappointing 19th in the final point standings (a distant 827 points behind champion Alan Kulwicki).

The 1992 effort was the start of Jarrett's uneven performance with Gibbs Racing. The struggles of 1992 gave way to his first truly competitive season in 1993. He won the 1993 Daytona 500—thanks to a memorable last-lap pass on Dale Earnhardt—and contended for the Winston Cup title for the first time. He broke through with 13 Top 5s and 18 Top 10s, far exceeding his previous efforts, and spent nearly the entire season among the Top 4 in the championship point standings, including his first brief run as the Winston Cup points leader.

All of the gains made in 1993 were washed out in 1994, however. Qualifying, never a Jarrett strength, created tremendous

problems for the No. 18 team. Jarrett needed provisionals to make three of the season's first four races, including the Daytona 500. Hitting rock bottom, he failed to make the October race at North Wilkesboro, the only DNQ of Jarrett's career since joining the Winston Cup series full-time in 1987. The inability to secure good starting positions produced a string of bad luck that bit Jarrett throughout the season. If there was a spin out, a tangle, a wreck, a piece of debris, or a mechanical gremlin in the vicinity, you could bet it found Jarrett. His never-ending bad luck was best exemplified in the inaugural Brickyard 400 at Indianapolis, where he got caught in the middle of the Fightin' Bodines. Geoffrey and Brett Bodine, who let a family dispute spill over onto the track, traded bumps 100 laps into the race and inadvertently wrecked Jarrett. An innocent victim yet again, Jarrett finished the first Brickyard in 40th place.

With 1994's dreadful qualifying and bad finishes came dashed championship hopes. Jarrett dipped as low as 30th in the point standings before ending the season in 16th. In the midst of his frustration, he met with

Robert Yates to discuss taking over the No. 28 Ford in 1995. Ernie Irvan, severely injured in a practice crash at Michigan in August 1994, was recovering quickly, but remained at least a year away from a return to racing. Despite being under contract with Gibbs for another two years, Jarrett accepted Yates' offer to drive the fabled but ill-fated No. 28. Gibbs released Jarrett reluctantly, doing so only after he was able to sign Bobby Labonte to take over the No. 18.

Driving the 28

For Jarrett, joining Robert Yates Racing meant facing high expectations for the first time in his career. While Gibbs was a high-profile owner, few insiders expected a rookie owner and a new team to make much of mark in their first few seasons. Similarly, the Wood Brothers, while an established team, had not seriously challenged for a title since David Pearson's amazing limited-schedule run in

Jarrett signed with Robert Yates in 1995 to drive the highly respected No. 28 Havoline Ford in place of the injured Ernie Irvan. The '95 season marked Jarrett's third tour of duty as a relief driver. Previously, he replaced Tommy Ellis in the Eric Freedlander Chevy in 1987 and took over for the injured Neil Bonnett in the Wood Brothers Ford in 1990.

Robert Yates Racing (1989–2001)

Driver	Seasons	Starts	Avg. Start	Avg. Finish	Wins	Top 5s	Top 10s	Poles	Laps Led	Money
Davey Allison	1989–1993*	132	12.1	13.6	15	45	64	6	3,657	5,463,777
Ernie Irvan	1993–1997	95	14.3	15.6	8	34	52	10	3,641	5,248,474
Dale Jarrett	1995–2001	231	12.5	11.2	25	116	152	14	5,870	29,609,088
Kenny Irwin	1998–1999	66	20.0	23.9	0	3	10	3	165	3,585,777
Ricky Rudd	2000–2001	70	12.9	12.4	2	26	41	3	931	7,831,397

* Does not include 1987–1988 seasons when Allison drove the No. 28 for Harry Rainer.

1973. The comfort of low expectations disappeared at RYR. Jarrett took over one of the most respected cars in NASCAR, one in which the driver seemed optional.

Davey Allison made a splash driving the No. 28 in 1987 for owner Harry Rainier (Yates built the team's engines). He won two races, five poles, and the Rookie of the Year award that season (far outdistancing another rookie: Dale Jarrett). When Yates acquired the team from Rainier in 1989, Allison thrived. Over the next five seasons, he won 15 races,

led the series in wins in 1991 and 1992, and finished as high as third in the point standings (just missing a shot at the 1992 title).

When Allison died in a helicopter accident at Talladega in July 1993, NASCAR was robbed of one of its true talents. If Davey had been anything like his father, Bobby, he probably had another 15 seasons and multiple championships in his future. Yates searched for a replacement for his star, including offering the ride to Jeff Gordon, before settling on Ernie Irvan. Another aggressive, talented driver, Irvan was a controversial figure in the Winston Cup series. Though his skills and desire were unquestioned, many in the garage—especially drivers—wondered about his sanity. He earned the nickname "Swervin' Irvan" thanks to a rash of on-track incidents that seemed to defy explanation. One of Irvan's most famous incidents occurred at Darlington in 1990. Ten laps off the pace—yes, 10 laps—he collided with race leader Ken Schrader on a restart with 150 laps to go. In taking out the leader, Irvan also ignited a multicar pile-up that knocked Neil Bonnett out of racing for years with blurred vision (leading to Jarrett taking over Bonnett's No. 21 Ford). When his fellow drivers reached a

Robert Yates endured 14 hellish months in 1993 and 1994. In July of 1993, his driver Davey Allison died in a helicopter crash at Talladega. At Michigan in August of 1994 he nearly lost Irvan in a practice crash. Yates' hiring of Jarrett in 1995 – criticized at the time – turned out to be one of the best decisions in his storied NASCAR career.

boiling point in 1991, Irvan voluntarily issued an apology expressing regret for his on-track actions.

A more patient Irvan joined Yates in 1993 and became an instant hit. He won his fourth race in the No. 28 at Martinsville. Two races later, he led 328 of 334 laps at Charlotte and recorded his second Yates win. In his first nine RYR races, he had six Top-10 finishes. He followed with more success in 1994, running neck-and-neck with Earnhardt for the

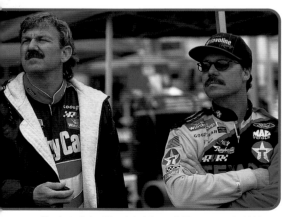

Thanks to Robert Yates' decision to field two teams in 1996, Jarrett and Irvan became teammates. Jarrett shocked the NASCAR world by emerging as the Yates' lead driver.

Jarrett rose to prominence during the late 1990s, establishing himself as one of NASCAR's most dominant drivers. He challenged – and often trumped – Dale Earnhardt's mastery of restrictor-plate racing. And Jarrett nearly derailed Jeff Gordon's bid for the Winston Cup title in 1997. Jarrett lost the 1997 points race to Gordon by just 14 points, the fourth closest finish in NASCAR history.

with the multicar reality and already possessing two experienced drivers, Yates' decision was easy. He offered Jarrett a second RYR car and used Irvan's comeback to begin building the new No. 88 team.

The key to Yates' second team was the hiring of Todd Parrott, a former member of Rusty Wallace's Penske South Racing team. Yates installed Parrott as crew chief of Irvan's interim team at Phoenix and watched his new hire make an impressive debut: Parrott helped Irvan march to the front of the field that day and stay in the lead for 111 laps. Engine trouble eventually cut Irvan's race short, but Yates had comforting proof that his "second" team was coming together.

Jarrett and Parrott joined forces in November to prepare for the 1996 season and clicked immediately. Eager to put 1995 behind him, Jarrett announced his arrival among the Winston Cup elite well before

championship. Irvan saw his hopes cut off, however, by a tremendous crash at Michigan in August 1994 that left him in a coma for nearly two weeks. Illustrating just how dominant he had been before his crash, Irvan still finished the season in 22nd place in the final point standings, despite having as many as 11 fewer starts than the next 14 drivers in the standings.

Given Allison's and Irvan's experience in the No. 28 Ford, most fans and insiders concluded that any driver with a modicum of talent could compete for a championship in a Yates car. Jarrett would test the theory. In his first eight seasons, he finished better than 16th in the points only one time. Thanks to Irvan's astonishing recovery from the Michigan wreck, Jarrett appeared only to have one season in which to make an impression. If he

wanted to show the NASCAR world his talent, he didn't have much time to do it.

Racing to the Top

Jarrett steered the No. 28 car for just one season, and that was probably long enough. His roller coaster 1995 season finally started to improve when Irvan returned to racing with an emotional start at North Wilkesboro in September (just 13 months after his life-threatening crash). Spurred by Irvan's recovery and Jarrett's promising rebound from a dismal first half of the season, Yates decided to pursue his interest in the burgeoning multicar concept that was sweeping the Winston Cup series. Best exemplified by Gordon and Hendrick Motorsports, multicar teams enjoyed testing and information-sharing advantages over the single-car teams. Faced

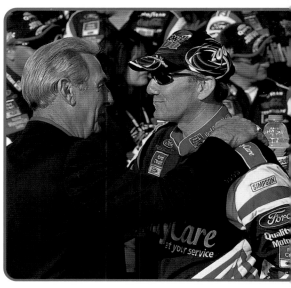

Jarrett's record at Daytona places him among the best drivers in NASCAR history. As a television commentator, Ned Jarrett has been able to participate in many of his son's magic moments.

most fans were ready to listen. In the season's opening weekend at Daytona, he and his new team won their first race together, the Busch Clash (now called the Bud Shootout), then followed up with a win in their first points race, the Daytona 500. For the second time in his career, Jarrett used a Daytona 500 victory as a springboard to a breakthrough season. He led the points standings for two months, the longest leader stretch of his career, and won three of the four biggest events of the season: in addition to the 500, he won the Coca-Cola 600 at Charlotte and the Brickyard 400; he finished 14th in the Southern 500 at Darlington. With his victories at Daytona and Charlotte, Jarrett gave one of the most determined runs for the Winston Million since the bonus's inception in 1985.

When Jarrett backed up his 1996 performance with the best year of his career in 1997, his place among the Winston Cup series' top drivers was confirmed. In seasons past, he had followed success with a step backwards. In 1994, he fell well off of the standard he had set in 1993. In 1992, he failed to win a race after getting his first victory in 1991. Jarrett broke the pattern in 1997. By any measure, his effort was title-worthy. He won seven races, had 20 Top 5s, and became just the ninth driver in the Modern Era to lead 2,000 or more laps in a season. He displayed the power and consistency to win a championship, and came close, falling just 14 points short of Gordon in the final standings.

In 1999, Jarrett finally reached the highest level of stock car racing. Building one of the most consistent seasons in NASCAR history, he dominated the series and won the championship by 201 points, the eighth largest margin since the implementation of the current point system. Jarrett established himself as the driver to beat early in the season, stringing together 19 consecutive Top

10 finishes. That run propelled him to a new Modern Era record for Top 10s in a single season (29) and helped him amass 5,262 championship points, the second highest total ever under the current point system. He also held the points lead for 24 straight weeks, the longest stretch since Earnhardt led 28 consecutive weeks in 1987.

Hoisting the Winston Cup trophy on that warm November afternoon at Homestead-Miami Speedway, the 43-year-old Jarrett became the second oldest first-time champ in Winston Cup history (only the 46-year-old Bobby Allison won his first title later). Capping a 13-year quest, the championship allowed Jarrett to join his father as a NASCAR champion. Only Lee and Richard Petty can match the Jarretts as father-son champs. Perhaps most amazing was Jarrett's ability to transform Robert Yates Racing. Ten successful and tragic years after acquiring the No. 28 car, Yates' first championship came from his "other" team.

By winning the 1999 Winston Cup title, Jarrett and his father Ned became just the second father-son pair to win championships in NASCAR history (joining Lee and Richard Petty).

Jarrett vs. the Winston Cup Series (1996–1999)

Category	Jarrett's Total	Jarrett's Rank	Category Leader*
Avg. start	10.3	3rd	Jeff Gordon—7.5
Avg. finish	9.1	1st	(Jeff Gordon—9.4)
Wins	18	2nd	Jeff Gordon—40
Top 5s	80	2nd	Jeff Gordon—87
Top 10s	95	3rd	Mark Martin—99
Total points	19,145	2nd	Jeff Gordon—19,278
Pole starts	7	5th	Jeff Gordon—20
Laps led	4,702	2nd	Jeff Gordon—6,997
Races led	86	2nd	Jeff Gordon—101
Times led	230	2nd	Jeff Gordon—322
Laps completed	38,451	1st	(Dale Earnhardt—38,433)

* 2nd-place driver listed in parentheses if Jarrett is category leader

Between 1996 and 1999, Jarrett's performance was nearly unsurpassed. Only Gordon, involved in a simultaneous magic ride, kept up with Jarrett's effort.

Grizzled and gray, Jarrett has become an elder statesmen of American racing. Like his father, he is one of NASCAR's foremost ambassadors. His new sponsorship deal with United Parcel Service and his lead role in the company's aggressive marketing campaign have made him one of the most recognizable sports figures in the world.

Distinguished Career

Pinpointing which accomplishments will most distinguish Dale Jarrett's Winston Cup career is difficult, though a few obvious examples spring to mind.

By winning the 1999 championship, he gained automatic entry into the Winston Cup history books as one of just 24 drivers ever to win a title.

His magical run between 1996 and 1999 put Jarrett at the very top of the Winston Cup series during some of its most competitive seasons. Only Gordon compares statistically during that four-year period. In fact, had Gordon's reign not corresponded with Jarrett's rise, Jarrett may have won another championship in 1997.

His record in the Daytona 500 places him in historic company. With three 500 victories, only Richard Petty (seven), Cale Yarborough (four), and Bobby Allison (three) have as many or more wins.

Also in the Daytona 500, the "Dale and Dale" show offered two of the greatest finishes in 500 history. Jarrett beat Daytona's greatest racer, Dale Earnhardt, twice. In 1993, he topped Earnhardt with a gripping last-lap pass. In 1996, he led Earnhardt for 60 miles and blocked four moves by the late legend on the final lap.

His overpowering performances at Indianapolis have earned him a top spot in the hallowed track's history. Even when he ran out of gas in 1998 and fell four laps behind the leader, he seemed to control the race.

Or, perhaps Jarrett's true distinguishing feature is an unfailing strength of character. He was the champion's son who never seemed to get favored treatment. He stayed in late models about a year longer and in the Busch series about three years longer than other well-connected kids. He took hand-me-down rides for years while trying to establish himself. He endured what must have felt like two of the longest years—1994 with Gibbs and 1995 with Yates—in recorded time. He missed out on a championship in 1997 by 14 points. For 13 years, when his career seemed ready to implode, he kept his chin up and methodically rebuilt what had been torn down. Jarrett's is a story of perseverance. When times grew difficult, he needed to think only of his late-model days, when $25 was the reward for a night's work. Yes, Dale Jarrett's considerable accomplishments will be remembered for a long time by race fans, but his character will ultimately distinguish him. Is there a greater compliment?

A Statistical Breakdown of Dale Jarrett's Career Performance

Racecar drivers often say, "Finishing second just means you're the first loser." Winston Cup racing may be the most austere of all sports. Winning is everything. The following section offers the bottom line statistical view of Jarrett's career.

Jarrett pops the cork on another victory at Daytona. His 2000 Daytona 500 win earned a No Bull Million dollar bonus, the second such prize of his career.

Dale Jarrett's Career Statistics

Year	Final Standing	Races Run	Wins	Top 5's	Top 10's	Poles	Avg. Start	Avg. Finish	DNF's	Total Points	Total Bonus Points	Points per Race	Total Winnings	Races Led	Laps Led	Pct. Led	On Lead Lap	Miles Driven
1984	—	3	0	0	0	0	30.0	24.7	1	267	0	89.0	7,345	0	0	0.0	0	798
1986	—	1	0	0	0	0	28.0	29.0	1	76	0	76.0	990	0	0	0.0	0	37
1987	25th	24	0	0	2	0	27.7	24.1	11	2,177	0	90.7	143,405	0	0	0.0	0	5,680
1988	23rd	29	0	0	1	0	24.5	24.3	14	2,622	10	90.4	118,640	2	5	0.1	4	8,161
1989	24th	29	0	2	5	0	24.2	22.7	11	2,789	15	96.2	232,317	3	99	1.0	3	9,178
1990	25th	24	0	1	7	0	15.2	19.4	9	2,558	20	106.6	214,495	4	73	0.9	4	7,699
1991	17th	29	1	3	8	0	16.4	19.4	9	3,124	35	107.7	444,256	7	47	0.5	9	9,438
1992	19th	29	0	2	8	0	16.5	17.8	5	3,251	30	112.1	418,648	6	103	1.1	8	10,295
1993	4th	30	1	13	18	0	19.7	12.4	5	4,000	75	133.3	1,242,394	15	263	2.6	17	11,335
1994	16th	30	1	4	9	0	22.7	18.7	7	3,298	40	109.9	881,754	8	55	0.6	8	10,441
1995	13th	31	1	9	14	1	18.4	17.4	6	3,584	45	115.6	1,363,158	8	324	3.3	16	10,417
1996	3rd	31	4	17	21	2	12.1	8.8	3	4,568	110	147.4	2,985,418	20	746	7.7	23	11,180
1997	2nd	32	7	20	23	2	7.2	9.6	1	4,696	145	146.8	3,240,542	22	2,083	21.2	24	12,652
1998	3rd	33	3	19	22	2	8.7	11.2	3	4,619	120	140.0	4,019,657	22	812	8.2	25	12,361
1999	1st	34	4	24	29	0	13.2	6.8	1	5,262	130	154.8	6,649,596	22	1,061	10.5	28	12,989
2000	4th	34	2	15	24	3	13.1	11.1	2	4,684	90	137.8	5,984,475	15	333	3.3	24	12,712
2001	5th	36	4	12	19	4	14.8	13.9	4	4,612	90	128.1	5,366,242	17	511	4.7	27	14,050
Totals		**459**	**28**	**141**	**210**	**14**	**16.7**	**15.5**	**93**	**56,187**	**955**	**122.4**	**33,313,332**	**171**	**6,515**	**4.46**	**220**	**159,423**

Bold indicates series-leading total

Though he has expressed displeasure with NASCAR's aerodynamics rules at Talladega and Daytona, Jarrett has developed into one of the most adept draftsmen in the Winston Cup series. Here, he leads the field during the 2000 DieHard 500.

Career Start Breakdown

Pos.	No. of Starts	Pct.
Pole*	16	3.49
2	15	3.27
3	25	5.45
4	16	3.49
5	14	3.05
6	11	2.40
7	12	2.61
8	10	2.18
9	22	4.79
10	18	3.92
11	14	3.05
12	9	1.96
13	17	3.70
14	20	4.36
15	6	1.31
16	11	2.40
17	19	4.14
18	20	4.36
19	8	1.74
20	14	3.05
21	15	3.27
22	12	2.61
23	12	2.61
24	8	1.74
25	9	1.96
26	13	2.83
27	9	1.96
28	9	1.96
29	7	1.53
30	4	0.87
31	11	2.40
32	9	1.96
33	9	1.96
34	1	0.22
35	6	1.31
36	7	1.53
37	6	1.31
38	4	0.87
39	3	0.65
40	3	0.65
41	5	1.09
42	0	—
43	0	—

Career Start Statistics

Total Races	459
Average Start	16.67
Front Row Starts (Pct.)	31 (6.8)
Top 5	86 (18.7)
Top 10	159 (34.6)
Top 20	297 (64.7)
Top 30	395 (86.1)
Pos. 31–43	64 (13.9)

Career Finish Breakdown

Pos.	No. of Finishes	Pct.
Win	28	6.10
2	30	6.54
3	27	5.88
4	29	6.32
5	27	5.88
6	16	3.49
7	16	3.49
8	11	2.40
9	9	1.96
10	17	3.70
11	16	3.49
12	16	3.49
13	4	0.87
14	8	1.74
15	10	2.18
16	14	3.05
17	6	1.31
18	10	2.18
19	5	1.09
20	8	1.74
21	9	1.96
22	4	0.87
23	12	2.61
24	6	1.31
25	9	1.96
26	6	1.31
27	4	0.87
28	8	1.74
29	6	1.31
30	7	1.53
31	8	1.74
32	12	2.61
33	2	0.44
34	8	1.74
35	9	1.96
36	6	1.31
37	6	1.31
38	8	1.74
39	6	1.31
40	6	1.31
41	7	1.53
42	3	0.65
43	0	—

Career Finish Statistics

Average Finish	15.5
Top 2 (Pct.)	58 (12.6)
Top 5	141 (30.7)
Top 10	210 (45.8)
Top 20	307 (66.9)
Top 30	378 (82.4)
Pos. 31–43	81 (17.6)
DNF	93 (20.3)

* — Indicates pole starts, not poles won (see Career Pole Starts)

Dale Jarrett's Career Pole Starts

Year	Career Race	Pole No.	Track – Race	Speed	Fin.
1995	229	1	Daytona—Daytona 500	193.498	5
1996	282	2	Darlington—Southern 500	170.934	14
	288	3	Rockingham—AC Delco 400	157.194	2
1997	295	4	Darlington—TranSouth Financial 400	171.095	1
	296	*	Texas—Interstate Batteries 500	Field set by points	2
	304	5	Michigan—Miller 400	183.669	6
1998	325	6	Las Vegas—Las Vegas 400	168.224	40
	346	7	Darlington—Southern 500	168.879	3
2000	390	8	Daytona—Daytona 500	191.091	1
	393	9	Atlanta—Cracker Barrel Old Country Store 500	192.574	36
	406	10	Daytona—Pepsi 400	187.547	2
2001	426	11	Las Vegas—UAW-DaimlerChrysler 400	172.106	2
	427	12	Atlanta—Cracker Barrel Old Country Store 500	192.748	4
	436	*	Dover—MBNA Platinum 400	Field set by points	5
	445	13	Watkins Glen—Global Crossing @ The Glen	122.698[1]	31
	450	14	Dover—MBNA Cal Ripken Jr. 400	154.919	12

[1]—track record

Pole Statistics

No. of Poles	14
Avg. Finished after Pole Starts	10.38
Wins from the Pole	2
No. of Track Records	1
Fastest Pole Speed	193.498
Slowest Pole Speed	122.698

Though he needed 229 tries to win his first pole, Jarrett has been a regular No. 1 starter since. He won 13 poles between 1996 and 2001.

Dale Jarrett's Career Victories

Year	Career Race	Win No.	Track–Race	Start Pos.	Laps	/	Led	Pct. Led	Money
1991	129	1	Michigan—Champion Spark Plug 400	11	200	/	12	6.0	74,150
1993	169	2	Daytona—Daytona 500	2	200	/	8	4.0	238,200
1994	225	3	Charlotte—Mello Yello 500	22	334	/	4	1.2	106,800
1995	245	4	Pocono—Miller 500	15	200	/	26	13.0	72,970
1996	260	5	Daytona—Daytona 500	7	200	/	40	20.0	360,775
	270	6	Charlotte—Coca-Cola 600	15	400	/	199	49.8	165,250
	278	7	Indianapolis—Brickyard 400	24	160	/	11	6.9	564,035
	280	8	Michigan—Goodwrench Services 400	11	200	/	8	4.0	83,195
1997	294	9	Atlanta—Primestar 500	9	328	/	253	77.1	137,650
	295	10	Darlington—TranSouth Financial 400	1	293	/	171	58.4	142,860
	308	11	Pocono—Pennsylvania 500	4	200	/	108	54.0	104,570
	312	12	Bristol—Goody's Headache Powder 500	3	500	/	210	42.0	101,550
	314	13	Richmond—Exide 400	23	400	/	39	9.8	91,490
	318	14	Charlotte—UAW-GM Quality 500	5	334	/	85	25.4	130,000
	321	15	Phoenix—Dura-Lube 500	9	312	/	73	23.4	99,830
1998	327	16	Darlington—TranSouth Financial 400	3	293	/	68	23.2	110,035
	334	17	Dover—MBNA Platinum 400	4	400	/	8	2.0	89,950
	351	18	Talladega—Winston 500	3	188	/	16	8.5	1,110,125
1999	366	19	Richmond—Pontiac Excitement 400	21	400	/	32	8.0	169,715
	369	20	Michigan—Kmart 400	6	200	/	150	75.0	151,240
	372	21	Daytona—Pepsi 400	12	160	/	40	25.0	164,965
	375	22	Indianapolis—Brickyard 400	4	160	/	117	73.1	712,240
2000	390	23	Daytona—Daytona 500	1	200	/	89	44.5	2,277,975
	420	24	Rockingham—Pop Secret 400	21	393	/	43	10.9	125,850
2001	428	25	Darlington—Carolina Dodge Dealers 400	2	293	/	16	5.5	214,612
	430	26	Texas—Harrah's 500	3	334	/	122	36.5	444,527
	431	27	Martinsville—Virginia 500	13	500	/	6	1.2	170,027
	442	28	New Hampshire—New England 300	9	300	/	92	30.7	238,027

Victory Statistics

No. of Victories	28
Avg. Starting Position	9.39
Favorite Starting Spot in Victories	3 (4 times)
Total Victory Earnings	$8,452,613
Laps Led (Pct.)	2,046 (25.32)
Fewest Laps Led in a Win	4
Most Laps Led in a Win	253
Highest Pct. Led	77.1
Lowest Pct. Led	1.2

Winning a Winston Cup race can make grown men do unusual things. At Indianapolis, they kiss bricks and, sometimes, each other. Here, crew chief Todd Parrott plants one on his driver after his victory in the 1996 Brickyard 400.

Dale Jarrett's Career Performance on Current and Former Winston Cup Tracks

Track	Track Length	No. of Races	Wins	Win Pct.	Top 5s	Top 10s	Poles	Avg. Start	Avg. Finish	DNFs	Total Winnings	Races Led	Laps Led	Pct. Led	Total Points	Points/ Race
Short Tracks																
Bristol	.533	31	1	3.2	8	16	0	17.8	14.8	8	$ 981,044	12	543	3.5	3,864	124.6
Martinsville	.526	31	1	3.2	8	15	0	16.1	14.2	4	909,429	4	144	0.9	3,847	124.1
North Wilkesboro	.626	19	0	0.0	1	5	0	17.9	16.4	3	205,515	3	111	1.5	2,196	115.6
Richmond	.750	28	2	7.1	11	12	0	17.8	14.0	4	1,083,199	6	385	3.4	3,554	126.9
Totals		**109**	**4**	**3.7**	**28**	**48**	**0**	**17.3**	**14.7**	**19**	**3,179,187**	**25**	**1,183**	**2.4**	**13,461**	**123.5**
1-mile Ovals																
Dover	1.0	30	1	3.3	9	11	1	15.1	18.8	12	$1,047,239	10	516	3.7	3,348	111.6
New Hampshire	1.058	14	1	7.1	6	10	0	9.6	10.6	0	1,023,654	8	263	6.3	1,953	139.5
Phoenix	1.0	14	1	7.1	2	7	0	18.1	15.9	3	532,309	5	175	4.1	1,673	119.5
Rockingham	1.017	29	1	3.4	11	14	1	18.5	13.5	5	1,106,829	10	1,019	7.8	3,756	129.5
Totals		**87**	**4**	**4.6**	**28**	**42**	**2**	**15.9**	**15.3**	**20**	**3,710,031**	**33**	**1,973**	**5.5**	**10,730**	**123.3**
Speedways (1–2 miles)																
Atlanta	1.54	28	1	3.6	10	15	2	19.5	14.3	5	$1,183,559	10	431	4.8	3,543	126.5
Charlotte	1.5	30	3	10.0	11	15	0	20.5	17.1	10	1,468,039	12	525	4.8	3,537	117.9
Chicagoland	1.5	1	0	0.0	1	1	0	11.0	4.0	0	101,300	0	0	0.0	160	160.0
Darlington	1.366	28	3	10.7	10	12	3	15.4	15.5	6	1,327,108	16	479	5.2	3,473	124.0
Homestead-Miami	1.5	3	0	0.0	1	1	0	12.3	21.0	0	243,917	1	1	0.1	312	104.0
Las Vegas	1.5	4	0	0.0	1	2	2	4.3	15.0	1	511,017	2	82	8.6	499	124.8
Kansas	1.5	1	0	0.0	0	0	0	18.0	30.0	1	91,827	0	0	0.0	73	73.0
Texas	1.5	5	1	20.0	3	3	1	6.8	9.8	0	1,089,477	5	272	16.3	739	147.8
Totals		**100**	**8**	**8.0**	**37**	**49**	**8**	**17.1**	**15.5**	**23**	**6,016,244**	**46**	**1,790**	**5.4**	**12,336**	**123.4**
SuperSpeedways (2 miles or greater)																
California	2.0	5	0	0.0	1	3	0	17.0	17.4	1	$338,417	3	52	4.2	581	116.2
Daytona	2.5	29	4	13.8	8	12	3	16.7	16.5	6	4,314,947[1]	12	332	6.5	3,477	119.9
Indianapolis	2.5	8	2	25.0	4	5	0	10.5	10.4	1	2,186,157	4	186	14.5	1,136	142.0
Michigan	2.0	30	3	10.0	11	16	1	18.0	15.3	5	1,182,047	12	262	4.4	3,711	123.7
Pocono	2.5	30	2	6.7	11	16	0	16.1	14.0	4	1,220,014	15	472	7.9	3,861	128.7
Talladega	2.66	30	1	3.3	9	11	0	16.5	17.9	8	2,170,824[1]	15	222	4.0	3,473	115.8
Totals		**132**	**12**	**9.1**	**44**	**63**	**4**	**16.4**	**15.6**	**25**	**11,412,406**	**61**	**1,526**	**6.1**	**16,239**	**123.0**
Road Courses																
Sears Point	1.99	13	0	0.0	1	3	0	20.1	19.5	3	$409,042	3	8	0.7	1,390	106.9
Riverside, CA	2.63	3	0	0.0	0	1	0	33	14.3	0	16,135	1	4	1.3	368	122.7
Watkins Glen	2.45	15	0	0.0	3	4	1	11.1	18.2	3	411,892	2	31	2.4	1,663	110.9
Totals		**31**	**0**	**0.0**	**4**	**8**	**1**	**17.0**	**18.4**	**6**	**837,069**	**6**	**43**	**1.6**	**3,421**	**110.4**

[1]—Includes No Bull Million bonus

Jarrett on the Short Tracks

Dale Jarrett started his career at Martinsville Speedway in 1984. Seventeen years and 30 tries later he finally won a race there. Such has been the stand-offish relationship between the 1999 champion and Winston Cup short tracks. In 109 starts at Martinsville, Bristol, North Wilkesboro, and Richmond, Jarrett has just four wins and has yet to win a pole or a front row starting position. In fact, the low point of Jarrett's career came at North Wilkesboro in the fall of 1994 when he failed to make the race at all, his only missed start since joining the series full-time in 1987.

Jarrett and the short tracks have a complicated relationship, however, one that cannot easily be cast as good driver versus evil ovals. Even though victories and top finishes have been difficult to secure, Jarrett has done pretty well on the shorties. Though wins are scarce, his 28 Top 5s are 15th in the modern era (by comparison, he ranks 22nd in short-track starts). More important, the half-miles helped Jarrett get a steady job in the Winston Cup series back when he was a Busch series regular. He was called on to fill in for departed drivers in 1987 and 1990. Both times, solid efforts at Bristol and North Wilkesboro helped him win confidence and earn full-time rides.

Not surprisingly, Jarrett's short-track fortunes improved in 1996 with the formation of the No. 88 Robert Yates Racing team. Since then, his effort at Bristol compares well with the performances of Jeff Gordon, Mark Martin, Rusty Wallace, and Terry Labonte, the current masters of the high banks. His victory in the 1997 Bristol night race was his first short-track victory in 83 starts. He also rebounded at North Wilkesboro to become a consistent finisher. When the .625-mile track was pushed off of NASCAR's schedule in 1996, Jarrett made his peace with the track by getting his best North Wilkesboro finish in its final race.

Martinsville, meanwhile offered Jarrett some of his earliest highlights. Besides his first career Winston Cup start, he also scored his first career Top 5 there in 1989. At Virginia's other short track, Richmond International Raceway, Jarrett celebrated three wins, even if NASCAR only gives him credit for two. A controversial red flag cost him a victory in 1998. But Jarrett proved he doesn't need much help on the .75-mile track, winning Richmond races fair-and-square in 1997 and 1999.

Short Track Definition

What is a short track?
A short track is any track measuring less than 1 mile long.

Which tracks are short tracks?
Bristol
Martinsville
North Wilkesboro*
Richmond
* —no longer on the Winston Cup schedule

Short Tracks Stats Chart

Short Tracks Record Book—Modern Era (min. 25 starts)

Category	Jarrett's Total	Jarrett's Rank	Modern Era Short Tracks Leader
Starts	109	22nd	Darrell Waltrip—225
Total points[1]	13,461	19th	Darrell Waltrip—31,149
Avg. start	17.3	40th	Cale Yarborough—4.1
Avg. finish	14.7	23rd	Cale Yarborough—6.4
Wins	4	14th	Darrell Waltrip—47
Winning pct.	3.7	20th	Cale Yarborough—35.4
Top 5s	28	15th	Darrell Waltrip—113
Top 10s	48	17th	Darrell Waltrip—141
DNFs	19	36th	J. D. McDuffie—61
Poles	0	—	Darrell Waltrip—35
Front row starts	0	—	Darrell Waltrip—57
Laps led	1,183	21st	Darrell Waltrip—14,840
Pct. laps led	2.4	22nd	Cale Yarborough—37.6
Races led	25	20th	Darrell Waltrip—133
Times led	46	20th	Darrell Waltrip—343
Times led most laps	4	13th	Darrell Waltrip—37
Bonus points[1]	145	19th	Darrell Waltrip—840
Laps completed	43,797	21st	Darrell Waltrip—92,033
Pct. laps completed	88.5	32nd	Bobby Labonte—95.8
Points per race[1]	123.5	21st	Cale Yarborough—157.9
Lead-lap finishes	41	9th	Darrell Waltrip—101

[1]—Since implementation of current point system in 1975

Jarrett on the 1-Mile Ovals

NASCAR's 1-mile ovals just seem to be longer short tracks for Dale Jarrett. Like their shorter brethren, the 1-milers haven't always been kind. Three of the four tracks that fit into this category have inflicted pain—physical, mental, and medical—on the Winston Cup veteran. In 1994, he broke a wrist at Dover in the third of his three wrecks that day; at Rockingham, he endured the mental anguish of six second-place finishes in a seven-race stretch before getting a win; at Phoenix, he suffered a gallstone attack that left him hospitalized for five days. If the periodic abuses were offset by consistently strong performances, Jarrett might have an easier time accepting his fate. Unfortunately, the 1-mile ovals have been almost as stingy as the short tracks with top finishes.

Jarrett can't complain too loudly, of course. While Dover has been one of his worst tracks—with 12 DNFs in his first 30 starts and a never-ending supply of bad luck—he can point to a few positives. His victory in 1998 was memorable for being a fuel-mileage gamble that actually came through for Jarrett. Efficient use of fuel has never been a Robert Yates Racing strength, so beating fuel-mileage king Jeff Gordon—at Dover, no less—gave Jarrett one of the most satisfying wins of his career.

Similar satisfaction was felt at Rockingham when Jarrett won the 2000 Pop Secret 400. In the preceding five seasons, no driver even approached Jarrett's dominance at the 1.017-mile track. He led 323 of 393 laps in 1997, only to lose to Gordon in a late-race pass. In 1998, he led 195 laps and finished second to Gordon again. In 2000, Jarrett turned the tables. He took the lead for the first time with just 43 laps to go and beat Gordon by 2.2 seconds. Phoenix, one of the blandest tracks in

> **1-Mile Oval Definition**
>
> *Which tracks are 1-mile ovals?*
> Dover
> New Hampshire
> Phoenix
> Rockingham

One-mile ovals haven't been too kind to Jarrett during his career, especially Dover. He didn't get his first front-row start at the Delaware track until 1999 when he started next to pole winner Bobby Labonte.

Jarrett's career, was important for introducing Todd Parrott as a new Yates crew chief. The mechanical brains behind Jarrett's amazing run from 1996 to 2001, Parrott debuted as crew chief for Ernie Irvan in October 1995 at Phoenix. Three months later, he helped Jarrett win the Daytona 500 for the second time. Two years later, he directed Jarrett to his only Phoenix victory.

Then there's New Hampshire International Speedway, the New England flat track that has become one of Jarrett's best tracks. He has 10 Top 10 finishes in 14 NHIS starts. The real story is qualifying, Jarrett's career-long Achilles' heel. Though he has a starting average of 16.7 in his career, his average is 9.6 at New Hampshire.

1-Mile Oval Stats Chart

1-Mile Ovals Record Book—All-Time (min. 25 starts)

Category	Jarrett's Total	Jarrett's Rank	Modern Era Short Tracks Leader
Starts	87	15th	Darrell Waltrip—133
Total points[1]	10,730	11th	Dale Earnhardt—15,405
Avg. start	15.9	23rd	David Pearson—5.1
Avg. finish	15.3	14th	Cale Yarborough—11.1
Wins	4	14th	Jeff Gordon—11
Winning pct.	4.6	21st	David Pearson—31
Top 5s	28	8th	Dale Earnhardt—39
Top 10s	42	9th	Dale Earnhardt—68
DNFs	20	16th	J. D. McDuffie—43
Poles	2	23rd	M. Martin, R. Wallace—11
Front row starts	6	18th	Mark Martin—19
Laps led	1,973	15th	Cale Yarborough—4,951
Pct. laps led	5.5	15th	David Pearson—25.9
Races led	33	13th	Dale Earnhardt—63
Times led	75	15th	Dale Earnhardt—181
Times led most laps	5	12th	Cale Yarborough—13
Bonus points[1]	190	10th	Dale Earnhardt—350
Laps completed	30,507	16th	Darrell Waltrip—53,580
Pct. laps completed	85.8	35th	Jeff Gordon—95.5
Points per race[1]	123.3	11th	Cale Yarborough—139.7
Lead-lap finishes	39	4th	Mark Martin—50

[1]—Since implementation of current point system in 1975

The New Hampshire one-mile oval has been one of Jarrett's best tracks. His starting average at NHIS – 9.6 – is better than at any other Winston Cup track.

The steady stream of new 1.5-mile tracks in Winston Cup racing plays right into the hands of Jarrett, who excels on speedways. He has already shown strength at Texas, Las Vegas, and Chicagoland. Homestead, with characteristics similar to New Hampshire, should quickly fall into line.

Jarrett on the Speedways

The unending construction of semi-banked, D-shaped, 1.5-mile ovals could play right into Dale Jarrett's hands. While fans' eyes glaze over as more cookie-cutter tracks are added to the Winston Cup schedule, Jarrett can bank on more strong finishes. He's already won at least one race on four of the speedways—Atlanta, Charlotte, Darlington, and Texas—and can set his sights on conquering the new asphalt at Las Vegas, Homestead (Florida), Chicago, and Kansas.

Jarrett needed some time to get comfortable on the older high-speed tracks. He won at Charlotte in his 16th start and in his 19th attempt at both Atlanta and Darlington. Each victory seemed to open the floodgates. At Darlington, he followed his first victory with 2 more wins, 7 Top 5s, and a pole in the next 9 races. He used his victory momentum at Charlotte to win twice more and claim 10 Top-10 finishes in 14 races. Atlanta, not wishing to be left out, donated four second-place finishes in the first five races after his 1997 win and two poles in 2000 and 2001.

Making Texas Motor Speedway so scary for the competition is the apparent absence of Jarrett's trademark learning curve. If his career demonstrates anything, it is that success takes time for Jarrett, the second oldest first-time Winston Cup champion in NASCAR history (he won his title in 1999 at age 43). At Texas, however, he showed an uncharacteristic impatience to win. He finished the inaugural race second in 1997 and matched that effort in 1999. In 2001, he won in his fifth Texas start, his fastest win at any track besides Indianapolis (where he won his third start).

Applying the same Texas style to the other new speedways, more Victory Lane celebrations can't be far away for Jarrett. At Vegas, he won two poles and finished as high as second. He also finished fourth in the inaugural Chicagoland Speedway event in 2001.

Speedway Definition

What is a speedway?

A speedway is any track longer than 1 mile but shorter than 2 miles.

Which tracks are speedways?

Atlanta
Charlotte
Chicagoland
Darlington
Homestead-Miami
Las Vegas
Kansas
Texas

Speedway Stats Chart

Speedways Record Book—Modern Era (min. 25 starts)

Category	Jarrett's Total	Jarrett's Rank	Modern Era Short Tracks Leader
Starts	100	20th	Darrell Waltrip—175
Total points[1]	12,336	14th	Bill Elliott—20,287
Avg. start	17.1	27th	David Pearson—4.4
Avg. finish	15.5	11th	Dale Earnhardt—12.0
Wins	8	8th	Dale Earnhardt—23
Winning pct.	8.0	10th	Jeff Gordon—20.3
Top 5s	37	8th	Dale Earnhardt—61
Top 10s	49	13th	Dale Earnhardt—83
DNFs	23	33rd	Dave Marcis—68
Poles	7	8th	David Pearson—25
Front row starts	9	16th	David Pearson—35
Laps led	1,790	12th	Dale Earnhardt—6,818
Pct. laps led	5.4	24th	David Pearson—15.1
Races led	46	13th	Dale Earnhardt—90
Times led	116	13th	Dale Earnhardt—362
Times led most laps	4	15th	Dale Earnhardt—24
Bonus points[1]	250	10th	Dale Earnhardt—570
Laps completed	29,029	18th	Darrell Waltrip—51,148
Pct. laps completed	87.7	25th	Tony Stewart—96.7
Points per race[1]	123.4	11th	Dale Earnhardt—136.7
Lead-lap finishes	46	4th	Dale Earnhardt—68

[1]—Since implementation of current point system in 1975

Jarrett on the SuperSpeedways

Jarrett distinguished himself on Winston Cup superspeedways – especially at Indianapolis, where he is one of just two drivers with more than one Brickyard 400 win. Here, he poses with the winners of the first four Brickyards, Jeff Gordon, Dale Earnhardt, and Ricky Rudd.

Dale Jarrett has defined himself on NASCAR's superspeedways. From his memorable defeat of Davey Allison at Michigan in 1991 to his memorable victories over Dale Earnhardt in the Daytona 500 to his overwhelming performance at Indianapolis, big tracks and big moments have drawn the best out of Jarrett. He has more wins, Top 5s, and Top 10s on the superspeedways than any other track type. The big tracks account for more than a third of his $33 million in winnings.

Without question, Jarrett's greatest accomplishments have come in the Daytona 500. With three career wins in NASCAR's Super Bowl, he is among an elite few who can say they've done the same. Only Richard Petty, Cale Yarborough, and Bobby Allison—legends, all—have equaled or bettered his feat. Enhancing Jarrett's Daytona 500 legend is the manner in which his victories were secured. He defeated Earnhardt, the acknowledged master of Daytona, twice in 1993 and 1996. He then displayed a nuanced grasp of Daytona's draft with a fine late-race pass on Johnny Benson to take the 500 in 2000.

If Daytona showcases Jarrett's finesse, Indianapolis reveals his ability to overpower the field. Aided by the horsepower of his Yates engines, he has earned a favored place in the stock car section of Indy's history book. Michigan, meanwhile, proves Jarrett's original talent on the superspeedways. Robert Yates' reputation as an engine builder and as an owner tends to overshadow the abilities of his drivers. No one has suffered from the guilt of his association with Yates quite like Jarrett. Big track success is attributable to horsepower, not the driver, critics say. Jarrett succeeded at Michigan before and after joining Robert Yates Racing, and no driver since Davey Allison has enjoyed the same success with Yates, not Irvan, Irwin, or Rudd (yet).

SuperSpeedway Stats Chart

SuperSpeedways Record Book—Modern Era (min. 25 starts)

Category	Jarrett's Total	Jarrett's Rank	Modern Era Short Tracks Leader
Starts	132	16th	Darrell Waltrip—213
Total points[1]	16,239	13th	Bill Elliott—25,176
Avg. start	16.4	28th	David Pearson—7.1
Avg. finish	15.6	12th	Jeff Gordon—11.0
Wins	12	8th	Dale Earnhardt—18
Winning pct.	9.1	11th	David Pearson—22.7
Top 5s	44	8th	Dale Earnhardt—70
Top 10s	63	11th	Dale Earnhardt—114
DNFs	25	39th	Dave Marcis—64
Poles	4	21st	Bill Elliott—23
Front row starts	12	16th	Bill Elliott—41
Laps led	1,526	12th	Dale Earnhardt—3,754
Pct. laps led	6.1	13th	Jeff Gordon—17.2
Races led	61	13th	Dale Earnhardt—122
Times led	139	17th	Dale Earnhardt—505
Times led most laps	7	13th	Dale Earnhardt—22
Bonus points[1]	340	13th	Dale Earnhardt—720
Laps completed	22,473	15th	Darrell Waltrip—34,703
Pct. laps completed	89.3	26th	Jeremy Mayfield—95.7
Points per race[1]	123.0	11th	Jeff Gordon—142.1
Lead-lap finishes	74	8th	Dale Earnhardt – 108

[1]—Since implementation of current point system in 1975

Speedway Definition

What is a superspeedway?
A superspeedway is any track measuring 2 miles or greater in length.

Which tracks are superspeedways?
California
Daytona
Indianapolis
Michigan
Pocono
Talladega

Jarrett on the Road Courses

The 2001 Watkins Glen race perfectly illustrated Dale Jarrett's frustrating development on NASCAR's road courses. After winning the pole with a record-setting lap, Jarrett built a two-second lead on the rest of the field, then saw his hopes of winning dashed when he ran his car off the road—by himself. The solo incident left him stuck in the gravel just off the first turn at Watkins Glen. Later in the race, he went off the road once more (this time with a little help from Mark Martin) and got stuck again. Inside of an hour, the very best and very worst of Jarrett's road course experience was on display for the world to see.

Much like short tracks, Jarrett cannot be painted with a broad brush when the subject is road course racing. With no wins and just four Top 5s in 31 road starts, it is difficult not to see his preference for ovals. At the Riverside, California, road course in 1988, however, he led a lap for the first time in his Winston Cup career and recorded one of his first Top 10 finishes. In the eight road course events between 1997 and 2000, he had six Top 10 finishes and appeared ready to become a credible threat to win. A poor finish in the 2001 race at Sears Point and the disaster at Watkins Glen, unfortunately, set his progress back a step.

Road Course Definition

What is a road course?
A road course is an enclosed, nonoval track that requires both left and right turns (oval tracks require only left turns).

Which tracks are road courses?
Riverside*
Sears Point
Watkins Glen
* —no longer on the Winston Cup schedule

The first time Jarrett led a race at Watkins Glen was in 1997, when he paced The Bud at the Glen for 14 laps. He set a track qualifying record in 2001, but is still searching for his first road course victory.

Road Course Stats Chart

Road Courses Record Book—Modern Era (min. 10 starts)

Category	Jarrett's Total	Jarrett's Rank	Modern Era Road Courses Leader
Starts	31	21	Darrell Waltrip—53
Total points[1]	3,421	17	Darrell Waltrip—6,598
Avg. start	17.0	29	Cale Yarborough—3.8
Avg. finish	18.4	26	Cale Yarborough—7.4
Wins	0	—	Jeff Gordon—7
Winning pct.	0.0	—	Jeff Gordon—38.9
Top 5s	4	21	Ricky Rudd—23
Top 10s	8	26	Dale Earnhardt—31
DNFs	6	28	Hershel McGriff—23
Poles	1	14	Darrell Waltrip—9
Front row starts	4	12	Darrell Waltrip—16
Laps led	43	23	Bobby Allison—820
Pct. laps led	1.6	23rd	Cale Yarborough—33.5
Races led	6	18	Darrell Waltrip—23
Times led	6	24	Bobby Allison—69
Times led most laps	0	—	Jeff Gordon—7
Bonus points[1]	30	19	Darrell Waltrip—140
Laps completed	2,530	21	Darrell Waltrip—4,743
Pct. laps completed	92.5	18	Johnny Benson Jr.—99.6
Points per race[1]	110.4	24	Cale Yarborough—163.0
Lead-lap finishes	20	12	Dale Earnhardt—40

[1]—Since implementation of current point system in 1975

The Record Book

Dale Jarrett's Standing in Winston Cup History— All-Time and the Modern Era

In 1972, NASCAR entered its "modern era" after striking a new series sponsorship deal with the R. J. Reynolds tobacco company. Most fundamental among the changes implemented as a result of the new deal was a significant reduction in the number of races staged on a reduced number of racetracks. Accompanied by the 1975 introduction of the current point system, which rewards consistency more than victories, NASCAR embarked on a new era of stability that in turn increased competitiveness and sparked an unprecedented boom in popularity through the 1980s and 1990s.

From a statistical point of view, the 1972 demarcation makes historical comparison a tap dance. Judging Jarrett's modern-era career in light of the cross-era career of a racer such as Richard Petty is fruitless. In 1967, Petty won 27 times in 48 starts, nearly equaling the number of victories in Jarrett's entire career. Petty was sometimes one of just a few Grand National regulars to enter a race, giving him an enormous advantage over the local Saturday night racers against whom he competed. Today's drivers face better competition in fewer events.

In recognition of these distinct eras and their fundamental differences, this section puts Jarrett's career in both contexts, all-time and modern era. All-time records include all drivers who have competed since NASCAR's inception in 1949; the modern era includes only results from 1972 to the present.

* Records through 2001

| All-Time Records | 29-31 |
| Modern Era Records | 32-39 |

Jarrett's rise in the Winston Cup series occurred as NASCAR experienced explosive growth during the 1990s. He topped $30 million in career winnings in 2001. His father Ned, a two-time champion, earned just under $350,000 during his 350-race career. Here, Dale leads the field to the green flag in the 1998 Southern 500 at Darlington.

All-Time Records

Championships

1	Dale Earnhardt	7
	Richard Petty	7
3	Jeff Gordon	4
4	David Pearson	3
	Lee Petty	3
	Darrell Waltrip	3
	Cale Yarborough	3
8	Buck Baker	2
	Tim Flock	2
	Ned Jarrett	2
	Terry Labonte	2
	Herb Thomas	2
	Joe Weatherly	2
14	Bobby Allison	1
	Red Byron	1
	Bill Elliott	1
	Bobby Isaac	1
	Dale Jarrett	**1**
	Alan Kulwicki	1
	Bobby Labonte	1
	Benny Parsons	1
	Bill Rexford	1
	Rusty Wallace	1
	Rex White	1

Career Starts

1	Richard Petty	1,184
2	Dave Marcis	881
3	Darrell Waltrip	809
4	Ricky Rudd	731
5	Bobby Allison	718
6	Terry Labonte	709
7	Buddy Baker	699
8	Dale Earnhardt	676
9	Bill Elliott	659
10	J. D. McDuffie	653
11	Buck Baker	636
12	Kyle Petty	609
13	James Hylton	601
14	David Pearson	574
15	Rusty Wallace	562
16	Buddy Arrington	560
17	Cale Yarborough	559
18	Geoffrey Bodine	554
19	Sterling Marlin	539
20	Elmo Langley	536
21	Ken Schrader	528
22	Benny Parsons	526
23	Michael Waltrip	498
24	Neil Castles	497
25	Wendell Scott	495
26	Mark Martin	494
27	Morgan Shepherd	481
28	Harry Gant	474
29	**Dale Jarrett**	**459**
30	Jimmy Means	455
31	Cecil Gordon	450
32	Brett Bodine	442
33	Lee Petty	427
34	Jim Paschal	422
35	G. C. Spencer	415
36	Lake Speed	402
37	Frank Warren	396
38	Henley Gray	374
39	Jimmy Spencer	370
40	Neil Bonnett	363

Career Wins

1	Richard Petty	200
2	David Pearson	105
3	Bobby Allison	85
4	Darrell Waltrip	84
5	Cale Yarborough	83
6	Dale Earnhardt	76
7	Jeff Gordon	58
8	Lee Petty	54
	Rusty Wallace	54
10	Junior Johnson	50
	Ned Jarrett	50
12	Herb Thomas	48
13	Buck Baker	46
14	Bill Elliott	41
15	Tim Flock	39
16	Bobby Isaac	37
17	Fireball Roberts	33
18	Mark Martin	32
19	**Dale Jarrett**	**28**
	Rex White	28
21	Fred Lorenzen	26
22	Jim Paschal	25
	Joe Weatherly	25
24	Ricky Rudd	22
25	Benny Parsons	21
	Jack Smith	21
	Terry Labonte	21
28	Speedy Thompson	20
29	Buddy Baker	19
	Davey Allison	19
	Fonty Flock	19
32	Geoffrey Bodine	18
	Harry Gant	18
	Neil Bonnett	18
	Bobby Labonte	18
36	Curtis Turner	17
	Marvin Panch	17
	Jeff Burton	17
39	Ernie Irvan	15
40	Dick Hutcherson	14
	LeeRoy Yarbrough	14

Winning Pct.

1	Herb Thomas	20.87
2	Tim Flock	20.86
3	Jeff Gordon	19.80
4	David Pearson	18.29
5	Richard Petty	16.89
6	Fred Lorenzen	16.46
7	Fireball Roberts	16.02
8	Junior Johnson	15.97
9	Cale Yarborough	14.85
10	Ned Jarrett	14.20
11	Dick Hutcherson	13.59
12	Lee Petty	12.65
13	Fonty Flock	12.34
14	Rex White	12.02
15	Bobby Isaac	12.01
16	Bobby Allison	11.84
17	Tony Stewart	11.54
18	Dale Earnhardt	11.24
19	Joe Weatherly	10.87
20	Darrell Waltrip	10.38
21	Dick Rathmann	10.16
22	Speedy Thompson	10.10
23	Davey Allison	9.95
24	Rusty Wallace	9.61
25	Curtis Turner	9.24
26	Jack Smith	7.98
27	Marvin Panch	7.87
28	Buck Baker	7.23
29	Paul Goldsmith	7.09
30	LeeRoy Yarbrough	7.07
31	Tim Richmond	7.03
32	Jim Reed	6.60
33	Jeff Burton	6.56
34	Mark Martin	6.48
35	Bill Elliott	6.22
36	Bobby Labonte	6.12
37	**Dale Jarrett**	**6.10**
38	Jim Paschal	5.92
39	Cotton Owens	5.63
40	A. J. Foyt	5.47

All-Time Records

Money Won

1	Jeff Gordon	45,008,022
2	Dale Earnhardt	41,473,589
3	**Dale Jarrett**	**33,313,332**
4	Rusty Wallace	29,432,672
5	Mark Martin	28,832,697
6	Bill Elliott	26,973,793
7	Terry Labonte	26,478,470
8	Bobby Labonte	25,631,984
9	Ricky Rudd	24,460,057
10	Darrell Waltrip	22,493,879
11	Jeff Burton	22,191,614
12	Sterling Marlin	19,814,283
13	Ken Schrader	17,931,458
14	Geoffrey Bodine	14,827,869
15	Kyle Petty	13,331,568
16	Michael Waltrip	13,280,246
17	Bobby Hamilton	12,738,653
18	Ward Burton	12,662,939
19	Jimmy Spencer	12,478,183
20	Tony Stewart	11,736,303
21	Jeremy Mayfield	11,634,821
22	Ernie Irvan	11,624,617
23	John Andretti	11,598,410
24	Brett Bodine	10,143,780
25	Joe Nemechek	9,859,452
26	Johnny Benson	9,533,583
27	Mike Skinner	9,142,142
28	Dale Earnhardt Jr.	8,782,033
29	Rick Mast	8,760,049
30	Morgan Shepherd	8,565,265
31	Richard Petty	8,541,218
32	Harry Gant	8,524,844
33	Ted Musgrave	8,464,192
34	Kenny Wallace	7,846,028
35	Bobby Allison	7,673,808
36	Robert Pressley	7,238,534
37	Dave Marcis	7,212,758
38	Steve Park	6,985,233
39	Ricky Craven	6,744,566
40	Jerry Nadeau	6,739,084

Top 5s

1	Richard Petty	555
2	Bobby Allison	336
3	David Pearson	301
4	Dale Earnhardt	281
5	Darrell Waltrip	276
6	Cale Yarborough	255
7	Buck Baker	246
8	Lee Petty	231
9	Buddy Baker	202
10	Benny Parsons	199
11	Mark Martin	188
12	Ned Jarrett	185
13	Rusty Wallace	182
14	Ricky Rudd	179
15	Terry Labonte	176
16	Bill Elliott	160
17	Jim Paschal	149
18	Jeff Gordon	147
19	**Dale Jarrett**	**141**
20	James Hylton	140
21	Bobby Isaac	134
22	Harry Gant	123
23	Herb Thomas	122
24	Junior Johnson	121
25	Rex White	110
26	Joe Weatherly	105
27	Tim Flock	102
28	Geoffrey Bodine	99
29	Marvin Panch	96
30	Dave Marcis	94
	Jack Smith	94
32	Fireball Roberts	93
33	Bobby Labonte	84
34	Neil Bonnett	83
35	Jeff Burton	81
36	Donnie Allison	78
	Speedy Thompson	78
38	Fred Lorenzen	75
39	Fonty Flock	72
40	Sterling Marlin	71

Top 10s

1	Richard Petty	712
2	Bobby Allison	446
3	Dale Earnhardt	428
4	Darrell Waltrip	390
5	Buck Baker	372
6	David Pearson	366
7	Ricky Rudd	344
8	Terry Labonte	340
9	Lee Petty	332
10	Cale Yarborough	318
11	Buddy Baker	311
12	James Hylton	301
13	Bill Elliott	294
14	Mark Martin	293
15	Rusty Wallace	292
16	Benny Parsons	283
17	Ned Jarrett	239
18	Jim Paschal	230
19	Dave Marcis	222
20	**Dale Jarrett**	**210**
21	Harry Gant	208
22	Elmo Langley	193
23	Jeff Gordon	190
24	Geoffrey Bodine	188
25	Neil Castles	178
	Sterling Marlin	178
27	Ken Schrader	176
28	Bobby Isaac	170
29	Morgan Shepherd	168
30	Kyle Petty	167
31	Rex White	163
32	Herb Thomas	156
	Neil Bonnett	156
34	Joe Weatherly	153
35	Dick Brooks	150
36	Junior Johnson	148
37	Wendell Scott	147
38	Bobby Labonte	142
39	Jack Smith	141
40	G. C. Spencer	138

Poles

1	Richard Petty	126
2	David Pearson	113
3	Cale Yarborough	70
4	Bobby Allison	59
	Darrell Waltrip	59
6	Bill Elliott	51
7	Bobby Isaac	50
8	Junior Johnson	47
9	Buck Baker	44
10	Mark Martin	41
11	Buddy Baker	40
12	Jeff Gordon	39
	Tim Flock	39
14	Herb Thomas	38
15	Geoffrey Bodine	37
16	Rex White	36
17	Fireball Roberts	35
	Ned Jarrett	35
	Rusty Wallace	35
20	Fonty Flock	33
	Fred Lorenzen	33
22	Ricky Rudd	27
23	Terry Labonte	26
24	Alan Kulwicki	24
	Jack Smith	24
26	Ken Schrader	23
27	Bobby Labonte	22
	Dale Earnhardt	22
	Dick Hutcherson	22
30	Marvin Panch	21
31	Benny Parsons	20
	Neil Bonnett	20
33	Ernie Irvan	19
	Joe Weatherly	19
35	Donnie Allison	18
	Lee Petty	18
	Speedy Thompson	18
38	Curtis Turner	17
	Harry Gant	17
40	**Dale Jarrett**	**14**

All-Time Records

Laps Led

1	Richard Petty	52,194
2	Cale Yarborough	31,776
3	Bobby Allison	27,539
4	Dale Earnhardt	25,714
5	David Pearson	25,425
6	Darrell Waltrip	23,130
7	Rusty Wallace	18,823
8	Bobby Isaac	13,229
9	Jeff Gordon	13,018
10	Junior Johnson	12,651
11	Bill Elliott	10,495
12	Mark Martin	9,760
13	Buddy Baker	9,748
14	Ned Jarrett	9,468
15	Geoffrey Bodine	8,680
16	Harry Gant	8,445
17	Fred Lorenzen	8,131
18	Ricky Rudd	7,441
19	Tim Flock	6,937
20	Benny Parsons	6,860
21	Terry Labonte	6,807
22	**Dale Jarrett**	**6,515**
23	Neil Bonnett	6,383
24	Herb Thomas	6,197
25	Fireball Roberts	5,970
26	Buck Baker	5,662
27	Ernie Irvan	5,484
28	Davey Allison	4,991
29	Lee Petty	4,787
30	Curtis Turner	4,771
31	Fonty Flock	4,682
32	Donnie Allison	4,642
33	Jim Paschal	4,591
34	Rex White	4,583
35	Jeff Burton	4,570
36	Dick Hutcherson	3,995
37	Kyle Petty	3,848
38	Speedy Thompson	3,667
39	Joe Weatherly	3,487
40	LeeRoy Yarbrough	3,421

Races Led

1	Richard Petty	599
2	Bobby Allison	414
3	Dale Earnhardt	405
4	Darrell Waltrip	402
5	Cale Yarborough	340
6	David Pearson	329
7	Rusty Wallace	255
8	Mark Martin	246
9	Buddy Baker	242
10	Bill Elliott	241
11	Terry Labonte	237
12	Geoffrey Bodine	220
13	Ricky Rudd	212
14	Jeff Gordon	201
15	Dave Marcis	195
16	Benny Parsons	192
	Harry Gant	192
18	**Dale Jarrett**	**171**
19	Bobby Isaac	155
	Neil Bonnett	155
21	Sterling Marlin	144
22	Junior Johnson	138
23	Ken Schrader	136
24	Bobby Labonte	130
25	Ernie Irvan	124
26	Ned Jarrett	111
27	Donnie Allison	105
28	Morgan Shepherd	104
29	Buck Baker	103
30	Kyle Petty	99
31	Davey Allison	97
32	Jeff Burton	94
33	Lee Petty	93
34	Fireball Roberts	90
35	Michael Waltrip	85
36	Herb Thomas	84
37	Fred Lorenzen	83
38	Tim Flock	82
39	Alan Kulwicki	77
40	Jim Paschal	76
	Tim Richmond	76

Modern Era Records

(minimum 100 Career Starts)

Championships

1	Dale Earnhardt	7
2	Jeff Gordon	4
	Richard Petty	4
4	Darrell Waltrip	3
	Cale Yarborough	3
6	Terry Labonte	2
7	Bobby Allison	1
	Bill Elliott	1
	Dale Jarrett	**1**
	Alan Kulwicki	1
	Bobby Labonte	1
	Benny Parsons	1
	Rusty Wallace	1

Starts

1	Darrell Waltrip	809
2	Dave Marcis	759
3	Ricky Rudd	731
4	Terry Labonte	709
5	Dale Earnhardt	676
6	Bill Elliott	659
7	Richard Petty	619
8	Kyle Petty	609
9	Rusty Wallace	562
10	Geoffrey Bodine	554
11	Sterling Marlin	539
12	Ken Schrader	528
13	Michael Waltrip	498
14	Mark Martin	494
15	Morgan Shepherd	478
16	Bobby Allison	476
17	Harry Gant	474
18	**Dale Jarrett**	**459**
19	Jimmy Means	455
20	J. D. McDuffie	443
21	Brett Bodine	442
22	Benny Parsons	441
23	Buddy Arrington	426
24	Lake Speed	402
25	Buddy Baker	391
26	Jimmy Spencer	370
27	Cale Yarborough	366
28	Neil Bonnett	363
29	Derrike Cope	355
	Rick Mast	355
31	Bobby Hamilton	337
32	Bobby Hillin Jr.	334
33	James Hylton	325
34	Ernie Irvan	313
35	Hut Stricklin	306
36	Cecil Gordon	300
37	Ted Musgrave	299
38	Dick Trickle	298
39	Bobby Labonte	294
40	Jeff Gordon	293

Victories

1	Darrell Waltrip	84
2	Dale Earnhardt	76
3	Cale Yarborough	69
4	Richard Petty	60
5	Jeff Gordon	58
6	Bobby Allison	55
7	Rusty Wallace	54
8	David Pearson	45
9	Bill Elliott	41
10	Mark Martin	32
11	**Dale Jarrett**	**28**
12	Ricky Rudd	22
13	Terry Labonte	21
14	Benny Parsons	20
15	Davey Allison	19
16	Geoffrey Bodine	18
	Harry Gant	18
	Bobby Labonte	18
	Neil Bonnett	18
20	Jeff Burton	17
21	Ernie Irvan	15
	Buddy Baker	15
23	Tim Richmond	13
24	Tony Stewart	12
25	Sterling Marlin	8
	Kyle Petty	8
27	Dale Earnhardt Jr.	5
	Alan Kulwicki	5
	Dave Marcis	5
30	Donnie Allison	4
	Bobby Hamilton	4
	Ken Schrader	4
	Morgan Shepherd	4
34	Ward Burton	3
	Jeremy Mayfield	3
36	Derrike Cope	2
	A. J. Foyt	2
	Steve Park	2
	John Andretti	2
	Kevin Harvick	2
	Jimmy Spencer	2
	Joe Nemechek	2

Modern Era Records

Winning Pct.

1	David Pearson	21.84
2	Jeff Gordon	19.80
3	Cale Yarborough	18.85
4	Bobby Allison	11.55
5	Tony Stewart	11.54
6	Dale Earnhardt	11.24
7	Darrell Waltrip	10.38
8	Davey Allison	9.95
9	Richard Petty	9.69
10	Rusty Wallace	9.61
11	Tim Richmond	7.03
12	Jeff Burton	6.56
13	Mark Martin	6.48
14	Bill Elliott	6.22
15	Bobby Labonte	6.12
16	**Dale Jarrett**	**6.10**
17	Neil Bonnett	4.96
18	Ernie Irvan	4.79
19	Benny Parsons	4.54
20	Buddy Baker	3.84
21	Harry Gant	3.80
22	Geoffrey Bodine	3.25
23	Ricky Rudd	3.01
24	Terry Labonte	2.96
25	Donnie Allison	2.52
26	Alan Kulwicki	2.42
27	Steve Park	1.75
28	Sterling Marlin	1.48
29	Kyle Petty	1.31
30	Jeremy Mayfield	1.27
31	Ward Burton	1.20
32	Bobby Hamilton	1.19
33	Morgan Shepherd	0.84
34	Joe Nemechek	0.79
35	John Andretti	0.76
36	Ken Schrader	0.76
37	Dave Marcis	0.66
38	Derrike Cope	0.56
39	Jimmy Spencer	0.54

Money Won

1	Jeff Gordon	$45,008,022
2	Dale Earnhardt	41,473,589
3	**Dale Jarrett**	**33,313,332**
4	Rusty Wallace	29,432,672
5	Mark Martin	28,832,697
6	Bill Elliott	26,973,793
7	Terry Labonte	26,478,470
8	Bobby Labonte	25,631,984
9	Ricky Rudd	24,460,057
10	Darrell Waltrip	22,493,879
11	Jeff Burton	22,191,614
12	Sterling Marlin	19,814,283
13	Ken Schrader	17,931,458
14	Geoffrey Bodine	14,827,869
15	Kyle Petty	13,331,568
16	Michael Waltrip	13,280,246
17	Bobby Hamilton	12,738,653
18	Ward Burton	12,662,939
19	Jimmy Spencer	12,478,183
20	Tony Stewart	11,736,303
21	Jeremy Mayfield	11,634,821
22	Ernie Irvan	11,624,617
23	John Andretti	11,598,410
24	Brett Bodine	10,143,780
25	Joe Nemechek	9,859,452
26	Johnny Benson	9,533,583
27	Mike Skinner	9,142,142
28	Dale Earnhardt Jr.	8,782,033
29	Rick Mast	8,760,049
30	Morgan Shepherd	8,565,265
31	Harry Gant	8,524,844
32	Ted Musgrave	8,464,192
33	Kenny Wallace	7,846,028
34	Robert Pressley	7,238,534
35	Steve Park	6,985,233
36	Ricky Craven	6,744,566
37	Jerry Nadeau	6,739,084
38	Davey Allison	6,689,154
39	Wally Dallenbach Jr.	6,144,988
40	Derrike Cope	6,104,549

Average Start

1	David Pearson	5.58
2	Cale Yarborough	7.15
3	Bobby Allison	8.44
4	Jeff Gordon	8.89
5	Benny Parsons	9.05
6	Mark Martin	9.83
7	Donnie Allison	9.97
8	Buddy Baker	10.73
9	Neil Bonnett	11.93
10	Alan Kulwicki	12.00
11	Davey Allison	12.38
12	Tim Richmond	12.46
13	Harry Gant	12.51
14	Rusty Wallace	12.60
15	Dale Earnhardt	12.90
16	Bill Elliott	13.12
17	Geoffrey Bodine	13.33
18	Richard Petty	13.40
19	Ricky Rudd	13.58
20	Darrell Waltrip	13.71
21	Bobby Labonte	14.66
22	Coo Coo Marlin	15.04
23	Ron Bouchard	15.12
24	Terry Labonte	15.34
25	Ken Schrader	15.38
26	Lennie Pond	15.43
27	Tony Stewart	15.50
28	Dick Brooks	15.92
29	Ernie Irvan	16.21
30	**Dale Jarrett**	**16.72**
31	Joe Ruttman	17.39
32	Sterling Marlin	17.96
33	Morgan Shepherd	17.96
34	Richard Childress	18.43
35	Mike Skinner	18.45
36	Jody Ridley	18.53
37	Ward Burton	18.82
38	Joe Nemechek	19.30
39	Rick Wilson	19.74
40	Bruce Hill	19.77

Modern Era Records

Average Finish

1	Dale Earnhardt	11.06
2	Cale Yarborough	11.45
3	Bobby Allison	11.58
4	Jeff Gordon	11.63
5	Tony Stewart	11.74
6	Mark Martin	12.74
7	David Pearson	13.45
8	Rusty Wallace	14.05
9	Richard Petty	14.15
10	Davey Allison	14.25
11	Benny Parsons	14.39
12	Terry Labonte	14.73
13	Bill Elliott	14.75
14	Bobby Labonte	14.77
15	Darrell Waltrip	15.12
16	Tim Richmond	15.18
17	Ricky Rudd	15.37
18	**Dale Jarrett**	**15.51**
19	Buddy Baker	15.52
20	Jeff Burton	15.75
21	Harry Gant	15.87
22	Alan Kulwicki	16.41
23	Neil Bonnett	16.52
24	Jody Ridley	16.58
25	Richard Childress	17.21
26	Ron Bouchard	17.23
27	Ken Schrader	17.25
28	James Hylton	17.34
29	Ernie Irvan	17.35
30	Sterling Marlin	17.58
31	Lennie Pond	17.78
32	Dick Brooks	17.80
33	Buddy Arrington	17.84
34	Cecil Gordon	17.84
35	Geoffrey Bodine	18.08
36	Elmo Langley	18.12
37	Morgan Shepherd	18.24
38	David Sisco	18.53
39	Donnie Allison	18.67
40	Walter Ballard	18.88

Top 5s

1	Dale Earnhardt	281
2	Darrell Waltrip	276
3	Richard Petty	221
4	Bobby Allison	217
5	Cale Yarborough	197
6	Mark Martin	188
7	Rusty Wallace	182
8	Ricky Rudd	179
9	Terry Labonte	176
10	Benny Parsons	172
11	Bill Elliott	160
12	Jeff Gordon	147
13	**Dale Jarrett**	**141**
14	Buddy Baker	128
15	Harry Gant	123
16	David Pearson	108
17	Geoffrey Bodine	99
18	Bobby Labonte	84
19	Neil Bonnett	83
20	Jeff Gordon	81
21	Dave Marcis	75
22	Sterling Marlin	71
23	Ernie Irvan	68
24	Davey Allison	66
25	Ken Schrader	64
26	Morgan Shepherd	63
27	Kyle Petty	51
28	Donnie Allison	42
	Tim Richmond	42
30	Tony Stewart	39
	Lennie Pond	39
32	Alan Kulwicki	38
33	Jeremy Mayfield	33
34	Dick Brooks	30
35	Jimmy Spencer	25
36	Michael Waltrip	21
	Ward Burton	21
38	Ted Musgrave	20
	Bobby Hamilton	20
	Cecil Gordon	20

Top 10s

1	Dale Earnhardt	428
2	Darrell Waltrip	390
3	Ricky Rudd	344
4	Terry Labonte	340
5	Richard Petty	311
6	Bobby Allison	300
7	Bill Elliott	294
8	Mark Martin	293
9	Rusty Wallace	292
10	Benny Parsons	239
11	Cale Yarborough	231
12	**Dale Jarrett**	**210**
13	Harry Gant	208
14	Buddy Baker	199
15	Jeff Gordon	190
16	Geoffrey Bodine	188
17	Dave Marcis	180
18	Sterling Marlin	178
19	Ken Schrader	176
20	Morgan Shepherd	168
21	Kyle Petty	167
22	Neil Bonnett	156
23	Bobby Labonte	142
24	David Pearson	124
	Ernie Irvan	124
26	Jeff Burton	119
27	Dick Brooks	108
28	Davey Allison	92
29	Lennie Pond	88
30	James Hylton	87
31	Michael Waltrip	85
32	Tim Richmond	78
33	Richard Childress	76
34	Lake Speed	75
	Alan Kulwicki	75
36	Cecil Gordon	71
37	Jimmy Spencer	70
38	Buddy Arrington	68
39	Donnie Allison	67
	Ward Burton	67

Modern Era Records

Modern Era Records, continued

Poles

1	Darrell Waltrip	59
2	David Pearson	56
3	Bill Elliott	51
	Cale Yarborough	51
5	Mark Martin	41
6	Jeff Gordon	39
7	Geoffrey Bodine	37
8	Bobby Allison	36
9	Rusty Wallace	35
10	Buddy Baker	30
11	Ricky Rudd	27
12	Terry Labonte	26
13	Alan Kulwicki	24
14	Richard Petty	23
	Ken Schrader	23
16	Dale Earnhardt	22
	Bobby Labonte	22
18	Neil Bonnett	20
19	Ernie Irvan	19
	Benny Parsons	19
21	Harry Gant	17
22	**Dale Jarrett**	**14**
	Davey Allison	14
	Tim Richmond	14
25	Dave Marcis	12
26	Sterling Marlin	11
27	Donnie Allison	9
	Bobby Isaac	9
29	Kyle Petty	8
30	Morgan Shepherd	7
31	Jeremy Mayfield	6
	Joe Nemechek	6
	Ward Burton	6
34	Ted Musgrave	5
	Mike Skinner	5
	Lennie Pond	5
	Bobby Hamilton	5
	A. J. Foyt	5
	Brett Bodine	5

Front Row Starts

1	Darrell Waltrip	115
2	Cale Yarborough	96
3	Bill Elliott	91
4	Bobby Allison	87
6	Mark Martin	81
5	David Pearson	86
7	Geoffrey Bodine	79
8	Jeff Gordon	73
9	Ricky Rudd	69
10	Rusty Wallace	66
12	Dale Earnhardt	58
11	Richard Petty	60
14	Terry Labonte	54
15	Benny Parsons	52
16	Harry Gant	45
	Buddy Baker	58
17	Ken Schrader	39
	Neil Bonnett	38
18	Bobby Labonte	38
20	Alan Kulwicki	37
21	Ernie Irvan	36
22	**Dale Jarrett**	**31**
23	Davey Allison	27
	Tim Richmond	27
25	Sterling Marlin	23
26	Donnie Allison	21
27	Dave Marcis	18
28	Bobby Isaac	16
	Brett Bodine	16
30	Kyle Petty	14
	Morgan Shepherd	14
	Ward Burton	14
33	Joe Nemechek	11
	Joe Ruttman	11
	Bobby Hamilton	11
36	John Andretti	10
	Mike Skinner	10
38	Ricky Craven	9
	Jeff Burton	9
	A. J. Foyt	9

Total Points[1]

1	Darrell Waltrip	96,545
2	Dale Earnhardt	93,962
3	Ricky Rudd	88,959
4	Terry Labonte	87,943
6	Rusty Wallace	71,977
5	Bill Elliott	81,834
7	Dave Marcis	69,550
8	Kyle Petty	65,619
9	Mark Martin	65,442
10	Richard Petty	65,333
12	Sterling Marlin	61,252
11	Geoffrey Bodine	62,845
14	Harry Gant	56,949
15	**Dale Jarrett**	**56,187**
16	Morgan Shepherd	53,234
13	Ken Schrader	60,389
17	Bobby Allison	53,199
19	Benny Parsons	44,146
18	Michael Waltrip	50,845
20	Neil Bonnett	43,072
21	Jimmy Means	42,573
22	Brett Bodine	42,386
23	Cale Yarborough	41,910
24	Lake Speed	40,791
25	Jeff Gordon	40,658
26	Buddy Arrington	39,861
27	Buddy Baker	39,546
28	Jimmy Spencer	37,442
29	Bobby Labonte	36,710
30	Ernie Irvan	36,434
31	J. D. McDuffie	35,061
32	Bobby Hamilton	34,344
33	Bobby Hillin Jr.	33,690
34	Rick Mast	32,611
35	Derrike Cope	31,960
36	Jeff Burton	31,535
37	Ted Musgrave	31,240
38	Hut Stricklin	27,942
39	Dick Trickle	26,773
40	Dick Brooks	26,628

[1] – Since current point system was implemented in 1975

Modern Era Records

Modern Era Records, continued

Points Per Race[1]

1	Dale Earnhardt	139.0
2	Jeff Gordon	138.8
3	Cale Yarborough	138.3
4	Bobby Allison	136.1
5	Tony Stewart	135.6
6	Mark Martin	132.5
7	Rusty Wallace	128.1
8	Davey Allison	127.5
9	David Pearson	125.9
10	Benny Parsons	125.8
11	Darrell Waltrip	125.5
12	Bobby Labonte	124.9
13	Bill Elliott	124.2
14	Terry Labonte	124.0
15	Richard Petty	123.3
16	Tim Richmond	123.0
17	**Dale Jarrett**	**122.4**
18	Jeff Burton	121.8
19	Ricky Rudd	121.7
20	Harry Gant	121.2
21	Buddy Baker	120.6
22	Neil Bonnett	119.3
23	Alan Kulwicki	118.5
24	Richard Childress	117.9
25	Jody Ridley	116.4
26	Ernie Irvan	116.4
27	Dick Brooks	114.8
28	Ken Schrader	114.4
29	Donnie Allison	113.9
30	Ron Bouchard	113.9
31	Sterling Marlin	113.6
32	Geoffrey Bodine	113.4
33	Lennie Pond	112.9
34	Morgan Shepherd	111.4
35	Buddy Arrington	109.8
36	Kyle Petty	107.7
37	James Hylton	107.3
38	Cecil Gordon	105.4
39	Johnny Benson Jr.	104.7
40	Joe Ruttman	104.6

[1] – Since current point system was implemented in 1975

DNFs

1	Dave Marcis	230
2	J. D. McDuffie	200
3	Richard Petty	189
4	Darrell Waltrip	176
5	Jimmy Means	172
6	Buddy Baker	159
7	Ricky Rudd	157
8	Geoffrey Bodine	156
	Benny Parsons	156
10	Kyle Petty	148
11	Harry Gant	146
12	Morgan Shepherd	141
13	Terry Labonte	140
14	Neil Bonnett	138
15	Lake Speed	128
16	Dick Brooks	126
17	Derrike Cope	123
18	Bobby Allison	122
19	Greg Sacks	118
20	Sterling Marlin	108
	Rusty Wallace	108
22	Cale Yarborough	105
23	Michael Waltrip	104
24	Lennie Pond	103
25	Bill Elliott	99
26	Buddy Arrington	98
27	Ronnie Thomas	95
	Dale Earnhardt	95
29	D. K. Ulrich	94
	Dick Trickle	94
31	**Dale Jarrett**	**93**
32	Ed Negre	90
33	Joe Ruttman	88
34	Donnie Allison	87
35	Brett Bodine	86
36	Richard Childress	85
	Mark Martin	85
38	Bobby Hillin Jr.	84
39	David Pearson	82
	Rick Wilson	82

Laps Led

1	Cale Yarborough	27,260
2	Dale Earnhardt	25,714
3	Darrell Waltrip	23,130
4	Rusty Wallace	18,823
5	Bobby Allison	18,502
6	Richard Petty	16,902
7	Jeff Gordon	13,018
8	Bill Elliott	10,495
9	David Pearson	10,079
10	Mark Martin	9,760
11	Geoffrey Bodine	8,680
12	Harry Gant	8,445
13	Ricky Rudd	7,441
14	Terry Labonte	6,807
15	Buddy Baker	6,580
16	Benny Parsons	6,552
17	**Dale Jarrett**	**6,515**
18	Neil Bonnett	6,383
19	Ernie Irvan	5,484
20	Davey Allison	4,991
21	Jeff Burton	4,570
22	Kyle Petty	3,848
23	Sterling Marlin	3,334
24	Bobby Labonte	3,202
25	Tony Stewart	2,904
26	Alan Kulwicki	2,686
27	Tim Richmond	2,537
28	Ken Schrader	2,373
29	Dave Marcis	2,332
30	Donnie Allison	2,297
31	Morgan Shepherd	2,141
32	Bobby Hamilton	1,975
33	Jeremy Mayfield	1,697
34	Ward Burton	1,491
35	Bobby Isaac	1,399
36	Dale Earnhardt Jr.	1,194
37	Jimmy Spencer	1,100
38	Brett Bodine	1,037
39	Mike Skinner	1,016
40	Steve Park	963

Modern Era Records

Pct. Led			Races Led			No. of Times Led		
1	Cale Yarborough	22.80	1	Dale Earnhardt	405	1	Dale Earnhardt	1,398
2	David Pearson	15.93	2	Darrell Waltrip	402	2	Darrell Waltrip	1,227
3	Jeff Gordon	14.33	3	Bobby Allison	306	3	Cale Yarborough	1,179
4	Dale Earnhardt	11.68	4	Richard Petty	289	4	Bobby Allison	1,112
5	Bobby Allison	11.55	5	Cale Yarborough	271	5	Richard Petty	975
6	Rusty Wallace	10.43	6	Rusty Wallace	255	6	Buddy Baker	720
7	Tony Stewart	9.32	7	Mark Martin	246	7	Rusty Wallace	671
8	Darrell Waltrip	8.65	8	Bill Elliott	241	8	David Pearson	663
9	Richard Petty	8.08	9	Terry Labonte	237	9	Jeff Gordon	607
10	Davey Allison	7.93	10	Geoffrey Bodine	220	10	Mark Martin	585
11	Mark Martin	6.16	11	Ricky Rudd	212	11	Bill Elliott	570
12	Jeff Burton	5.76	12	Jeff Gordon	201	12	Terry Labonte	501
13	Ernie Irvan	5.49	13	Harry Gant	192	13	Geoffrey Bodine	477
14	Neil Bonnett	5.34	14	Dave Marcis	183	14	Neil Bonnett	460
15	Harry Gant	5.30	15	Benny Parsons	182	15	Benny Parsons	457
16	Buddy Baker	5.14	16	Buddy Baker	178	16	Harry Gant	454
17	Bill Elliott	4.99	**17**	**Dale Jarrett**	**171**	17	Ricky Rudd	397
18	Geoffrey Bodine	4.81	18	Neil Bonnett	155	**18**	**Dale Jarrett**	**382**
19	Benny Parsons	4.53	19	Sterling Marlin	144	19	Dave Marcis	326
20	**Dale Jarrett**	**4.46**	20	David Pearson	140	20	Ernie Irvan	320
21	Donnie Allison	4.35	21	Ken Schrader	136	21	Ken Schrader	284
22	Tim Richmond	4.16	22	Bobby Labonte	130	22	Sterling Marlin	269
23	Alan Kulwicki	3.84	23	Ernie Irvan	124	23	Bobby Labonte	265
24	Bobby Labonte	3.51	24	Morgan Shepherd	104	24	Davey Allison	263
25	Ricky Rudd	3.14	25	Kyle Petty	99	25	Donnie Allison	252
26	Terry Labonte	2.95	26	Davey Allison	97	26	Jeff Burton	207
27	Steve Park	2.85	27	Jeff Burton	94	27	Morgan Shepherd	190
28	Jeremy Mayfield	2.34	28	Michael Waltrip	85	28	Tim Richmond	188
29	Ward Burton	1.95	29	Alan Kulwicki	77	29	Kyle Petty	171
30	Kyle Petty	1.94	30	Tim Richmond	76	30	Alan Kulwicki	157
31	Mike Skinner	1.94	31	Jimmy Spencer	74	31	Jeremy Mayfield	113
32	Sterling Marlin	1.94	32	Donnie Allison	69	32	A. J. Foyt	110
33	Bobby Hamilton	1.86	33	Brett Bodine	64	33	Tony Stewart	109
34	Ken Schrader	1.40	34	Ward Burton	55	34	Michael Waltrip	106
35	Morgan Shepherd	1.36	35	Lennie Pond	53	35	Bobby Hamilton	103
36	Jerry Nadeau	1.34	36	Bobby Hamilton	51		Ward Burton	103
37	Ricky Craven	1.22	37	Jeremy Mayfield	49	37	Jimmy Spencer	99
38	Joe Ruttman	1.15	38	John Andretti	46	38	Lennie Pond	93
39	Lennie Pond	1.12	39	Tony Stewart	45	39	Bobby Isaac	88
40	Jimmy Spencer	0.94	40	Mike Skinner	43	40	Brett Bodine	86

Modern Era Records

	No. of Times Led Most Laps			Bonus Points[1]				Laps Completed	
1	Cale Yarborough	88	1	Dale Earnhardt	2,445	1	Darrell Waltrip	237,772
2	Dale Earnhardt	84	2	Darrell Waltrip	2,310	2	Ricky Rudd	211,452
3	Darrell Waltrip	69	3	Rusty Wallace	1,595	3	Terry Labonte	208,187
4	Rusty Wallace	64	4	Cale Yarborough	1,465	4	Dave Marcis	205,554
5	Bobby Allison	61	5	Bobby Allison	1,400	5	Dale Earnhardt	202,888
6	Jeff Gordon	53	6	Bill Elliott	1,395	6	Bill Elliott	193,282
7	Richard Petty	41	7	Mark Martin	1,390	7	Richard Petty	175,097
8	David Pearson	39	8	Terry Labonte	1,290	8	Kyle Petty	170,711
9	Bill Elliott	37	9	Jeff Gordon	1,270	9	Rusty Wallace	163,524
10	Mark Martin	32	10	Geoffrey Bodine	1,225	10	Geoffrey Bodine	155,915
11	Buddy Baker	28	11	Richard Petty	1,220	11	Ken Schrader	154,252
12	Geoffrey Bodine	25	12	Ricky Rudd	1,160	12	Sterling Marlin	153,362
13	Harry Gant	23	13	Harry Gant	1,075	13	Mark Martin	144,686
14	Ernie Irvan	22	**14**	**Dale Jarrett**	**955**	14	Michael Waltrip	141,407
15	Terry Labonte	21	15	Dave Marcis	905	15	Bobby Allison	139,780
16	**Dale Jarrett**	**20**	16	Benny Parsons	870	16	Harry Gant	133,628
	Jeff Burton	20	17	Neil Bonnett	855	17	Morgan Shepherd	129,983
18	Ricky Rudd	19	18	Buddy Baker	795	**18**	**Dale Jarrett**	**128,336**
19	Davey Allison	17	19	Sterling Marlin	775	19	Brett Bodine	124,953
20	Neil Bonnett	16	20	Ernie Irvan	730	20	Buddy Arrington	123,604
21	Benny Parsons	14	21	Ken Schrader	700	21	Benny Parsons	116,905
22	Kyle Petty	11	22	Bobby Labonte	685	22	Jimmy Means	113,948
	Tim Richmond	11	23	Jeff Burton	580	23	J. D. McDuffie	105,874
24	Tony Stewart	10	24	Davey Allison	570	24	Lake Speed	105,738
	Sterling Marlin	10	25	Kyle Petty	550	25	Jimmy Spencer	103,123
26	Alan Kulwicki	7	26	Morgan Shepherd	535	26	Cale Yarborough	102,924
	Bobby Labonte	7	27	David Pearson	525	27	Rick Mast	100,128
28	Dale Earnhardt Jr.	6	28	Tim Richmond	435	28	Bobby Hamilton	97,614
29	Donnie Allison	5	29	Michael Waltrip	430	29	Buddy Baker	97,394
	Jeremy Mayfield	5	30	Alan Kulwicki	420	30	Neil Bonnett	96,119
31	A. J. Foyt	4	31	Jimmy Spencer	380	31	Derrike Cope	90,783
	Ken Schrader	4	32	Brett Bodine	330	32	Bobby Hillin Jr.	90,070
	Mike Skinner	4	33	Ward Burton	290	33	James Hylton	89,291
34	Morgan Shepherd	3	34	Donnie Allison	285	34	Ernie Irvan	88,656
	Steve Park	3	35	Tony Stewart	275	35	Ted Musgrave	88,104
	Ward Burton	3	36	Jeremy Mayfield	270	36	Bobby Labonte	85,296
	Bobby Isaac	3		Bobby Hamilton	270	37	Jeff Gordon	85,221
	Bobby Hamilton	3	38	Mike Skinner	235	38	Hut Stricklin	83,947
				Lennie Pond	235	39	Dick Trickle	82,630
			40	John Andretti	230	40	Cecil Gordon	80,137

[1] – Since current point system was implemented in 1975

Modern Era Records

Modern Era Records, continued

Pct. of Laps Completed

1	Tony Stewart	95.25
2	Steve Park	93.83
3	Jeff Gordon	93.80
4	Bobby Labonte	93.50
5	Johnny Benson Jr.	93.12
6	Ted Musgrave	93.11
7	Elliott Sadler	92.87
8	Jeff Burton	92.31
9	Dale Earnhardt	92.14
10	Bobby Hamilton	92.03
11	Bill Elliott	91.93
12	Jerry Nadeau	91.72
13	Jeremy Mayfield	91.71
14	Mark Martin	91.37
15	Ken Schrader	91.26
16	Joe Nemechek	91.15
17	Kevin Lepage	90.83
18	Rusty Wallace	90.62
19	Mike Skinner	90.30
20	Terry Labonte	90.17
21	Steve Grissom	90.07
22	Ricky Rudd	89.11
23	Sterling Marlin	89.10
24	Davey Allison	89.04
25	Darrell Waltrip	88.94
26	Michael Waltrip	88.79
27	Ernie Irvan	88.74
28	Brett Bodine	88.69
29	Jimmy Spencer	88.23
30	Alan Kulwicki	88.09
31	Ward Burton	87.96
32	Wally Dallenbach Jr.	87.94
33	**Dale Jarrett**	**87.86**
34	John Andretti	87.84
35	Mike Wallace	87.47
36	Bobby Allison	87.29
37	Chad Little	86.80
38	Kenny Wallace	86.77
39	Rick Mast	86.75
40	Ricky Craven	86.46

The Seasons

A Season-by-Season Look at Dale Jarrett's Career

This section gives details of Jarrett's career, season by season. Every race started by Jarrett since he joined the Winston Cup series full-time in 1987 is presented, listing his start, finish, total laps, laps completed, race-ending condition, and amount of money won. His championship performance in each season is also charted, including championship and bonus points earned for each race, his position in the points standings, and how far he trailed the points leader. If Jarrett is the points leader at any point, the second place driver in the standings is listed in parentheses along with the margin of Jarrett's lead. The context of each race is also available with the "Career Race" column, which indicates the number of races in which Jarrett competed at any point in his career.

Each season is given historical context with the inclusion of full statistics and a season summary. For each season, 20 statistical categories are cataloged. Jarrett's total for each category is listed, along with his rank and that category's leader. If Jarrett is the leader of a category, the second-place driver is listed in parentheses with his total. The season summary explores Jarrett's accomplishments and memorable moments and is often accompanied by tables that provide greater insight into his career.

In 1987, Jarrett became one of the first drivers to compete full-time in both the Busch Grand National and Winston Cup series. He raced in all 27 Busch races, finishing sixth in the final point standings. After taking over for Tommy Ellis, Jarrett ran the final 24 Winston Cup races. Here, Jarrett dispenses advice to Dale Earnhardt, Jr. at Michigan in 1997.

Though Dale Jarrett's success in Winston Cup racing is unquestioned, he still has a way to go before catching up with his dad. In eight seasons, Ned Jarrett won 50 races and two championships. Dale has about half as many of each, with 28 career wins through the 2001 season and a single championship.

1987: The Accidental Rookie

A full-time Winston Cup ride was not in Dale Jarrett's plans as the 1987 season began. Safely ensconced in the Busch Grand National series, which was still in its infancy since being established in 1982, he appeared to have his sights set on competing for the junior circuit's championship. Then, as happened regularly during the early years of Jarrett's career, events turned and circumstances developed.

In early 1987, the circumstance was Tommy Ellis, a fellow Busch series regular and budding Winston Cup driver. Just five races into the 1987 season, he quit his ride in the No. 18 Eric Freedlander Chevrolet, a car he had piloted the previous two seasons. Frustration was the cause of Ellis' sudden departure. He had opened the year with a violent, rolling wreck in the Twin 125s at Daytona, becoming airborne after being tapped. Worse than the damage to his car was seeing his chance to earn a spot in the Daytona 500 eliminated.

Ellis' bad luck continued after his Daytona disappointment. He crashed at Rockingham and Atlanta; at Richmond, he managed to keep his car in one piece, but finished six laps off the pace. Disgruntled, Ellis parked his car just three laps into the season's fifth race at Darlington, leaving Freedlander's team high and dry. (Ellis returned to the Busch series full-time, winning the 1988 championship. Yet he started just eight more Winston Cup races during the rest of his career.)

Facing 24 more races without a driver, Freedlander turned to Jarrett for relief. The eager Jarrett was a natural choice to fill a vacant Winston Cup driver's seat. The son of a former Winston Cup champion, Dale had shown promise against his Busch series competition. Though he never won a championship, he finished sixth or better in the final standings in each of the series' first five seasons. When Jarrett responded to his new Winston Cup opportunity by finishing 12th at North Wilkesboro and 10th at Bristol, an impressed Freedlander signed him for the remainder of the season.

Despite a strong start, the ultimate result of taking over a chaotic situation was a predictably uneven performance. Jarrett neither started nor finished a race better than 10th place. He never led a lap or even finished on the lead lap. Five consecutive DNFs ended any momentum gained from North Wilkesboro and Bristol. Nearly half (11) of Jarrett's 24 starts ended prematurely due to engine or mechanical problems. By the end of the season, all 28 of his career starts had ended at least two laps off of the race winner's pace.

The disorderly debut also denied Jarrett a chance to compete for the Rookie of the Year award, though few drivers could have competed successfully against 1987's rookie star, Davey Allison. Driving the No. 28 car that Jarrett would take over eight years later, Allison—with two wins and five poles in just 22 starts—put together a rookie campaign bettered in NASCAR history only by Tony Stewart in 1999.

Still, for Jarrett, the opportunity was golden. Every Sunday, he got to strap into a Winston Cup car and race against Earnhardt, Waltrip, Elliott, Petty, and the Allisons. By the end of the season, Jarrett climbed 21 spots in the championship point standings, finishing 25th.

Jarrett in 1987

Category	Total	Rank	1987 Leader*
Money	$143,405	25th	Dale Earnhardt—$2,099,243
Total points	2,177	25th	Dale Earnhardt—4,696
Avg. start	27.7	33rd	Bill Elliott—6.1
Avg. finish	24.1	29th	Dale Earnhardt—5.9
Wins	0	—	Dale Earnhardt—11
Top 5s	0	—	Dale Earnhardt—21
Top 10s	2	26th	Dale Earnhardt—24
DNFs	11	5th	Harry Gant—21
Poles	0	—	Bill Elliott—8
Front row starts	0	—	Bill Elliott—11
Laps led	0	—	Dale Earnhardt—3,358
Races led	0	—	Dale Earnhardt—27
Times led	0	—	Dale Earnhardt—116
Miles led	0	—	Dale Earnhardt—3,399
Times led most laps	0	—	Dale Earnhardt—13
Bonus points	0	—	Dale Earnhardt—200
Laps completed	4,788	26th	Dale Earnhardt—9,043
Miles completed	5,680	26th	Darrell Waltrip—11,034
Points per race	90.7	30th	Dale Earnhardt—161.9
Lead-lap finishes	0	—	Dale Earnhardt—23

Jarrett vs. the Rookie Class of 1987

Driver	Starts	Wins	Poles	Avg. Start	Avg. Finish	Laps Led	Total Points
Davey Allison*	22	2	5	9.1	14.2	710	2,824
Dale Jarrett	**24**	**0**	**0**	**27.7**	**24.1**	**0**	**2,177**
Brett Bodine	14	0	0	18.1	24.2	0	1,271
Derrike Cope	11	0	0	23.9	30.2	0	797

*Won 1987 Rookie of the Year Award

1987 Performance Chart

No. 18 Eric Freedlander Chevrolet

Career Race	Race No.	Date	Race	St.	Fin.	Total Laps	Laps Completed	Laps Led	Condition	Money	Pts.	Bonus Pts.	Current Standing	Behind Leader	Current Leader
5	6	Apr. 5	North Wilkesboro—First Union 400[1]	14	12	400	398	0	Running	$4,725	127	0	46	-898	Earnhardt
6	7	Apr. 12	Bristol—Valleydale Meats 500	24	10	500	497	0	Running	7,845	134	0	36	-944	Earnhardt
7	8	Apr. 26	Martinsville—Sovran Bank 500	14	29	500	113	0	DNF–Engine	4,135	76	0	34	-1,053	Earnhardt
8	9	May 3	Talladega—Winston 500	38	28	178	96	0	DNF–Engine	6,200	79	0	34	-1,139	Earnhardt
9	10	May 24	Charlotte—Coca-Cola 600	35	38	400	84	0	DNF–Engine	4,310	49	0	33	-1,193	Earnhardt
10	11	May 31	Dover—Budweiser 500	23	35	500	84	0	DNF–Transmission	3,200	58	0	32	-1,300	Earnhardt
11	12	June 14	Pocono—Miller High Life 500	24	35	200	103	0	DNF–Ignition	3,700	58	0	31	-1,402	Earnhardt
12	13	June 21	Riverside—Budweiser 400	41	18	95	93	0	Running	5,765	109	0	28	-1,439	Earnhardt
13	14	June 28	Michigan—Miller American 400	37	20	200	197	0	Running	7,060	103	0	27	-1,521	Earnhardt
14	15	July 4	Daytona—Pepsi Firecracker 400	41	23	160	156	0	Running	6,110	94	0	26	-1,582	Earnhardt
15	16	July 19	Pocono—Summer 500	28	12	200	198	0	Running	7,670	127	0	26	-1,640	Earnhardt
16	17	July 26	Talladega—Talladega 500	37	21	188	183	0	Running	7,210	100	0	25	-1,710	Earnhardt
17	18	Aug. 10	Watkins Glen—The Bud at the Glen	20	36	90	42	0	DNF–Transmission	4,280	55	0	25	-1,802	Earnhardt
18	19	Aug. 16	Michigan—Champion Spark Plug 400	37	39	200	25	0	DNF–Engine	4,400	46	0	25	-1,936	Earnhardt
19	20	Aug. 22	Bristol—Busch 500	23	12	500	491	0	Running	5,810	127	0	25	-1,994	Earnhardt
20	21	Sept. 6	Darlington—Southern 500	38	15	202	200	0	Running	9,110	118	0	25	-2,061	Earnhardt
21	22	Sept. 13	Richmond—Wrangler Jeans Indigo 400	18	27	400	109	0	DNF–Crash	2,430	82	0	25	-2,164	Earnhardt
22	23	Sept. 20	Dover—Delaware 500	17	38	500	45	0	DNF–Engine	3,175	49	0	25	-2,190	Earnhardt
23	24	Sept. 27	Martinsville—Goody's 500	10	10	500	492	0	Running	8,345	134	0	25	-2,236	Earnhardt
24	25	Oct. 4	North Wilkesboro—Holly Farms 400	14	18	400	394	0	Running	4,995	109	0	25	-2,302	Earnhardt
25	26	Oct. 11	Charlotte—Oakwood Homes 500	40	34	334	102	0	DNF–Engine	5,285	61	0	25	-2,373	Earnhardt
26	27	Oct. 25	Rockingham—AC Delco 500	20	16	492	486	0	Running	7,460	115	0	25	-2,433	Earnhardt
27	28	Nov. 8	Riverside—Winston Western 500	39	17	119	116	0	Running	5,370	112	0	25	-2,399	Earnhardt
28	29	Nov. 22	Atlanta—Atlanta Journal 500	33	36	328	84	0	DNF–Clutch	4,065	55	0	25	-2,519	Earnhardt

[1] —Took over No. 18 Chevrolet after Tommy Ellis quit.

1988: Musical Rides, Escorting a Legend

After his surprise ride in 1987, Dale Jarrett found himself in another unusual situation the following season when he signed with NASCAR legend Cale Yarborough. That is, Jarrett steered Yarborough's No. 29 Oldsmobile when Yarborough himself wasn't driving it.

The retiring Yarborough used the 1988 season as his farewell tour, bringing to an end one of the truly great American racing careers. In a 31-year career, Yarborough won three Winston Cup championships (consecutively in 1976, 1977, and 1978), 83 races, and 70 poles. His 1977 title-winning season, in which he became the first driver to reach the 5,000-point mark under NASCAR's current point system, was arguably the best season ever assembled by a NASCAR driver. Eleven years after that amazing season, the 49-year-old Yarborough committed to drive a limited 10-race schedule, focusing his attention on NASCAR's biggest tracks (Daytona, Atlanta, Charlotte, Talladega, and Michigan).

Though he was a part-time driver, Yarborough wanted to be a full-time owner. To drive his car in the season's other 19 races, he hired Jarrett. Fortunately for Jarrett, this unusual arrangement was supplemented with rides in the other 10 races, in effect allowing the 31-year-old to run a full schedule. In other words, Jarrett drove all 29 races, just not in the same car.

The result was a dizzying round of musical rides. Jarrett switched cars 15 times during the course of the season. Besides Yarborough's Olds, he also hopped into cars owned by Hoss Ellington, Buddy Arrington, and Ralph Ball. Despite the constant change, Jarrett saw improvement in his performance and enjoyed expanded opportunities. Most significantly, he competed in his first Daytona 500, an event on which he would make an indelible mark later in his career. In the 1988 Daytona 500, Jarrett started 36th but climbed to a 16th-place finish. Though a seemingly minor accomplishment, the race marked the first time Jarrett finished a race on the lead lap, ending his dubious 28-race lead-lapless streak.

At Riverside, Jarrett achieved two more first-time milestones by cracking the Top 10 (with an eighth-place finish) and by leading a lap. Considering his difficulties on road courses throughout his career, the fact that Jarrett hit these early marks at Riverside—a winding 2.63-mile track—should keep NASCAR trivia buffs stumped for years to come.

Though he tasted success in 1988, the constant car-hopping proved to be difficult to overcome. Jarrett ran five more races than he had the previous season but barely improved in point standings (he finished 23rd versus 25th in 1987). His 14 DNFs were the third highest total in the series.

Cale and Dale

Cale Yarborough drove a limited schedule during his farewell season in 1988, competing in 10 of 29 races. He hired Jarrett to drive his car in the other 19. Below is a look at the No. 29 team's season, broken down by driver.

Driver	Starts	Avg. Start	Avg. Finish	Laps Led	Money	Total Points
Dale Jarrett	19	22.3	21.7	4	$68,515	1,863
Cale Yarborough	10	26.9	23.5	6	66,065	940
No. 29 Team Totals	29	23.9	22.4	10	134,580	2,803

Cale vs. Dale

Jarrett had the opportunity to race against his boss in 10 races during the 1988 season. Here's a comparison of their head-to-head performances at Atlanta, Charlotte, Daytona, Michigan, and Talladega.

Driver	Best Finish	Avg. Start	Avg. Finish	Laps Led	Money	Total Points
Dale Jarrett	11th	28.6	29.2	1	42,125	759
Cale Yarborough	9th (twice)	26.9	23.5	6	66,065	940

Jarrett in 1988

Category	Total	Rank	1988 Leader
Money	$118,640	31st	Bill Elliott—$1,554,639
Total points	2,622	23rd	Bill Elliott—4,488
Avg. start	24.5	30th	Geoffrey Bodine—6.8
Avg. finish	24.3	32nd	Bill Elliott—6.6
Wins	0	—	Bill Elliott—6
Top 5s	0	—	Rusty Wallace—19
Top 10s	1	30th	Rusty Wallace—23
DNFs	14	3rd	Derrike Cope—16
Poles	0	—	Bill Elliott—6
Front row starts	0	—	Bill Elliott—10
Laps led	5	34th	Dale Earnhardt—1,808
Races led	2	30th	Earnhardt, Elliott—20
Times led	2	31st	Dale Earnhardt—63
Miles led	13	31st	Bill Elliott—1,851
Times led most laps	0	—	Dale Earnhardt—7
Bonus points	10	30th	Dale Earnhardt—135
Laps completed	6,556	25th	Bill Elliott—9,647
Miles completed	8,161	25th	Bill Elliott—11,521
Points per race	90.4	33rd	Bill Elliott—154.8
Lead-lap finishes	4	20th	Rusty Wallace—21

1988 Performance Chart
No. 29 Yarborough Motorsports Oldsmobile

Career Race	Race No.	Date	Race	St.	Total Fin.	Laps Laps	Laps Completed	Led	Condition	Money	Bonus Pts.	Point Pts.	Current Standing	Behind Leader	Current Leader
29	1	Feb. 14	Daytona—Daytona 500[1]	36	16	200	200	0	Running	$18,845	115	0	16	-70	B. Allison
30	2	Feb. 21	Richmond—Pontiac Excitement 400[2]	32	26	400	337	0	DNF—Crash	1,510	85	0	21	-145	Bonnett
31	3	Mar. 6	Rockingham—Goodwrench 500	7	16	492	488	0	Running	3,370	115	0	19	-215	Bonnett
32	4	Mar. 20	Atlanta—Motorcraft Quality Parts 500[3]	40	29	328	164	0	DNF—Brakes	2,175	76	0	20	-241	Bonnett
33	5	Mar. 27	Darlington—TranSouth 500[4]	32	12	367	362	0	Running	3,520	127	0	19	-240	Earnhardt
34	6	Apr. 10	Bristol—Valleydale Meats 500	25	28	500	129	0	DNF—Mechanical	1,360	79	0	22	-287	Earnhardt
35	7	Apr. 17	North Wilkesboro—First Union 400	21	21	400	393	0	Running	1,510	100	0	24	-362	Earnhardt
36	8	Apr. 24	Martinsville—Pannill Sweatshirts 500	13	13	500	491	0	Running	2,470	124	0	20	-423	Earnhardt
37	9	May 1	Talladega—Winston 500[5]	28	11	188	188	0	Running	9,790	130	0	19	-431	Earnhardt
38	10	May 29	Charlotte—Coca-Cola 600[6]	39	41	400	27	0	DNF—Engine	4,200	40	0	22	-515	Earnhardt
39	11	June 5	Dover—Budweiser 500[4]	35	20	500	492	0	Running	3,700	103	0	22	-527	Earnhardt
40	12	June 12	Riverside—Budweiser 400	19	8	95	95	4	Running	5,000	147	5	21	-549	R. Wallace
41	13	June 19	Pocono—Miller High Life 500	20	13	200	199	0	Running	5,950	124	0	20	-595	R. Wallace
42	14	June 26	Michigan—Miller High Life 400[5]	33	25	200	183	0	Running	3,255	88	0	20	-692	R. Wallace
43	15	July 2	Daytona—Pepsi Firecracker 400	17	14	160	159	0	Running	4,705	121	0	19	-698	R. Wallace
44	16	July 24	Pocono—AC Spark Plug 500[4]	21	25	200	188	0	Running	3,425	88	0	19	-701	R. Wallace
45	17	July 31	Talladega—Talladega DieHard 500[5]	26	37	188	141	1	DNF—Engine	2,795	57	5	21	-799	R. Wallace
46	18	Aug. 14	Watkins Glen—The Bud at the Glen[4]	18	11	90	90	0	Running	6,180	130	0	18	-844	R. Wallace
47	19	Aug. 21	Michigan—Champion Spark Plug 400[5]	11	41	200	50	0	DNF—Mechanical	2,210	40	0	20	-984	R. Wallace
48	20	Aug. 27	Bristol—Busch 500[4]	15	26	500	207	0	DNF—Crash	2,325	85	0	22	-1,053	Elliott
49	21	Sept. 4	Darlington—Southern 500	18	34	367	239	0	DNF—Engine	2,850	61	0	22	-1,177	Elliott
50	22	Sept. 11	Richmond—Miller High Life 400	33	15	400	395	0	Running	4,430	118	0	20	-1,210	Elliott
51	23	Sept. 18	Dover—Delaware 500	17	28	500	377	0	DNF—Crash	3,400	79	0	19	-1,316	Elliott
52	24	Sept. 25	Martinsville—Goody's 500	25	32	500	14	0	DNF—Engine	1,310	67	0	22	-1,404	Elliott
53	25	Oct. 9	Charlotte—Oakwood Homes 500[5]	22	37	334	78	0	DNF—Engine	1,530	52	0	22	-1,517	Elliott
54	26	Oct. 16	North Wilkesboro—Holly Farms 400[4]	19	23	400	395	0	Running	2,250	94	0	22	-1,583	Elliott
55	27	Oct. 23	Rockingham—AC Delco 500	22	32	492	255	0	DNF—Engine	2,450	67	0	23	-1,686	Elliott
56	28	Nov. 6	Phoenix—Checker 500	32	31	312	215	0	DNF—Engine	2,600	70	0	23	-1,776	Elliott
57	29	Nov. 20	Atlanta—Atlanta Journal 500[5]	34	41	328	5	0	DNF—Crash	1,525	40	0	23	-1,866	Elliott

[1] —Drove No. 1 Hoss Ellington Buick
[2] —Switched to No. 29 Yarborough Motorsports Olds
[3] —Switched to No. 99 Ralph Ball Chevrolet
[4] —Returned to No. 29 Yarborough Motorsports Olds
[5] —Returned to No. 1 Hoss Ellington Buick
[6] —Switched to No. 67 Arrington Racing Chevrolet

1989: A Ride of One's Own

The 1989 season presented Dale Jarrett with a career novelty: his own ride, for a full season, from beginning to end. After taking over a ride in-season in 1987, then splitting a ride with Cale Yarborough in 1988, Jarrett was retained by Yarborough as the full-time driver of the No. 29 Yarborough Motorsports Pontiac.

For Jarrett, the season saw more baby steps: continued improvement, but nothing like a breakthrough. The 32-year-old continued a natural, deliberate progression in his performance, cracking the Top 5 for the first time in his career and claiming a career-high of five Top 10 finishes. He also led many more laps—99—than he had in either of his previous seasons.

The highlight of Jarrett's season was the fall race at Martinsville, where he earned his first Top 5 finish in 81 career races. In fact, Jarrett even threatened to win the race. Starting 25th, he climbed steadily through the field and took the lead from Darrell Waltrip on lap 251. Jarrett led the next 96 laps consecutively, the longest sustained lead by any driver during the race.

Though he eventually faded to fifth, Jarrett had victory in his sight for the first time in his Winston Cup career (he had three Busch Grand National series wins by 1989). The setting for Jarrett's first strong run was fitting. He drove late models and Busch cars at Martinsville in the early 1980s (winning a BGN pole in 1983) and got his first Winston Cup start there in 1984 in Emanuel Zervakis' No. 2 Chevrolet. Of all the Winston Cup tracks, the tiny .526-mile Virginia oval most resembled his original home track, the claustrophobic .353-mile Hickory (North Carolina) Motor Speedway.

Following Martinsville, Jarrett needed just four more races to record his second career Top 5, this time at Phoenix. Starting 31st, he stayed on the lead lap and climbed to a fifth-place finish. Earlier in the season, Jarrett had knocked on the Top 5 door with a seventh-place finish at Pocono, a race he led for one lap.

Jarrett's bright spots in 1989 were special and rare, however. He qualified poorly throughout the season, starting just one race in the Top 10. Generally, he finished only slightly better than he started. His average finish of 22.7 was a marginal improvement on his 24.2 average during the previous two seasons. He finished outside of the Top 20 17 times in 29 races and ended 40th or worse three times. Equally discouraging was the number of Jarrett's DNFs—11—which reached double digits for the third time in his three Winston Cup seasons. The result was a worse points finish than in 1988 (Jarrett dropped one spot to 24th).

Though he had run up front in the Busch series for six seasons and then revealed signs of promise in inferior Winston Cup equipment, Jarrett was approaching his 100th start with depressingly little to show for his effort: zero wins, two Top 5s, and just eight Top 10s.

Being in the fishbowl environment of NASCAR stardom is nothing new for Jarrett, especially at Daytona. In 2000, he won the Bud Shootout, the Daytona 500 pole and the Daytona 500.

Jarrett in 1989

Category	Total	Rank	1989 Leader
Money	$232,317	22nd	Rusty Wallace—$2,237,950
Total points	2,789	24th	Rusty Wallace—4,176
Avg. start	24.2	29th	Mark Martin—5.3
Avg. finish	22.7	30th	Dale Earnhardt—10.2
Wins	0	—	D. Waltrip, R. Wallace—6
Top 5s	2	16th	Earnhardt, Martin, Waltrip—14
Top 10s	5	20th	Rusty Wallace—20
DNFs	11	5th	G. Sacks, J. Means—13
Poles	0	—	A. Kulwicki, M. Martin—6
Front row starts	0	—	Mark Martin—9
Laps led	99	15th	Dale Earnhardt—2,735
Races led	3	25th	Rusty Wallace—23
Times led	3	25th	Dale Earnhardt—88
Miles led	55	17th	Dale Earnhardt—2,624
Times led most laps	0	—	Rusty Wallace—9
Bonus points	15	25th	Rusty Wallace—160
Laps completed	7,798	22nd	Darrell Waltrip—9,333
Miles completed	9,178	26th	Ricky Rudd—11,075
Points per race	96.2	30th	Rusty Wallace—144.0
Lead-lap finishes	3	21st	Dale Earnhardt—19

1989 Performance Chart
No. 29 Yarborough Motorsports Pontiac

Career Race	Race No.	Date	Race	St.	Fin.	Total Laps	Laps Completed	Laps Led	Condition	Money	Pts.	Bonus Pts.	Point Standing	Behind Leader	Points Leader*
58	1	Feb. 19	Daytona—Daytona 500	20	32	200	131	0	Running	$15,000	67	0	31	-113	D. Waltrip
59	2	Mar. 5	Rockingham—Goodwrench 500	21	11	492	489	2	Running	8,525	135	5	19	-133	Earnhardt
60	3	Mar. 19	Atlanta—Motorcraft Quality Parts 500	10	9	328	324	0	Running	11,200	138	0	10	-170	Earnhardt
61	4	Mar. 26	Richmond—Pontiac Excitement 400	32	23	400	390	0	Running	4,025	94	0	14	-246	Earnhardt
62	5	Apr. 2	Darlington—TranSouth 500	9	40	367	83	0	DNF—Engine	3,645	43	0	24	-290	Kulwicki
63	6	Apr. 9	Bristol—Valleydale Meats 500	20	22	500	440	0	Running	4,520	97	0	24	-326	G. Bodine
64	7	Apr. 16	North Wilkesboro—First Union 400	18	19	400	383	0	Running	4,745	106	0	25	-374	Earnhardt
65	8	Apr. 23	Martinsville—Pannill Sweatshirts 500	23	15	500	495	0	Running	6,070	118	0	25	-431	Earnhardt
66	9	May 7	Talladega—Winston 500	28	40	188	37	0	DNF—Crash	5,375	43	0	24	-535	Earnhardt
67	10	May 28	Charlotte—Coca-Cola 600	24	28	400	331	0	DNF—Engine	5,200	79.	0	26	-559	D. Waltrip
68	11	June 4	Dover—Budweiser 500	14	11	500	494	0	Running	8,025	130	0	23	-567	D. Waltrip
69	12	June 11	Sears Point—Banquet Frozen Foods 300	33	42	74	8	0	DNF—Transmission	4,250	37	0	25	-688	Earnhardt
70	13	June 18	Pocono—Miller High Life 500	14	7	200	200	1	Running	11,150	151	5	23	-707	Earnhardt
71	14	June 25	Michigan—Miller High Life 400	18	22	200	197	0	Running	6,785	97	0	24	-722	Earnhardt
72	15	July 1	Daytona—Pepsi 400	30	31	160	108	0	DNF—Crash	5,510	70	0	25	-766	Earnhardt
73	16	July 23	Pocono—AC Spark Plug 500	17	18	200	198	0	Running	7,550	109	0	26	-800	Earnhardt
74	17	July 30	Talladega—Talladega DieHard 500	41	23	188	184	0	Running	7,235	94	0	25	-836	Earnhardt
75	18	Aug. 13	Watkins Glen—The Bud at the Glen	14	23	90	87	0	DNF—Engine	5,480	94	0	26	-912	Earnhardt
76	19	Aug. 20	Michigan—Champion Spark Plug 400	27	38	200	119	0	DNF—Mechanical	5,350	49	0	26	-975	Earnhardt
77	20	Aug. 26	Bristol—Busch 500	30	10	500	494	0	Running	10,975	134	0	25	-967	Earnhardt
78	21	Sept. 3	Darlington—Heinz Southern 500	26	20	367	361	0	Running	7,810	103	0	25	-1,049	Earnhardt
79	22	Sept. 10	Richmond—Miller High Life 400	26	35	400	17	0	DNF—Crash	3,675	58	0	25	-1,166	Earnhardt
80	23	Sept. 17	Dover—Peak Performance 500	28	23	500	472	0	DNF—Engine	5,400	94	0	25	-1,257	Earnhardt
81	24	Sept. 24	Martinsville—Goody's 500	25	5	500	500	96	Running	15,125	160	5	24	-1,240	Earnhardt
82	25	Oct. 8	Charlotte—All Pro Auto Parts 500	29	24	334	328	0	Running	5,450	91	0	24	-1,221	R. Wallace
83	26	Oct. 15	North Wilkesboro—Holly Farms 400	25	27	400	218	0	DNF—Overheating	3,830	82	0	24	-1,285	R. Wallace
84	27	Oct. 22	Rockingham—AC Delco 500	32	39	492	74	0	DNF—Clutch	4,450	46	0	25	-1,419	R. Wallace
85	28	Nov. 5	Phoenix—Autoworks 500	31	5	312	312	0	Running	22,112	155	0	24	-1,384	R. Wallace
86	29	Nov. 19	Atlanta—Atlanta Journal 500	37	16	328	324	0	Running	6,850	115	0	24	-1,387	.R. Wallace

1990: Providing Relief .... Again

Christmas time at the Jarrett household was often spent discussing Dale's next racing opportunity, or lack thereof. Since starting his Winston Cup career in 1987, Jarrett rarely possessed firm plans for the upcoming season. Christmas 1989 was no different.

Any sense of stability enjoyed by Dale Jarrett during the 1989 campaign, his first full-time Winston Cup ride, disappeared during the off-season when his car owner, Cale Yarborough, dropped him in favor of Dick Trickle. Jarrett started the 1990 Winston Cup season on the sidelines, returning to the Busch series and appearing once again to be at a starting point in his career.

Then history repeated itself, kind of. Five races into the 1990 season, fan favorite Neil Bonnett suffered severe head injuries in a wreck at Darlington. The accident occurred 212 laps into the TranSouth 500 when Ernie Irvan, who was 10 laps down at the time, collided with race leader Ken Schrader on a restart and ignited a wreck that included Bonnett. Though it initially did not appear serious, the crash would sideline Bonnett for nearly three years. (When Bonnett attempted to make a full comeback in 1994, he lost control of his car and was killed while practicing for the Daytona 500.)

With the extent of Bonnett's injuries unknown, the No. 21 Wood Brothers Ford suddenly found itself driverless. The legendary Wood brothers looked to Jarrett for relief. Out of Winston Cup racing for the first time in three years, he eagerly accepted the opportunity.

For Jarrett, the scenario was all too familiar. As in 1987, he was taking over a driverless team six races into the season. Also similar to 1987, he earned the right to stay in the car for the rest of the season by making a favorable impression immediately.

In his first race for the Wood Brothers, the Valleydale Meats 500 at Bristol, Jarrett qualified 12th, took the lead on lap 90, led 39 laps, and finished 11th. After staying with the Top 5 for much of the race, Jarrett's hopes for a top finish were dashed when he and Irvan, his future teammate, got together while battling on lap 354. Despite the clash with Irvan, Jarrett's effort matched the Wood Brothers' best finish of the season (Bonnett had finished 11th in the Daytona 500). That finish helped him secure the confidence of his new team.

Perhaps the most crucial aspect of Jarrett's 1990 experience was his exposure to an experienced and successful ownership team that offered better equipment than he had ever enjoyed. His performance reflected this new reality. Following Bristol, Jarrett managed a 14th at North Wilkesboro and added Top 10s at Daytona (8th), again at Bristol (7th), and at Dover (6th). He closed the season with the best race of his Winston Cup career, a fourth-place finish in the season-ending Atlanta race.

The best indication of Jarrett's stronger, more reliable cars was his improved qualifying and finishes. He bettered his average start by an astonishing 10 positions per race, and finished an average of four positions higher in the final race order. When the Wood Brothers offered Jarrett a full-time ride for the 1991 season, fans and insiders wondered: Could Dale contend for wins and a championship with one of NASCAR's most storied teams?

Making Gains

A comparison of Jarrett's performance in 1990 versus his first three seasons on the Winston Cup circuit

Year	Starts	Avg. Start	Avg. Finish	DNFs
1990	24	15.2	19.4	8
1987-89	82	25.3	23.7	36

Jarrett in 1990

Category	Total	Rank	1990 Leader
Money	$214,495	26th	Dale Earnhardt—3,083,056
Total points	2,558	25th	Dale Earnhardt—4,430
Avg. start	15.2	15th	Mark Martin—5.4
Avg. finish	19.4	20th	Mark Martin—6.6
Wins	0	—	Dale Earnhardt—9
Top 5s	1	22nd	Dale Earnhardt—18
Top 10s	7	19th	Earnhardt, Martin—23
DNFs	9	7th	Rick Wilson, Rob Moroso—15
Poles	0	—	Dale Earnhardt—4
Front row starts	0	—	Mark Martin—11
Laps led	73	18th	Dale Earnhardt—2,438
Races led	4	20th	Dale Earnhardt—22
Times led	5	22nd	Dale Earnhardt—84
Miles led	44	21st	Dale Earnhardt—3,203
Times led most laps	0	—	Dale Earnhardt—10
Bonus points	20	20th	Dale Earnhardt—160
Laps completed	6,802	28th	Mark Martin—9,636
Miles completed	7,699	29th	Mark Martin—11,487
Points per race	106.6	20th	Dale Earnhardt—152.8
Lead-lap finishes	4	20th	Mark Martin—22

1990 Performance Chart
No. 21 Wood Brothers Ford

Career Race	Race No.	Date	Race	St.	Fin.	Total Laps	Laps Completed	Laps Led	Condition	Money	Pts.	Bonus Pts.	Current Standing	Behind Leader	Current Leader
87	6	Apr. 8	Bristol—Valleydale Meats 500[1]	12	11	500	493	39	Running	$8,300	135	5	41	-810	Earnhardt
88	7	Apr. 22	North Wilkesboro—First Union 400	16	14	400	399	0	Running	5,975	121	0	37	-859	Earnhardt
89	8	Apr. 29	Martinsville—Hanes Activewear 500	5	30	500	171	0	DNF–Clutch	4,050	73	0	35	-946	Earnhardt
90	9	May 6	Talladega—Winston 500	16	34	188	103	0	DNF–Crash	7,230	61	0	35	-1,070	Earnhardt
91	10	May 27	Charlotte—Coca-Cola 600	19	32	400	241	4	DNF–Engine	7,120	72	5	33	-1,071	Earnhardt
92	11	June 3	Dover—Budweiser 500	17	12	500	498	0	Running	8,425	127	0	31	-1,073	Shepherd
93	12	June 10	Sears Point—Banquet Frozen Foods 300	10	14	74	74	0	Running	5,800	121	0	30	-1,090	Martin
94	13	June 17	Pocono—Miller Genuine Draft 500	13	31	200	171	0	DNF–Crash	6,425	70	0	30	-1,146	Martin
95	14	June 24	Michigan—Miller Genuine Draft 400	26	34	200	101	0	DNF–Transmission	7,010	61	0	30	-1,250	Martin
96	15	July 7	Daytona—Pepsi 400	24	8	160	160	0	Running	13,500	142	0	29	-1,238	Martin
97	16	July 19	Pocono—AC Spark Plug 500	18	18	200	198	0	Running	7,950	109	0	29	-1,279	Martin
98	17	July 26	Talladega—DieHard 500	22	39	188	51	0	DNF–Engine	7,005	46	0	29	-1,371	Martin
99	18	Aug. 12	Watkins Glen—The Bud at the Glen	26	20	90	89	0	Running	7,445	103	0	29	-1,428	Martin
100	19	Aug. 19	Michigan—Champion Spark Plug 400	16	10	200	200	0	Running	14,825	134	0	29	-1,479	Martin
101	20	Aug. 25	Bristol—Busch 500	9	7	500	499	29	Running	9,850	151	5	29	-1,493	Martin
102	21	Sept. 2	Darlington—Heinz Southern 500	18	28	367	241	1	DNF–Crash	6,655	84	5	29	-1,559	Martin
103	22	Sept. 9	Richmond—Miller Genuine Draft 400	13	29	400	272	0	DNF–Crash	4,355	76	0	29	-1,658	Martin
104	23	Sept. 16	Dover—Peak AntiFreeze 500	11	6	500	499	0	Running	13,675	150	0	28	-1,683	Martin
105	24	Sept. 23	Martinsville—Goody's 500	6	10	500	497	0	Running	10,725	34	0	28	-1,719	Martin
106	25	Sept. 30	North Wilkesboro—Tyson/Holly Farms 400	4	19	400	396	0	Running	5,150	106	0	28	-1,793	Martin
107	26	Oct. 7	Charlotte—Mello Yello 500	11	10	334	333	0	Running	14,625	134	0	27	-1,780	Martin
108	27	Oct. 21	Rockingham—AC Delco 500	10	16	492	489	0	Running	8,525	115	0	27	-1,795	Martin
109	28	Nov. 4	Phoenix—Checker 500	21	30	312	299	0	DNF–Accident	6,395	73	0	26	-1,862	Earnhardt
110	29	Nov. 18	Atlanta—Atlanta Journal 500	21	4	328	328	0	Running	17,225	160	0	25	-1,872	Earnhardt

[1]—Took over No. 21 Ford for Neil Bonnett, who suffered head injuries in a crash during Race No. 5 at Darlington

In 1990, Jarrett took over the No. 21 Citgo Ford after its driver, Neil Bonnett, was injured at Darlington. Jarrett immediately endeared himself with his new car owners, the storied Wood Brothers, when he led 39 laps and finished 11th at Bristol in his first start.

1991: First Career Win

With Neil Bonnett still sidelined by blurred vision (due to his 1990 wreck at Darlington), the Wood Brothers turned to Dale Jarrett once again to fill the driver's seat of their No. 21 Citgo Ford. It was an easy decision considering Jarrett's promising performance after taking over for Bonnett the previous season.

Jarrett repaid the Wood Brothers' loyalty with the best performance of his career. The 34-year-old won his first Winston Cup race in 1991, a stirring victory over wunderkind Davey Allison at Michigan. Accompanying the victory was creeping consistency and the first string of Top 10 finishes in his career—four, to be exact.

"The Streak" got started at Pocono, where Jarrett finished sixth. The following week, he finished eighth at Talladega (after starting 40th). On the road course at Watkins Glen, he steered his Ford to a fifth-place finish.

At Michigan, all signs pointed to just "another" solid Top 10 finish for Jarrett, nothing more. But when the caution flag waved with 12 laps to go, Jarrett and his crew gambled. As one of just nine cars on the lead lap, they decided to pit for gas only, a good news/bad news strategy that gave Jarrett the lead, but also forced him to drive the final nine-lap dash on old tires.

Allison, the race's dominant driver and the leader before the caution, took on new tires but dropped back to sixth place in the running order. After the restart, Allison navigated to the front of the field and caught Jarrett with two laps remaining. The two pedigreed drivers raced side by side over the final 4 miles of the race before Jarrett inched ahead, literally, for the win. Jarrett's car crossed the finish line less than a foot ahead of Allison's No. 28 Ford.

The win was the first Winston Cup/Grand National victory for a driver named Jarrett since 1965 when Dale's father, Ned, claimed the last of his 50 wins in the Tidewater 300 at Dog Track Speedway, a 1/3-mile oval located in Moyock, North Carolina.

Besides his milestone victory, Jarrett enjoyed career highs in Top-5 and Top-10 finishes. He started his season on a high note, finishing a career-best sixth in the Daytona 500. In typical Jarrett fashion, however, the season was ultimately a mini-breakthrough, a solid step forward, but still one in a line of baby steps he had taken since joining the Winston Cup series full-time in 1987. Though his performance was improving, he was not getting much closer to a championship or anything like a championship effort. Despite having a career year, Jarrett finished the season well outside of the Top 10 in points: 15th, 1,163 points behind champion Dale Earnhardt. Similarly, he didn't crack the Top 10 in any major statistical category, except one, DNFs. His nine DNFs were eighth most in the Winston Cup series in 1991.

Luckily for Jarrett, car owners look past yesterday's struggles while searching for upside potential. Like investors, they seek high-return deals before they have reached their peak. In 1991, a new car owner name Joe Gibbs was looking for the right kind of driver. He was looking for a driver who appeared to be on the verge of realizing his potential. Jarrett was Gibbs' man.

Slow Starter

Dale Jarrett needed 129 starts before getting his first victory, many more than other recent Winston Cup champions.

Driver	No. of Starts	First Victory
Dale Jarrett	129	1991 Michigan
Alan Kulwicki	85	1988 Phoenix
Bobby Labonte	74	1995 Charlotte
Rusty Wallace	72	1986 Bristol
Terry Labonte	59	1980 Darlington
Jeff Gordon	42	1994 Charlotte
Dale Earnhardt	16	1979 Bristol

Jarrett in 1991

Category	Total	Rank	1991 Leader
Money	$444,256	15th	Dale Earnhardt—2,416,685
Total points	3,124	17th	Dale Earnhardt—4,287
Avg. start	16.4	15th	Alan Kulwicki—6.8
Avg. finish	19.4	19th	Dale Earnhardt—8.6
Wins	1	8th	D. Allison, Gant – 5
Top 5s	3	16th	Harry Gant – 15
Top 10s	8	16th	Dale Earnhardt—21
DNFs	9	8th	D. Cope, J. Spencer—14
Poles	0	—	Mark Martin—5
Front row starts	0	—	Kulwicki, Martin—8
Laps led	47	21st	Harry Gant—1,684
Races led	7	14th	Davey Allison—23
Times led	9	17th	Davey Allison—72
Miles led	80	20th	Davey Allison—1,879
Times led most laps	0	—	D. Allison, Gant—5
Bonus points	35	15th	Davey Allison—140
Laps completed	7,767	26th	Ricky Rudd—9,561
Miles completed	9,438	25th	Dale Earnhardt—11,435
Points per race	107.7	18th	Dale Earnhardt—147.8
Lead-lap finishes	9	11th	Dale Earnhardt—17

1991 Performance Chart
No. 21 Wood Brothers Ford

Career Race	Race No.	Date	Race	St.	Fin.	Total Laps	Laps Completed	Laps Led	Condition	Money	Pts.	Bonus Pts.	Current Standing	Behind Leader	Current Leader*
111	1	Feb. 17	Daytona—Daytona 500 by STP	17	6	200	199	0	Running	$74,900	150	0	6	-30	Irvan
112	2	Feb. 24	Richmond—Pontiac Excitement 400	13	21	400	392	0	Running	5,825	100	0	9	-90	Earnhardt
113	3	Mar. 3	Rockingham—GM Goodwrench 500	18	11	492	488	0	Running	11,100	130	0	8	-102	Earnhardt
114	4	Mar. 18	Atlanta—Motorcraft Quality Parts 500	22	20	328	325	0	Running	10,470	103	0	12	-169	Earnhardt
115	5	Apr. 4-7	Darlington—TranSouth 500	14	39	367	30	0	DNF– Crash	5,670	46	0	19	-279	Rudd
116	6	Apr. 17	Bristol—Valleydale Meats 500	18	7	500	500	0	Running	10,775	146	0	17	-298	Rudd
117	7	Apr. 21	North Wilkesboro—First Union 400	6	25	400	369	0	DNF–Crash	5,500	88	0	17	-340	Rudd
118	8	Apr. 28	Martinsville—Hanes 500	7	12	500	495	0	Running	7,900	127	0	17	-343	Rudd
119	9	May 6	Talladega—Winston 500	22	35	188	70	0	DNF–Crash	7,850	58	0	21	-418	Earnhardt
120	10	May 26	Charlotte—Coca-Cola 600	12	5	400	400	3	Running	27,400	160	5	15	-428	Earnhardt
121	11	June 2	Dover—Budweiser 500	20	35	500	18	0	DNF–Crash	5,600	58	0	17	-550	Earnhardt
122	12	June 9	Sears Point—Banquet Frozen Foods 300	21	41	74	46	1	DNF–Ignition	5,475	45	5	20	-651	Earnhardt
123	13	June 16	Pocono—Champion Spark Plug 500	25	19	200	200	0	Running	8,250	106	0	20	-720	Earnhardt
124	14	June 23	Michigan—Miller Genuine Draft 400	14	12	200	199	0	Running	12,825	127	0	17	-758	Earnhardt
125	15	July 6	Daytona—Pepsi 400	31	18	160	160	0	Running	9,810	109	0	18	-800	Earnhardt
126	16	July 21	Pocono—Miller Genuine Draft 500	12	6	179	179	3	Running	13,700	155	5	17	-742	Earnhardt
127	17	July 28	Talladega—DieHard 500	40	8	188	188	8	Running	14,400	147	5	17	-780	Earnhardt
128	18	July 11	Watkins Glen—The Bud at the Glen	14	5	90	90	0	Running	18,565	155	0	15	-748	Earnhardt
129	19	Aug. 18	Michigan—Champion Spark Plug 400	11	1	200	200	12	Running	74,150	180	5	13	-659	Earnhardt
130	20	Aug. 24	Bristol—Bud 500	16	28	500	253	0	DNF–Crash	5,500	79	0	15	-726	Earnhardt
131	21	Sept. 1	Darlington—Heinz Southern 500	8	25	367	350	1	Running	7,545	93	5	14	-780	Earnhardt
132	22	Sept. 7	Richmond—Miller Genuine Draft 400	25	20	400	396	0	Running	6,925	103	0	15	-812	Earnhardt
133	23	Sept. 15	Dover—Peak AntiFreeze 500	8	34	500	68	0	DNF–Crash	5,800	61	0	16	-874	Earnhardt
134	24	Sept. 22	Martinsville—Goody's 500	20	18	500	496	0	Running	6,755	109	0	16	-935	Earnhardt
135	25	Sept. 29	North Wilkesboro—Tyson/Holly Farms 400	5	9	400	400	0	Running	7,975	138	0	16	-977	Earnhardt
136	26	Oct. 6	Charlotte—Mello Yello 500	22	26	334	302	0	DNF–Valve	6,388	85	0	16	-985	Earnhardt
137	27	Oct. 20	Rockingham—AC Delco 500	8	25	492	479	0	Running	7,275	88	0	17	-1,043	Earnhardt
138	28	Nov. 3	Phoenix—Pyroil 500	17	35	312	151	19	DNF–Engine	6,000	63	5	17	-1,118	Earnhardt
139	29	Nov. 17	Atlanta—Hardee's 500	10	16	328	324	0	Running	8,750	115	0	17	-1,163	Earnhardt

A consistently strong competitor at Michigan, Jarrett scored his first career victory on the two-mile oval in 1991 when he beat Davey Allison to the finish line by less than a foot. Here, Jarrett edges ahead of Dale Earnhardt during the 2000 Pepsi 400.

1992: Driving for the Coach

In 1992, Joe Gibbs enjoyed perhaps the grandest entrance of any new Winston Cup owner in series history. Less than a month after winning his third Super Bowl as head coach of the Washington Redskins, he witnessed his first Daytona 500 as the proud owner of the No. 18 Interstate Batteries Chevy Lumina.

While preparing his new NASCAR enterprise, Gibbs displayed an instant understanding of NASCAR's family-oriented culture, hiring brothers-in-law Jimmy Makar and Dale Jarrett to assume the two highest profile jobs in his fledgling organization: Makar as crew chief and Jarrett as driver.

For Jarrett, the situation was ideal. Now with his fourth Winston Cup organization in six seasons, he finally had his *own* team. Gibbs' team and, more important, his cars would be built around him. Dale Jarrett was no longer a relief driver, a convenient substitute, or simply the best alternative. He was a *real* Winston Cup driver, possessing the same focus and resources that other top drivers enjoyed.

Despite the anticipation and favorable circumstances, the rookie reality of Gibbs Racing's first season quickly set in. At Speedweeks in Daytona, Jarrett crashed out of his Twin 125 qualifying race and was forced to start the Daytona 500 in 35th position. In the 500, Jarrett got caught in the race's field-thinning wreck on lap 91. He finished 36th.

When Jarrett finished 37th the following week at Rockingham, he and Gibbs Racing suddenly found themselves mired in 35th place in the championship point standings. Jarrett could not escape bad luck. At the second Talladega race, he took the lead on lap 125 (of 188), only to run out of gas four laps later. He finished two laps down as a result of the miscalculation and ended in 21st place.

A month later at Michigan, another strong run was nullified when Jarrett was caught on pit road when the caution flag came out. He made up the lap but settled for eighth place. The following week in the Southern 500, Jarrett started 17th, marched to fifth by lap 60, led 21 laps, and appeared to be a contender. Then it rained … and kept on raining. The final 100 miles of the race were never run, leaving a dejected Jarrett in sixth place (his career-best Southern 500 finish until 1997).

When he escaped the effects of bad luck, Jarrett enjoyed strong finishes at Bristol (where he led a season-high 38 laps and finished second) and Daytona in July. By leading 26 laps and finishing third in the Pepsi 400, Jarrett gave his best early indication that he could compete with the best at the legendary 2.5-mile track.

Jarrett also logged Top 10 finishes at Talladega, Pocono, North Wilkesboro, and Atlanta. His most positive signs in 1992 were fundamental improvements: He finished more races and finished them well. Gibbs' cars were the most reliable of Jarrett's career (he had a career-low five DNFs in 1992) and his average finish improved to a career-best 17.8.

Despite a handful of bright spots, Jarrett took a step back from most of the gains he made with the Wood Brothers in 1991. He dropped two spots in the point standings (finishing 19th), failed to win a race, and finished in the Top 5 one fewer time. Underscoring Jarrett regression was the comparative success of Morgan Shepherd, who took over for Jarrett in the No. 21 Wood Brothers Ford and thrived. Shepherd (14th) beat Jarrett in the final point standings and bettered Jarrett's average start and finish.

Jarrett in 1992

Category	Total	Rank	1992 Leader
Money	$418,648	20th	Alan Kulwicki—2,322,561
Total points	3,251	19th	Alan Kulwicki—4,078
Avg. start	16.5	17th	Ernie Irvan—7.1
Avg. finish	17.8	19th	Alan Kulwicki—10.6
Wins	0	—	D. Allison, Elliott—5
Top 5s	2	19th	Davey Allison—15
Top 10s	8	19th	Ricky Rudd—18
DNFs	5	19th	Dave Marcis—14
Poles	0	—	Alan Kulwicki—6
Front row starts	0	—	Kulwicki, Marlin, Martin, Rudd—6
Laps led	103	15th	Davey Allison—1,377
Races led	6	14th	Alan Kulwicki—20
Times Led	12	14th	Alan Kulwicki—51
Miles led	150	15th	Davey Allison—2,315
Times led most laps	0	—	Davey Allison—6
Bonus points	30	14th	Alan Kulwicki—125
Laps completed	8,586	15th	Ted Musgrave—9,253
Miles completed	10,295	12th	Harry Gant—11,220
Points per race	112.1	19th	Alan Kulwicki—140.6
Lead-lap finishes	8	16th	Alan Kulwicki—17

1992 Performance Chart

No. 18 Joe Gibbs Chevrolet

Career Race	Race No.	Date	Race	St.	Fin.	Total Laps	Laps Completed	Laps Led	Condition	Money	Pts.	Bonus Pts.	Point Standing	Behind Leader	Points Leader*
140	1	Feb. 16	Daytona—Daytona 500 by STP	35	36	200	91	0	DNF–Crash	$19,780	55	0	37	-130	D. Allison
141	2	Mar. 1	Rockingham—GM Goodwrench 500	18	37	492	73	0	DNF–Cam Shaft	4,075	52	0	35	-253	D. Allison
142	3	Mar. 8	Richmond—Pontiac Excitement 400	21	13	400	398	0	Running	4,800	124	0	30	-294	D. Allison
143	4	Mar. 15	Atlanta—Motorcraft Quality Parts 500	17	11	328	328	0	Running	7,670	130	0	25	-334	D. Allison
144	5	Mar. 29	Darlington—TranSouth 500	9	21	367	328	0	Running	4,950	100	0	26	-404	D. Allison
145	6	Apr. 5	Bristol—Food City 500	4	2	500	500	38	Running	29,835	175	5	21	-313	D. Allison
146	7	Apr. 12	North Wilkesboro—First Union 400	24	17	400	399	0	Running	3,885	112	0	18	-381	D. Allison
147	8	Apr. 26	Martinsville—Hanes 500	21	28	500	351	0	Running	5,225	79	0	22	-387	D. Allison
148	9	May 3	Talladega—Winston 500	15	7	188	188	0	Running	19,215	146	0	21	-426	D. Allison
149	10	May 24	Charlotte—Coca-Cola 600	23	12	400	397	1	Running	15,400	132	5	18	-459	D. Allison
150	11	May 31	Dover—Budweiser 500	28	27	500	308	0	DNF–Engine	6,490	82	0	21	-507	D. Allison
151	12	June 7	Sears Point—SaveMart 300K	23	39	74	52	0	DNF–Transmission	4,750	46	0	23	-540	D. Allison
152	13	June 14	Pocono—Champion Spark Plug 500	7	22	200	187	0	Running	10,150	97	0	23	-603	D. Allison
153	14	June 21	Michigan—Miller Genuine Draft 400	13	24	200	191	0	Running	11,425	91	0	22	-697	D. Allison
154	15	July 4	Daytona—Pepsi 400	10	3	160	160	26	Running	37,200	170	5	20	-666	D. Allison
155	16	July 19	Pocono—Miller Genuine Draft 500	18	10	200	200	0	Running	15,190	134	0	20	-615	Elliott
156	17	July 26	Talladega—DieHard 500	8	21	188	186	13	Running	12,270	105	5	20	-671	D. Allison
157	18	Aug. 9	Watkins Glen—The Bud at the Glen	7	15	51	51	0	Running	11,420	118	0	20	-673	Elliott
158	19	Aug. 16	Michigan—Champion Spark Plug 400	14	8	200	200	4	Running	18,265	147	5	20	-701	Elliott
159	20	Aug. 29	Bristol—Bud 500	14	17	500	492	0	Running	10,525	112	0	20	-739	Elliott
160	21	Sept. 6	Darlington—Mountain Dew Southern 500	17	6	298	298	21	Running	19,055	155	5	18	-754	Elliott
161	22	Sept. 12	Richmond—Miller Genuine Draft 400	16	25	400	397	0	Running	8,855	88	0	19	-787	Elliott
162	23	Sept. 20	Dover—Peak AntiFreeze 500	11	12	500	490	0	Running	12,505	127	0	19	-840	Elliott
163	24	Sept. 28	Martinsville—Goody's 500	13	23	500	477	0	Running	8,150	94	0	19	-819	Elliott
164	25	Oct. 5	North Wilkesboro—Tyson/Holly Farms 400	10	10	400	397	0	Running	12,755	134	0	19	-770	Elliott
165	26	Oct. 11	Charlotte—Mello Yello 500	7	24	334	324	0	DNF–Clutch	9,640	91	0	19	-757	Elliott
166	27	Oct. 25	Rockingham—AC Delco 500	27	15	492	488	0	Running	12,550	118	0	19	-804	Elliott
167	28	Nov. 1	Phoenix—Pyroil 500	17	20	312	309	0	Running	10,485	103	0	19	-811	D. Allison
168	29	Nov. 15	Atlanta—Hooters 500	32	10	328	326	0	Running	16,950	134	0	19	-827	Kulwicki

Dale Jarrett vs. Morgan Shepherd

In 1992, Jarrett joined rookie car owner Joe Gibbs' organization, while Morgan Shepherd took over Jarrett's former ride with the veteran Wood Brothers team. Here's a comparison of their 1992 performance.

Driver	Final Standing	Total Points	Avg. Start	Avg. Finish	Top 5s	Top 10s	Laps Led	Laps Completed	Winnings
Dale Jarrett	19th	3,251	16.5	17.8	2	8	103	8,586	$418,648
Morgan Shepherd	14th	3,549	13.5	14.3	3	11	60	9,093	634,222

Jarrett joined the brand-new Joe Gibbs Racing team in 1992. Gibbs learned the ropes during 1992 while also head coaching the NFL Washington Redskins.

1993: Running with the Lead Pack

Beginning with his triumphant Speedweeks at Daytona—capped by a dramatic win in the Daytona 500 over Dale Earnhardt—Dale Jarrett experienced a true breakthrough in 1993. He maintained a level of excellence throughout the season that he had previously hinted at but could never produce. And, unlike 1991, his improvement was accompanied by prolonged championship contention.

Beginning with his first Daytona 500 win, Jarrett recorded career-best finishes at 9 of the first 12 tracks the Winston Cup series visited in 1993. He scored nearly twice as many Top 5s in 1993 alone as he had in his previous six seasons combined. He also topped the $1 million mark in earnings for the first time in his career.

In the race for the championship, Jarrett battled the Winston Cup elite from beginning to end. He never dropped below eighth in the point standings and only rarely fell below fourth. For the first time in his career, Jarrett was a contender. He revealed an ability to sustain a Top 5 car, and he got a sense for just how much effort is required to win a Winston Cup title. Indicating his racing maturity, the 36-year-old showed he could recover quickly from bad luck and poor finishes; only twice in 1993 did Jarrett go more that two races outside of the Top 10.

While the step-change improvement in Jarrett's performance was an interesting career development, the highlight of 1993 was his victory at Daytona. With his father in the CBS-TV booth calling the nationally televised race, Dale chased and caught the front-running cars of Dale Earnhardt and Jeff Gordon with two laps to go. He passed Earnhardt on the last lap and edged the late Winston Cup legend by two-tenths of a second at the finish. The victory was the second of his career and the first for owner Joe Gibbs.

Among the interesting facts embedded in Jarrett's Daytona adventure are:
- The combined margin of victory in Jarrett's first two Winston Cup wins was less than one second; this includes his narrow 1991 victory over Davey Allison at Michigan.
- The 1993 Daytona 500 marked the first time Jarrett earned a front-row starting position. Still pole-less after 169 starts, he qualified second in the 500.

After Daytona, Jarrett continued to break ground. He followed his victory with career-best finishes at Rockingham (sixth) and Richmond (fourth). Three weeks into the season, he led Earnhardt in the championship point standings—his first-ever tour as Winston Cup points leader. Shortly after, a bout of bad luck knocked Jarrett from his points perch, however. At the first Atlanta race, pneumonia and a late-race spin forced him out of the race early (he finished 31st). At Bristol, after looking strong and climbing through the field, Jarrett was wrecked by Bobby Hillin with 300 laps to go. When Jarrett reacted by throwing his helmet at Hillin's car—and connecting—NASCAR punished him by ordering his crew to load the still-drivable No. 18 car on to the team trailer. Jarrett officially finished the race in 32nd. The following week at North Wilkesboro, old-fashioned engine trouble precipitated another 32nd-place finish.

That run of bad finishes left Jarrett in eighth place in the point standings. He climbed back to second by midseason, but Earnhardt was well on his way to his seventh Winston Cup title. Despite the setbacks, Jarrett gave his strongest indication yet that championship aspirations were not unreasonable. He also previewed his 1996 run at the Winston Million with strong efforts in each of the bonus program's designated races. (The Winston Million was a $1 million bonus paid by R. J. Reynolds to any driver who could win three of NASCAR's four biggest races.) Besides winning the Daytona 500, he finished third in the Winston 500 at Talladega and third in the Coca-Cola 600 at Charlotte (he wasn't a factor in the Southern 500 at Darlington, finishing 12th).

Jarrett in 1993

Category	Total	Rank	1993 Leader
Money	$1,242,394	5th	Dale Earnhardt—3,353,789
Total points	4,000	4th	Dale Earnhardt—4,526
Avg. start	19.7	19th	Ernie Irvan—7.7
Avg. finish	12.4	4th	Dale Earnhardt—8.2
Wins	1	5th	Rusty Wallace—10
Top 5s	13	3rd	Rusty Wallace—19
Top 10s	18	4th	Earnhardt, Wallace—21
DNFs	5	25th	Jeff Gordon—11
Poles	0	—	Ken Schrader—6
Front row starts	1	12th	Ernie Irvan—9
Laps led	263	10th	Rusty Wallace—2,860
Races led	15	5th	Dale Earnhardt—21
Times led	28	7th	Dale Earnhardt—81
Miles led	466	6th	Dale Earnhardt—2,485
Times led most laps	0	—	Earnhardt, Wallace—9
Bonus points	75	5th	Dale Earnhardt—150
Laps completed	9,149	11th	Dale Earnhardt—9,787
Miles completed	11,335	3rd	Dale Earnhardt—11,808
Points per race	133.3	4th	Dale Earnhardt—150.9
Lead-Lap finishes	17	4th	Rusty Wallace—23

1993 Performance Chart

No. 18 Joe Gibbs Chevrolet

Career Race	Race No.	Date	Race	St.	Fin.	Total Laps	Laps Completed	Laps Led	Condition	Money	Pts.	Bonus Pts.	Current Standing	Behind Leader	Current Leader
169	1	Feb. 14	Daytona—Daytona 500	2	1	200	200	8	Running	$238,200	180	5	1	0	(Earnhardt)
170	2	Feb. 28	Rockingham—GM Goodwrench 500	22	6	492	492	0	Running	21,885	150	0	2	-25	Earnhardt
171	3	Mar. 7	Richmond—Pontiac Excitement 400	9	4	400	400	0	Running	29,050	160	0	1	1	(Earnhardt)
172	4	Mar. 20	Atlanta—Motorcraft Quality Parts 500	33	31	328	247	0	Running	15,145	70	0	4	-59	Earnhardt
173	5	Mar. 28	Darlington—TranSouth 500	4	3	367	367	1	Running	30,685	170	5	4	-74	Earnhardt
174	6	Apr. 4	Bristol—Food City 500	22	32	500	207	30	DNF—Crash	15,420	72	5	6	-177	Earnhardt
175	7	Apr. 18	North Wilkesboro—First Union 400	11	32	400	311	1	DNF—Engine	12,155	72	5	8	-238	R. Wallace
176	8	Apr. 25	Martinsville—Hanes 500	11	3	500	500	0	Running	30,350	165	0	8	-258	R. Wallace
177	9	May 2	Talladega—Winston 500	3	3	188	188	35	Running	44,870	170	5	4	-243	R. Wallace
178	10	May 16	Sears Point—SaveMart Supermarket 300K	32	13	74	74	0	Running	16,610	124	0	6	-193	Earnhardt
179	11	May 30	Charlotte—Coca-Cola 600	32	3	400	400	114	Running	73,100	170	5	3	-208	Earnhardt
180	12	June 6	Dover—Budweiser 500	29	2	500	500	0	Running	42,435	170	0	3	-223	Earnhardt
181	13	June 13	Pocono—Champion Spark Plug 500	21	19	200	195	1	Running	15,815	111	5	3	-247	Earnhardt
182	14	June 20	Michigan—Miller Genuine Draft 400	17	4	200	200	0	Running	29,590	160	0	2	-213	Earnhardt
183	15	July 3	Daytona—Pepsi 400	13	8	160	160	3	Running	21,150	147	5	2	-251	Earnhardt
184	16	July 11	New Hampshire—Slick 50 300	9	4	300	300	1	Running	33,850	165	5	2	-171	Earnhardt
185	17	July 18	Pocono—Miller Genuine Draft 500	23	8	200	200	47	Running	19,915	147	5	2	-209	Earnhardt
186	18	July 25	Talladega—DieHard 500	15	5	188	188	5	Running	30,390	160	5	2	-234	Earnhardt
187	19	Aug. 8	Watkins Glen—Bud at the Glen	14	32	90	61	0	DNF—Clutch	13,650	67	0	2	-281	Earnhardt
188	20	Aug. 15	Michigan—Champion Spark Plug 400	27	4	200	200	0	Running	29,045	160	0	2	-259	Earnhardt
189	21	Aug. 28	Bristol—Bud 500	33	31	500	199	0	DNF—Rear End	15,600	70	0	4	-354	Earnhardt
190	22	Sept. 5	Darlington—Mountain Dew Southern 500	27	12	351	348	0	Running	16,510	127	0	4	-392	Earnhardt
191	23	Sept. 11	Richmond—Miller Genuine Draft 400	13	14	400	398	0	Running	14,955	121	0	4	-436	Earnhardt
192	24	Sept. 19	Dover—SplitFire Spark Plug 500	26	4	500	500	2	Running	31,035	165	5	4	-353	Earnhardt
193	25	Sept. 26	Martinsville—Goody's 500	17	5	500	499	0	Running	22,675	155	0	3	-274	Earnhardt
194	26	Oct. 3	North Wilkesboro—Tyson/Holly Farms 400	24	9	400	397	2	Running	14,455	143	5	3	-306	Earnhardt
195	27	Oct. 10	Charlotte—Mello Yello 500	38	26	334	325	0	Running	13,160	85	0	4	-391	Earnhardt
196	28	Oct. 24	Rockingham—AC Delco 500	21	30	492	454	1	DNF—Broken Pinion Gear	15,675	78	5	4	-488	Earnhardt
197	29	Oct. 31	Phoenix—Slick 50 500	14	16	312	311	0	Running	15,320	115	0	4	-538	Earnhardt
198	30	Nov. 14	Atlanta—Hooters 500	29	7	328	328	12	Running	23,380	151	5	4	-526	Earnhardt

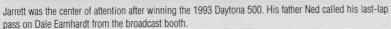

Jarrett was the center of attention after winning the 1993 Daytona 500. His father Ned called his last-lap pass on Dale Earnhardt from the broadcast booth.

Besides being one of the biggest wins of his career, the 1993 Daytona 500 marked the first time Jarrett started a race on the front row. He started second, lining up next to pole winner Kyle Petty. Jarrett's first pole came two years later when he started the 1995 Daytona 500 in the No. 1 position.

1994: One Step Back

The two steps forward taken by Dale Jarrett in his quest for a championship in 1993 were offset by one large step back in 1994. After a sustained run among the leaders in 1993, Jarrett dropped to a midpack 16th in the final point standings in 1994.

Similar to seasons past, a slow start spelled early doom for Jarrett. He relied on provisionals to make the field in three of the season's first four races, including the Daytona 500. A blown engine forced him out of competition just a single lap into his Twin 125 qualifying race. Three days later, starting the Daytona 500 in 41st position, he suffered more engine troubles, this time a burned piston, and finished the Great American Race a dismal 35th.

Season-long qualifying problems led to one of the lowest points in Jarrett's career. At North Wilkesboro in the fall, the 37-year-old failed to qualify for the Tyson Holly Farms 400. Since joining the series as a full-time driver in 1987, Jarrett had never missed a race. While certainly not a great qualifier, he had been good enough to start 219 consecutive races. On October 2, 1994, however, Jarrett watched Winston Cup racing like the rest of us: at home, sitting on the couch, staring at the TV.

North Wilkesboro pointed out the danger of relying on provisionals. After failing to make the field on speed, Jarrett was locked out of the race by two other drivers, Morgan Shepherd and Lake Speed. While Jarrett was stuck in 18th place in the standings, Shepherd was 6th and Speed was 14th. Given priority, Speed and Shepherd happily gobbled up the race's remaining starting spots.

To Jarrett and his team's credit, they rebounded from their DNQ (Did Not Qualify) with an inspired victory the following week at Charlotte—Jarrett's third career win. Nothing, however, could remove the level of frustration that had been building all season long. No matter where he steered his Chevy, bad luck lurked. Among the incidents were the following:

- He crashed out of the Bristol spring race just 66 laps into the event, finishing 36th.
- He lost power steering at Martinsville (of all places) and fell six laps off the pace in 21st.
- He got caught in the "big one" in the spring Talladega race, ending up in 21st.
- He was collected in Jeff Burton's crash at Dover and finished 29th.
- A faulty transmission at Pocono filled his car with noxious fumes and forced an unscheduled pit stop with eight laps to go, dropping him from 6th to 20th.
- When Geoffrey and Brett Bodine staged their family feud in the inaugural Brickyard 400 at Indianapolis, they inadvertently collected and crashed Jarrett, who ended in 40th place.
- He crashed out of the Bristol night race while battling for ninth place.
- He was involved in three wrecks in the fall Dover race, the third of which broke a bone in his wrist.

All of the above occurred before his failure to qualify at North Wilkesboro. In the face of his frustration, or perhaps because of it, Jarrett agreed to meet with Robert Yates to discuss taking over Yates' coveted No. 28 Havoline Ford. Yates' car had been vacated in August when driver Ernie Irvan suffered severe head and chest injuries in a vicious crash during practice at Michigan. Yates offered Jarrett the job in the fall of 1994. The two formalized their new partnership in November.

While an incredible opportunity for Jarrett, the Yates deal left Joe Gibbs driverless and disappointed. Gibbs pointed to the fact that Jarrett still had two years remaining on his contract to drive the No. 18 car. Gibbs agreed to release Jarrett from his obligation only after he was able to sign another up-and-coming driver—Bobby Labonte—to take over the Interstate Batteries Chevy.

Jarrett in 1994

Category	Total	Rank	1994 Leader
Money	$881,754	13th	Dale Earnhardt—$3,400,733
Total points	3,298	16th	Dale Earnhardt—4,694
Avg. start	22.7	28th	Ernie Irvan—6.6
Avg. finish	18.7	16th	Dale Earnhardt—8.0
Wins	1	9th	Rusty Wallace—8
Top 5s	4	13th	Dale Earnhardt—20
Top 10s	9	16th	Dale Earnhardt—25
DNFs	7	14th	Geoffrey Bodine—15
Poles	0	—	G. Bodine, Irvan—5
Front row starts	0	—	Geoffrey Bodine—10
Laps led	55	19th	Rusty Wallace—2,141
Races led	8	11th	Dale Earnhardt—23
Times led	9	16th	Ernie Irvan—79
Miles led	69	20th	Ernie Irvan—2,419
Times led most laps	0	—	Ernie Irvan—10
Bonus points	40	12th	Ernie Irvan—135
Laps completed	8,410	22nd	Darrell Waltrip—9,905
Miles completed	10,441	21st	Ricky Rudd—12,046
Points per race	109.9	17th	Dale Earnhardt—151.4
Lead-lap finishes	8	14th	Dale Earnhardt—22

1994 Performance Chart
No. 18 Joe Gibbs Chevrolet

Career Race	Race No.	Date	Race	St.	Fin.	Total Laps	Laps Completed	Laps Led	Condition	Money	Pts.	Bonus Pts.	Current Standing	Behind Leader	Current Leader
199	1	Feb. 20	Daytona—Daytona 500	41	35	200	146	3	DNF–Piston	$38,325	63	5	34	-117	Marlin
200	2	Feb. 27	Rockingham—Goodwrench Service 500	41	18	492	485	0	Running	20,635	109	0	30	-183	Marlin
201	3	Mar. 6	Richmond—Pontiac Excitement 400	22	10	400	399	0	Running	21,825	134	0	19	-214	Irvan
202	4	Mar. 13	Atlanta—Purolator 500	36	35	328	205	2	DNF–Engine	19,820	63	5	23	-336	Irvan
203	5	Mar. 27	Darlington—TranSouth Financial 400	14	4	293	293	9	Running	27,550	165	5	18	-326	Irvan
204	6	Apr. 10	Bristol—Food City 500	36	36	500	66	0	DNF–Crash	12,025	55	0	22	-375	Earnhardt
205	7	Apr. 17	North Wilkesboro—First Union 400	31	25	400	394	0	Running	16,275	88	0	24	-442	Earnhardt
206	8	Apr. 24	Martinsville—Hanes 500	20	21	500	494	0	Running	16,475	100	0	23	-497	Irvan
207	9	May 1	Talladega—Winston Select 500	9	21	188	186	0	Running	20,860	100	0	23	-577	Irvan
208	10	May 15	Sears Point—Save Mart Supermarkets 300	20	12	74	74	0	Running	20,755	127	0	23	-635	Irvan
209	11	May 29	Charlotte—Coca-Cola 600	16	4	400	400	9	Running	54,600	165	5	17	-630	Irvan
210	12	June 5	Dover—Budweiser 500	13	29	500	424	0	Running	19,665	76	0	16	-734	Irvan
211	13	June 12	Pocono—UAW-GM Teamwork 500	22	20	200	198	5	Running	20,860	108	5	16	-777	Irvan
212	14	June 19	Michigan—Miller Genuine Draft 400	35	14	200	199	0	Running	22,675	121	0	17	-770	Irvan
213	15	July 2	Daytona—Pepsi 400	11	11	160	160	0	Running	24,265	130	0	16	-820	Irvan
214	16	July 10	New Hampshire—Slick 50 300	31	14	300	300	0	Running	23,775	121	0	16	-786	Earnhardt
215	17	July 17	Pocono—Miller Genuine Draft 500	17	10	200	199	0	Running	24,510	134	0	15	-798	Earnhardt
216	18	July 24	Talladega—DieHard 500	13	39	188	34	0	DNF–Piston	20,690	46	0	17	-834	Irvan
217	19	Aug. 6	Indianapolis—Brickyard 400	14	40	160	99	0	DNF–Crash	33,225	43	0	19	-935	Earnhardt
218	20	Aug. 14	Watkins Glen—The Bud at the Glen	14	11	90	90	0	Running	20,250	130	0	19	-975	Earnhardt
219	21	Aug. 21	Michigan—GM Goodwrench Dealer 400	31	30	200	133	0	Running	19,965	73	0	21	-954	Earnhardt
220	22	Aug. 27	Bristol—Goody's 500	29	26	500	388	19	DNF–Crash	19,285	90	5	22	-1,034	Earnhardt
221	23	Sept. 4	Darlington—Mountain Dew Southern 500	35	9	367	365	0	Running	23,370	138	0	20	-1,071	Earnhardt
222	24	Sept. 10	Richmond—Miller Genuine Draft 400	25	16	400	397	0	Running	18,830	115	0	18	-1,126	Earnhardt
223	25	Sept. 18	Dover—SplitFire Spark Plug 500	19	34	500	323	0	DNF–Crash	19,405	61	0	22	-1,240	Earnhardt
224	26	Sept. 25	Martinsville—Goody's 500	8	5	500	500	0	Running	26,775	155	0	18	-1,260	Earnhardt
—	27	Oct. 2	North Wilkesboro—Tyson Holly Farms 400	Did Not Qualify									21	-1,411	Earnhardt
225	28	Oct. 9	Charlotte—Mello Yello 500	22	1	334	334	4	Running	106,800	180	5	19	-1,401	Earnhardt
226	29	Oct. 23	Rockingham—AC Delco 500	27	12	492	489	0	Running	21,850	127	0	19	-1459	Earnhardt
227	30	Oct. 30	Phoenix—Slick 50 300	5	9	312	310	4	Running	21,920	143	5	17	-1,359	Earnhardt
228	31	Nov. 13	Atlanta—Hooters 500	23	9	328	326	0	Running	23,325	138	0	16	-1,396	Earnhardt

Gibbs Racing (1992–2001)

A look at the drivers hired by Winston Cup owner Joe Gibbs and their performances

Driver	W. C. Titles	Starts	Avg. Start	Avg. Finish	Wins	Top 5s	Top 10s	Poles	Money
Dale Jarrett	0	89	19.7	16.2	2	19	35	0	$2,542,796
Bobby Labonte	1	231	12.9	13.1	18	83	134	21	24,677,670
Tony Stewart	0	104	15.5	11.7	12	39	66	4	11,736,303
Totals	**1**	**424**	**15.0**	**13.4**	**32**	**141**	**235**	**25**	**38,956,769**

Jarrett's third career win came at Charlotte in 1994, one week after he failed to qualify for the Tyson 400 at North Wilkesboro. The DNQ ended his 219-consecutive-start streak.

1995: Providing Relief . . . For the Last Time

Dale Jarrett faced enormous pressure when he took over the No. 28 Robert Yates Racing Ford in 1995. Though in a familiar role (Jarrett was a relief driver for the third time in his career), his new situation was drastically different. He was taking over for an extremely successful driver (Ernie Irvan) and occupying the driver's seat of a car many felt was destined for championship greatness but cursed by fate.

Thanks to Irvan's miraculous, quicker-than-expected recovery, Jarrett appeared to have only one season in which to make an impression. Once Irvan was ready to return, it seemed, Jarrett was out.

Dogging Jarrett was his inconsistency with various car owners over the previous eight seasons. Though he had provided brief glimpses of championship potential, particularly in 1993, he had finished higher than 13th in the point standings just once.

When his title hopes began to wane just 10 races into the 1995 season, the pressure on Jarrett intensified. Allison and Irvan had won early and often in the No. 28, but Jarrett couldn't seem to find Victory Lane. Though he started the year strong by scoring five Top 10s in the first eight races, he soon suffered the kind of discouraging run that had become a hallmark of his career. This time, it started with suspension problems at Talladega (where he finished 19th) and continued the following week at Sears Point where, after being forced off the track by Rusty Wallace, Jarrett's car tumbled and ended up on its right side. Track workers had to tip Jarrett's Ford back on to its wheels before he could resume (and finish 23rd).

Two races later, just two laps into the Miller 500 at Dover, Jarrett was the innocent victim of a John Andretti–Ricky Craven crash-and-spin and finished 40th. A 38th-place finish at Pocono and a 42nd at Daytona dropped Jarrett to 16th in the point standings, 616 points out of the top spot.

By the time the Winston Cup series made its second stop at Pocono in July, Jarrett was investigating his options for 1996, including starting his own team. Making the situation more difficult was the success of Jarrett's old team. New driver Bobby Labonte took advantage of the hyper-successful re-introduction of the Chevy Monte Carlo, driving the No. 18 car to three wins, two poles, and a 10th-place finish in the point standings. This was all better than Jarrett could muster in the vaunted No. 28.

In the intense heat of Pocono, where temperatures reached 130 degrees on the track, Jarrett finally got a break: He won. Starting 15th, he and crew chief Larry McReynolds gambled that fuel mileage could decide the race on the wide-open 2.5-mile track. They guessed right; Jarrett ran out of gas under the checkered flag, earning his first win with Robert Yates Racing and the fourth of his career. Finally, Jarrett could breathe again.

The only event of 1995 that was more important to Jarrett's career than that victory at Pocono was the emergence of Jeff Gordon. Though the success of one driver rarely improves the fate of another, Gordon's title run may have been the second biggest savior of Jarrett's season. Gordon and Hendrick Motorsports were the best illustration of the success of the multicar team concept, which blossomed in 1995. Thanks to testing and information-sharing advantages, multicar teams were beginning to dominate Winston Cup racing. One of the first single-car owners to take notice of the trend was Yates.

Believing Jarrett and the healing Irvan were the kind of experienced drivers who could make the multicar concept work, Yates approached Jarrett in August at Bristol and offered him the ride in his second, yet-to-be-formed team. Jarrett jumped at the opportunity. In September at Richmond, Irvan made a triumphant return to the Winston Cup series, driving a second Yates car, the No. 88 Ford. The following season, Jarrett would take over the No. 88 and hand the No. 28 back to Irvan.

Inside of two months, the 1995 season turned from pressure-filled frustration to career-nurturing stability. Jarrett was about to became a perennial contender. He would repay Yates' faith and loyalty many times over, starting in February 1996.

Jarrett in 1995

Category	Total	Rank	1995 Leader
Money	$1,363,158	8th	Jeff Gordon—4,347,343
Total points	3,584	13th	Jeff Gordon—4,614
Avg. start	18.4	16th	Jeff Gordon—5.0
Avg. finish	17.4	14th	Dale Earnhardt—9.2
Wins	1	8th	Dale Earnhardt—7
Top 5s	9	7th	Dale Earnhardt—19
Top 10s	14	8th	Earnhardt, Gordon—23
DNFs	6	13th	G. Sacks, D. Waltrip—11
Poles	1	7th	Jeff Gordon—9
Front row starts	1	11th	Jeff Gordon—12
Laps led	324	8th	Jeff Gordon—2,600
Races led	8	12th	Jeff Gordon—29
Times led	19	10th	Jeff Gordon—94
Miles led	373	9th	Jeff Gordon—3,458
Times led most laps	1	6th	Jeff Gordon—11
Bonus points	45	12th	Jeff Gordon—200
Laps completed	8,671	20th	Sterling Marlin—9,728
Miles completed	10,417	23rd	Sterling Marlin—11,936
Points per race	115.6	13th	Jeff Gordon—148.8
Lead-lap finishes	16	7th	Jeff Gordon—23

1995 Performance Chart

No. 28 Robert Yates Racing Ford

Career Race	Race No.	Date	Race	St.	Fin.	Total Laps	Laps Completed	Laps Led	Condition	Money	Pts.	Bonus Pts.	Current Standing	Behind Leader	Current Leader
229	1	Feb. 19	Daytona—Daytona 500	1	5	200	200	0	Running	$119,855	155	0	5	-30	Marlin
230	2	Feb. 26	Rockingham—Goodwrench 500	26	5	492	491	0	Running	34,075	155	0	4	-35	Earnhardt
231	3	Mar. 5	Richmond—Pontiac Excitement 400	13	25	400	393	0	Running	24,375	88	0	5	-122	Earnhardt
232	4	Mar. 12	Atlanta—Purolator 500	18	5	328	327	0	Running	33,725	155	0	5	-132	Earnhardt
233	5	Mar. 26	Darlington—TranSouth Financial 400	26	38	293	133	0	DNF—Transmission	22,809	49	0	9	-258	Earnhardt
234	6	Apr. 2	Bristol—Food City 500	19	6	500	500	0	Running	27,660	150	0	7	-196	Earnhardt
235	7	Apr. 9	North Wilkesboro—First Union 400	33	11	400	398	0	Running	22,140	130	0	2	-251	Earnhardt
236	8	Apr. 23	Martinsville—Hanes 500	10	7	356	356	0	Running	26,595	146	0	7	-181	Earnhardt
237	9	Apr. 30	Talladega—Winston 500	5	19	188	188	35	Running	27,240	111	5	7	-175	Gordon
238	10	May 7	Sears Point—SaveMart Supermarkets 300	9	23	74	74	0	Running	24,730	94	0	7	-261	Earnhardt
239	11	May 28	Charlotte—Coca-Cola 600	22	32	400	317	0	DNF—Engine	21,050	67	0	12	-349	Earnhardt
240	12	June 4	Dover—Miller 500	18	40	500	2	0	DNF—Crash	26,680	43	0	13	-466	Earnhardt
241	13	June 11	Pocono—UAW/GM 500	14	38	200	126	0	Running	22,610	49	0	17	-559	Earnhardt
242	14	June 18	Michigan—Miller 400	29	6	200	200	8	Running	33,500	155	5	14	-473	Marlin
243	15	July 1	Daytona—Pepsi 400	7	42	160	38	0	DNF—Engine	27,645	37	0	16	-616	Marlin
244	16	July 9	New Hampshire—Slick 50 300	14	30	300	296	0	Running	26,925	73	0	16	-721	Gordon
245	17	July 16	Pocono—Miller 500	15	1	200	200	26	Running	72,970	180	5	16	-716	Gordon
246	18	July 23	Talladega—DieHard 500	13	2	188	188	0	Running	65,895	170	0	14	-698	Gordon
247	19	Aug. 5	Indianapolis—Brickyard 400	26	3	160	160	0	Running	203,200	165	0	12	-688	Gordon
248	20	Aug. 13	Watkins Glen—Bud at the Glen	13	17	90	90	0	Running	25,100	112	0	13	-746	Gordon
249	21	Aug. 20	Michigan—Goodwrench Service 400	17	33	200	101	36	DNF—Engine	35,465	69	5	14	-852	Gordon
250	22	Aug. 26	Bristol—Goody's 500	16	3	500	500	99	Running	39,390	175	10	12	-832	Gordon
251	23	Sept. 3	Darlington—Mountain Dew Southern 500	12	28	367	331	0	Running	24,870	79	0	12	-933	Gordon
252	24	Sept. 9	Richmond—Miller 400	27	4	400	400	0	Running	40,605	160	0	12	-928	Gordon
253	25	Sept. 17	Dover—MBNA 500	26	30	500	410	1	DNF—Crash	29,765	78	5	14	-1,035	Gordon
254	26	Sept. 24	Martinsville—Goody's 500	14	10	500	500	11	Running	27,050	139	5	13	-1,047	Gordon
255	27	Oct. 1	North Wilkesboro—Tyson 400	6	7	400	400	108	Running	24,790	151	5	13	-1,066	Gordon
256	28	Oct. 8	Charlotte—UAW-GM Quality 500	31	5	334	334	0	Running	51,400	155	0	13	-989	Gordon
257	29	Oct. 22	Rockingham—AC Delco 400	27	23	393	390	0	Running	24,700	94	0	13	-1003	Gordon
258	30	Oct. 29	Phoenix—Dura-Lube 500	26	11	312	312	0	Running	26,070	130	0	12	-1,028	Gordon
259	31	Nov. 12	Atlanta—NAPA 500	38	31	328	316	0	Running	21,340	70	0	13	-1,030	Gordon

Winning Early in the 28

Davey Allison and Ernie Irvan won immediately in the No. 28 Ford.
Dale Jarrett needed a little more time.

Driver	No. of Starts	First Victory
Ernie Irvan	4	Martinsville—1993 Goody's 500
Davey Allison	6	Talladega—1987 Winston 500*
Dale Jarrett	17	Pocono—1995 Miller 500

*—No. 28 car owned by Harry Rainer; Robert Yates bought the team in 1989

As he had in his previous experiences as a relief driver, Jarrett made a quick impression with his new Robert Yates Racing team in 1995. He won the pole for the Daytona 500 and finished fifth in three of the season's first four races.

1996: Becoming a Champion

In 1996, Dale Jarrett became unrecognizable. He chucked the conservative driving style and incremental success that had marked his nine-year career, and instead adopted the dominating, move-to-the-front model of Gordon, Earnhardt, and his teammate, Ernie Irvan.

Piloting Robert Yates' new No. 88 Quality Care Ford, Jarrett entered the season with a new team and a rookie crew chief, Todd Parrott.

When Jarrett took over the No. 88, he and Parrott clicked immediately. They won their first race together—the 1996 Busch Clash—then went on to win their first points race, the Daytona 500. The victory was Jarrett's second in the Daytona 500, making him one of just seven drivers in NASCAR history to win the event more than once.

Besides putting him in the history books, the Daytona 500 also kicked off Jarrett's second serious run at the Winston Million. After a second-place finish in the Winston 500 at Talladega, he boosted his chances of winning the Million with a dominating victory in the Coca-Cola 600 at Charlotte. Jarrett's overpowering performance was remarkable: He led 199 of 400 laps and crossed the finish line 12 seconds ahead of second-place finisher Earnhardt.

Squarely in position to become just the second driver to win the Million (Bill Elliott was the first in 1985), Jarrett created excitement by winning the pole for the Southern 500. He led 23 of the race's first 46 laps and appeared to have the best car in the field when oil on the racetrack spoiled his run. Jarrett's famous "I'm in the wall" radio transmission back to his crew announced the end of his spirited run. He finished the race in 14th, two laps off the pace.

The run for the Winston Million highlighted a season of accomplishment for Jarrett. He finished with career highs in wins, Top 5s, Top 10s, money, poles, laps led, races led, and lead-lap finishes. With victories in some of the biggest, most prestigious races on the circuit—besides the Daytona 500 and Coca-Cola 600, Jarrett won the Brickyard 400—he was developing a reputation as a "big race" driver.

More important, Jarrett was also becoming a true title contender. For the second time in his career, he enjoyed a stint as the Winston Cup points leader, this time extending his stay until the third month of the season.

When Jarrett ultimately finished the season third in points—just 89 points behind champion Terry Labonte—his crashes at Dover and Pocono in June loomed large. At Dover, Jarrett led 82 laps and had one of the race's best cars when he hit oil left behind by Gary Bradberry's blown engine. In third place at the time, Jarrett nailed the wall on lap 362 and had to settle for 32nd place. Two weeks later at Pocono, Jarrett crashed in qualifying and suffered a cracked left rib and a broken bone in his right knee. The injuries did not force Jarrett out of the car on race day, but he didn't get a chance to compete, either. A blown engine on lap 38 dropped him to 38th place.

Those two mishaps pinned Jarrett in fourth place in the point standings, 233 points out of the lead. Despite his injuries, he rebounded from his painful Pocono weekend to score 15 Top 10s in the season's remaining 18 races, including 10 Top 3 finishes and two more wins. He got as close at 76 points with two races left in the season, but he could never catch the steady Labonte. The best indication of just how close Jarrett was to a championship was his average finish: Jarrett's average was 8.6, while Labonte's was 8.2.

If Jarrett came close to a Winston Cup title in 1996, he would suffer an even closer finish in 1997. In typical Jarrett fashion, reaching the next level of success would take time.

Jarrett in 1996

Category	Total	Rank	1996 Leader
Money	$2,985,418	3rd	Terry Labonte—4,030,648
Total points	4,568	3rd	Terry Labonte—4,657
Avg. start	12.1	5th	Jeff Gordon—6.3
Avg. finish	8.8	2nd	Terry Labonte—8.2
Wins	4	3rd	Jeff Gordon—10
Top 5s	17	3rd	J. Gordon, T. Labonte—21
Top 10s	21	4th	J. Gordon, T. Labonte—24
DNFs	3	28th	Andretti, Cope, D. Waltrip—11
Poles	2	5th	Jeff Gordon—5
Front row starts	4	5th	Jeff Gordon—15
Laps led	746	4th	Jeff Gordon—2,314
Races led	20	3rd	Jeff Gordon—25
Times led	49	4th	Jeff Gordon—97
Miles led	1,023	4th	Jeff Gordon—2,386
Times led most laps	2	6th	Jeff Gordon—10
Bonus points	110	3rd	Jeff Gordon—175
Laps completed	9,307	6th	Dale Earnhardt—9,530
Miles completed	11,180	7th	Dale Earnhardt—11,523
Points per race	147.4	3rd	Terry Labonte—150.2
Lead-lap finishes	23	3rd	J. Gordon, T. Labonte—24

1996 Performance Chart

No. No. 88 Robert Yates Racing Ford

Career Race	Race No.	Date	Race	St.	Fin.	Total Laps	Laps Completed	Laps Led	Condition	Money	Pts.	Bonus Pts.	Current Standing	Behind Leader	Current Leader
260	1	Feb. 18	Daytona—Daytona 500	7	1	200	200	40	Running	$360,775	180	5	1	+5	(Earnhardt)
261	2	Feb. 25	Rockingham—Goodwrench Service 400	13	2	393	393	8	Running	48,960	175	5	1	—	(Tie—Earnhardt)
262	3	Mar. 3	Richmond—Pontiac Excitement 400	11	2	400	400	23	Running	44,225	175	5	1	+86	(Earnhardt)
263	4	Mar. 10	Atlanta—Purolator 500	36	11	328	326	0	Running	20,820	130	0	1	+50	(Earnhardt)
264	5	Mar. 24	Darlington—TranSouth Financial 400	3	15	293	291	10	DNF—Out of Gas	22,950	123	5	1	+47	(Earnhardt)
265	6	Mar. 31	Bristol—Food City 500	7	6	342	342	0	Running	26,395	150	0	1	+37	(Earnhardt)
266	7	Apr. 14	North Wilkesboro—First Union 400	29	11	400	398	0	Running	16,615	130	0	1	+2	(Earnhardt)
267	8	Apr. 21	Martinsville—Goody's Headache Powder 500	12	29	500	458	0	Running	17,115	76	0	3	-82	Earnhardt
268	9	Apr. 28	Talladega—Winston Select 500	2	2	188	188	20	Running	64,145	175	5	2	-77	Earnhardt
269	10	May 5	Sears Point—SaveMart Supermarkets 300	20	12	74	74	0	Running	20,530	127	0	2	-115	Earnhardt
270	11	May 26	Charlotte—Coca-Cola 600	15	1	400	400	199	Running	165,250	185	10	2	-105	Earnhardt
271	12	June 2	Dover—Miller 500	6	36	500	374	82	DNF—Crash	22,055	60	5	4	-215	Earnhardt
272	13	June 16	Pocono—UAW/GM Teamwork 500	28	38	200	37	0	DNF—Crank-shaft	16,520	49	0	4	-233	Earnhardt
273	14	June 23	Michigan—Miller Genuine Draft 400	30	10	200	200	5	Running	27,850	139	5	4	-232	Earnhardt
274	15	July 6	Daytona—Pepsi 400	3	6	117	117	14	Running	30,910	155	5	4	-237	Earnhardt
275	16	July 14	New Hampshire—Jiffy Lube 300	10	2	300	300	2	Running	59,725	175	5	4	-212	T. Labonte
276	17	July 21	Pocono—Miller 500	20	3	200	200	2	Running	35,705	170	5	4	-157	T. Labonte
277	18	July 28	Talladega—DieHard 500	3	2	129	129	5	Running	55,070	175	5	4	-82	Gordon
278	19	Aug. 3	Indianapolis—Brickyard 400	24	1	160	160	11	Running	564,035	180	5	3	-63	T. Labonte
279	20	Aug. 11	Watkins Glen—Bud at the Glen	2	24	90	90	0	Running	18,105	91	0	4	-147	T. Labonte
280	21	Aug. 18	Michigan—Goodwrench Service 400	11	1	200	200	8	Running	83,195	180	5	4	-137	T. Labonte
281	22	Aug. 24	Bristol—Goody's 500	9	4	500	500	18	Running	32,980	165	5	3	-127	T. Labonte
282	23	Sept. 1	Darlington—Mountain Dew Southern 500	1	14	367	365	23	Running	128,165	126	5	3	-91	T. Labonte
283	24	Sept. 7	Richmond—Miller 400	8	4	400	400	11	Running	30,505	165	5	3	-86	T. Labonte
284	25	Sept. 15	Dover—MBNA 500	9	3	500	500	29	Running	40,880	170	5	3	-97	Gordon
285	26	Sept. 22	Martinsville—Hanes 500	4	16	500	498	0	Running	19,500	115	0	3	-162	Gordon
286	27	Sept. 29	North Wilkesboro—Tyson/Holly Farms 400	30	3	400	400	0	Running	35,790	165	0	3	-182	Gordon
287	28	Oct. 6	Charlotte—UAW/GM Quality 500	10	3	334	334	0	Running	58,300	165	0	3	-92	Gordon
288	29	Oct. 20	Rockingham—AC Delco 400	1	2	393	393	207	Running	62,125	180	10	3	-76	T. Labonte
289	30	Oct. 27	Phoenix—Dura-Lube 500	5	8	312	312	29	Running	22,055	147	5	3	-99	T. Labonte
290	31	Nov. 10	Atlanta—NAPA 500	5	2	328	328	0	Running	59,500	170	0	3	-89	T. Labonte

Becoming a Champion

Jarrett's drive for a championship took a huge step forward in 1996. His season performance compares strongly with that of 1996 champ Terry Labonte. Below is a look at their 1996 stats.

Driver	Point Standing	Wins	Top 5s	Top 10s	Avg. Fin	Races Led	Laps Led	Bonus Points	Total Points
Dale Jarrett	3rd	4	17	21	8.8	20	746	110	4,568
Terry Labonte	1st	2	21	24	8.2	22	969	130	4,657

The 1996 season proved to be one of Jarrett's best. Besides winning the Daytona 500, he won the Brickyard 400 (pictured) and the Coca-Cola 600.

1997: Champion Consistency

If Dale Jarrett was the old Dale Jarrett, the pre-Robert Yates Dale Jarrett, in 1997, he would have taken a step back after the success of 1996. Jarrett's history dictated that disaster and disappointment should follow a season in which he had finished just 89 points shy of the Winston Cup title. Instead, the new Dale Jarrett, the Jarrett transformed by Robert Yates' loyalty and confidence, took yet another major step forward.

By any measure, Jarrett's 1997 performance was championship caliber. He won seven races and was ranked first or second in 19 of 20 major statistical categories (the one category—DNFs—is better left unled). Illustrating the dependability of Yates' cars and Jarrett's burgeoning ability to nurture them, he completed all but 53 of the season's 9,822 laps, a reliability record bettered during NASCAR's modern era only by Bobby Labonte in 2000.

Unfortunately for Jarrett, his effort fell short of Jeff Gordon's. While Jarrett amassed career highs in wins (7), Top 5s (20), and Top 10s (23), Gordon had more of each. The young phenom outlasted a furious late-season charge by Jarrett and won the championship by 14 points, the fourth closest points race in NASCAR history.

Highlighting the No. 88 team's dominance, Jarrett became just the ninth driver in NASCAR's modern era to lead more than 2,000 laps in a single season. Nearly half of those pace-setting laps were logged in the first five races of the season, a show of early season dominance nearly unmatched in the modern era. In the year's second race, he led 323 of 393 laps at Rockingham, by far the most laps led since races at "The Rock" were shortened from 492 laps in October 1995. Typical of Jarrett's luck that season, he lost the race to Gordon.

Two races later, Jarrett led 253 of 328 laps at Atlanta to post his first victory of the season. When he followed with a win at Darlington the next week, it marked the first time Jarrett had ever won consecutive races. His dominance on the series' big tracks was evident in the list of venues where the No. 88 was victorious: Atlanta, Darlington, Pocono, Charlotte, and Phoenix. Also significant was his new-found success on short tracks. Jarrett posted his first career win on a track shorter than 1 mile when he took the checkered flag in Bristol's night race. Two races later, he won another short track race at Richmond.

Hurting Jarrett's championship hopes was a run of midseason trouble. At Talladega, he experienced engine problems on the race's second lap and finished 35th. In the Coca-Cola 600, his problems started when he was penalized on pit road for a stray tire and fell to 32nd in the running order. When he battled back to what looked like a solid finish, his engine failed on the race's final lap and knocked him back to 27th. At Dover the following week, he was in the lead when a wreck in front of him caused him to slow his car. Second-place driver Jeff Gordon couldn't slow down in time, however, and slammed into Jarrett's rear bumper. Jarrett escaped serious damage and maintained his lead but was forced out of the event seven laps later when his engine seized up. He finished in 32nd.

NASCAR contributed to Jarrett's bad luck two months later at Watkins Glen in a controversial call. Winston Cup officials black-flagged the 88 car on suspicion that it was dropping oil on the track. When Jarrett honored the flag and stopped on pit road, NASCAR's inspectors could find nothing wrong. The forced pit stop cost Jarrett tremendous track time. He ended up a lap down in 32nd.

The effect of the midseason slump on Jarrett's championship hopes was dramatic. Before the Talladega race, he held a 40-point lead. When he left Watkins Glen 10 races later, he was 260 points behind Gordon—a 300-point swing from which he never recovered.

Jarrett in 1997

Category	Total	Rank	1997 Leader
Money	$3,240,542	2nd	Jeff Gordon—6,375,658
Total points	4,696	2nd	Jeff Gordon—4,710
Avg. start	7.2	1st	(Jeff Gordon—9.4)
Avg. finish	9.6	2nd	Mark Martin—9.0
Wins	7	2nd	Jeff Gordon—10
Top 5s	20	2nd	Jeff Gordon—22
Top 10s	23	2nd	Mark Martin—24
DNFs	1	49th	Dallenbach, K. Wallace, R. Wallace—10
Poles	2	2nd	B. Labonte, Martin—3
Front row starts	6	T-1st	(J. Gordon, Martin—6)
Laps led	2,083	1st	(Jeff Gordon—1,647)
Races led	22	2nd	Jeff Gordon—24
Times led	71	1st	(Jeff Gordon—63)
Miles led	2,541	1st	(Jeff Gordon—1,838)
Times led most laps	7	1st	(J. Gordon, Martin—4)
Bonus points	145	1st	(Jeff Gordon—140)
Laps completed	9,769	1st	(Dale Earnhardt—9,693)
Miles completed	12,652	1st	(Johnny Benson—12,511)
Points per race	146.8	2nd	Jeff Gordon—147.2
Lead-lap finishes	24	T-1st	(J. Burton, Martin—24)

*—2nd-place driver listed if Jarrett is category leader

1997 Performance Chart
No. 88 Robert Yates Racing Ford

Career Race	Race No.	Date	Race	St.	Fin.	Total Laps	Laps Completed	Laps Led	Condition	Money	Pts.	Bonus Pts.	Current Standing	Behind Leader	Current Leader
291	1	Feb. 16	Daytona—Daytona 500	3	23	200	200	0	Running	$70,510	94	0	23	-86	Gordon
292	2	Feb. 23	Rockingham—Goodwrench Service 400	3	2	393	393	323	Running	68,760	180	10	7	-86	Gordon
293	3	Mar. 2	Richmond—Pontiac Excitement 400	3	3	400	400	172	Running	50,750	175	10	3	-76	Gordon
294	4	Mar. 9	Atlanta—Primestar 500	9	1	328	328	253	Running	137,650	185	10	1	+29	(T. Labonte)
295	5	Mar. 23	Darlington—TranSouth Financial 400	1	1	293	293	171	Running	142,860	185	10	1	+87	(Gordon)
296	6	Apr. 6	Texas—Interstate Batteries 500	1	2	334	334	42	Running	232,800	175	5	1	+95	(T. Labonte)
297	7	Apr. 13	Bristol—Food City 500	6	4	500	500	0	Running	39,265	160	0	1	+90	(T. Labonte)
298	8	Apr. 20	Martinsville—Goody's Headache Powder 500	23	16	500	499	0	Running	28,265	115	0	1	+45	(T. Labonte)
299	9	May 5	Sears Point—SaveMart Supermarkets 300	8	4	74	74	2	Running	50,135	165	5	1	+40	(T. Labonte)
300	10	May 10	Talladega—Winston 500	9	35	188	184	0	Running	31,365	58	0	3	-52	T. Labonte
301	11	May 25	Charlotte—Coca-Cola 600	3	27	333	332	24	Running	40,875	87	5	3	-112	T. Labonte
302	12	June 1	Dover—Miller 500	6	32	500	463	255	DNF—Engine	44,130	77	10	4	-156	T. Labonte
303	13	June 8	Pocono—Pocono 500	2	3	200	200	5	Running	53,245	170	5	4	-129	Gordon
304	14	June 15	Michigan—Miller 400	1	6	200	200	0	Running	46,525	150	5	4	-134	Gordon
305	15	June 22	California—California 500	9	8	250	250	49	Running	58,750	147	5	4	-172	Gordon
306	16	July 5	Daytona—Pepsi 400	16	5	160	160	0	Running	45,975	155	0	4	-122	Gordon
307	17	July 13	New Hampshire—Jiffy Lube 300	5	38	300	293	98	Running	51,900	54	5	4	-165	T. Labonte
308	18	July 20	Pocono—Pennsylvania 500	4	1	200	200	108	Running	104,570	185	10	4	-152	Gordon
309	19	Aug. 3	Indianapolis—Brickyard 400	3	6	160	160	31	Running	223,900	170	5	3	-147	Gordon
310	20	Aug. 10	Watkins Glen—Bud at the Glen	2	32	90	89	14	Running	28,365	72	5	3	-260	Gordon
311	21	Aug. 17	Michigan—DeVilbiss 400	4	5	200	200	0	Running	46,848	155	0	3	-280	Gordon
312	22	Aug. 23	Bristol—Goody's Headache Powder 500	3	1	500	500	210	Running	101,550	185	10	3	-171	Martin
313	23	Aug. 31	Darlington—Mountain Dew Southern 500	3	3	367	367	38	Running	47,505	170	5	3	-168	Gordon
314	24	Sept. 6	Richmond—Exide 400	23	1	400	400	39	Running	91,490	180	5	3	-153	Gordon
315	25	Sept. 14	New Hampshire—CMT 300	19	6	300	300	0	Running	52,125	150	0	3	-188	Gordon
316	26	Sept. 21	Dover—MBNA 400	3	5	400	399	0	Running	39,845	155	0	3	-184	Gordon
317	27	Sept. 29	Martinsville—Hanes 500	21	12	500	500	0	Running	28,800	127	0	3	-222	Gordon
318	28	Oct. 5	Charlotte—UAW-GM Quality 500	5	1	334	334	85	Running	130,000	180	5	3	-197	Gordon
319	29	Oct. 12	Talladega—DieHard 500	18	21	188	187	13	Running	39,930	105	5	3	-155	Gordon
320	30	Oct. 27	Rockingham—AC Delco 400	2	2	393	393	73	Running	65,175	175	5	3	-145	Gordon
321	31	Nov. 2	Phoenix—Dura-Lube 500	9	1	312	312	73	Running	99,830	180	5	2	-77	Gordon
322	32	Nov. 16	Atlanta—NAPA 500	3	2	325	325	5	Running	79,600	175	5	2	-14	Gordon

The 2,000 Club

Modern Era drivers who have led 2,000 laps or more in a single season

Driver	No. of Times Led 2,000+ Laps	Best Season
Darrell Waltrip	7	1982—3,027
Cale Yarborough	7	1976—3,791
Dale Earnhardt	4	1987—3,358
Jeff Gordon	3	1995—2,600
Richard Petty	3	1975—3,158
Rusty Wallace	3	1993—2,860
Bobby Allison	2	1972—4,343
Dale Jarrett	**1**	**1997—2,083**
David Pearson	1	1973—2,658

Quickly Dominant

Most laps led to start a season, Modern Era (first five races)

Driver	Year	Laps Led
Dale Earnhardt	1987	1,005
Dale Jarrett	**1997**	**919**
Richard Petty	1975	820
Jeff Gordon	1995	797
Cale Yarborough	1974	788

Finish What You Start

In 1997, Dale Jarrett had one of the most reliable cars in NASCAR history.

Driver	Year	Possible Laps	Laps Completed	Uncompleted Laps
Bobby Labonte	2000	10,167	10,158	9
Dale Jarrett	**1997**	**9,822**	**9,769**	**53**
Mark Martin	1990	9,720	9,636	84
Bobby Hamilton	1998	9,932	9,840	92

1998: Biding Time

Like every other Winston Cup driver, Dale Jarrett was forced to write off the 1998 season as Jeff Gordon sped away to one of the most impressive campaigns in NASCAR history. Gordon tied Richard Petty's Modern Era record for wins in a season (13) and set a new mark for most Top 5 finishes (26). Put simply, Gordon was too good and too consistent for the rest of the field in 1998.

The effect of Gordon's mastery on Jarrett's title hopes was best illustrated by a nine-race streak starting with Sears Point in June and ending with the Southern 500 at Darlington in September. In those nine races, Jarrett drove to seven Top 10 finishes and a streak of five consecutive Top 5s. Gordon, meanwhile, won seven of those nine races and finished his non-wins in third and fifth. Points-wise, what should have been a challenge from Jarrett became an also-ran fade. At Sears Point, he was 74 points behind Gordon in the point standings. In September, after Gordon's triumph in the Southern 500, that difference deepened to an insurmountable 248 points.

While 1998 was Gordon's year, Jarrett's season was also eventful. While trying to get a handle on the new Ford Taurus (which replaced the legendary and discontinued Thunderbird), he was embroiled in two controversies that built on the anger inspired by NASCAR's "phantom black flag" at Watkins Glen in 1997. At Richmond, with Jarrett in the lead with six laps to go, NASCAR red-flagged the Pontiac Excitement 400 after a messy four-car wreck threatened an unsatisfying finish under yellow. Because NASCAR rarely used red flags to ensure green-flag finishes, Jarrett felt victimized by an inconsistent policy. When the race resumed, Jarrett's fortunes turned even worse. He was tapped and nearly spun by Terry Labonte with two laps to go and lost the lead. In the night's final irony, the race ended under the yellow flag—with Labonte winning and Jarrett in second.

Two months later, Jarrett's unhappiness with NASCAR was exacerbated during the Brickyard 400 at Indianapolis. Once again, while in the lead, Jarrett saw his hopes for a win affected by Winston Cup officials. This time, on lap 81, with a 2.5-second lead, Jarrett ran out of gas on the backstretch. After coasting nearly 1.5 miles, he came to a stop at the entrance to pit road and needed crew members to push his car to his pit stall. By the time he got back out on to the track, Jarrett was four laps off the pace and wondering why a yellow flag had not been thrown. NASCAR, Jarrett claimed, had assured drivers that if they ran out of gas and stayed clear of the main racing groove, they "would be taken care of." Livid, Jarrett made up all four laps, thanks to caution flags, and then made an incredible climb from 30th to 16th in the final eight laps.

When not jousting with NASCAR officials, Jarrett and his No. 88 team were making important strides, giving unmistakable signs that, after three seasons together, they were ready to contend for a championship. Besides Jarrett's continued development, crew chief Todd Parrott revealed a growing flair for making correct strategic calls from atop the team's pit road war wagon. Likewise, the over-the-wall and behind-the-wall crews stepped forward with amazing efforts that hinted at championship potential.

The spring Martinsville race exemplified the 88 team's ability, and willingness, to change strategy quickly when necessary. Jarrett tested at the short track for three days in hopes of improving on a string of poor finishes. It didn't work. He qualified 23rd and was forced to pit on the backstretch. Though many teams are reluctant to undo a plan that took weeks and months to develop, Parrott and the crew rethought and reworked their car overnight. The shift in strategy, along with a risky, off-schedule pit strategy propelled Jarrett to a third-place finish, his first Martinsville Top 5 in four years.

Another example of the team's ability to salvage strong finishes out of dire circumstances was the second Pocono race. Riding in the Top 5, debris on the track knocked a hole in the oil pan of Jarrett's car. His car trailing smoke and oil, Jarrett brought his car down pit road under caution and watched as his crew quickly diagnosed the problem, plugged the hole, replenished the car's oil supply, and got their driver back in the race without losing a lap. Jarrett made up lost ground and finished an impressive fifth.

Gordon was too good in 1998, but Jarrett and his team showed that 1999 could be their year.

Jarrett in 1998

Category	Total	Rank	1998 Leader
Money	$4,019,657	3rd	Jeff Gordon—9,306,584
Total points	4,619	3rd	Jeff Gordon—5,328
Avg. start	8.7	2nd	Jeff Gordon—7.0
Avg. finish	11.2	3rd	Jeff Gordon—5.7
Wins	3	3rd	Jeff Gordon—13
Top 5s	19	3rd	Jeff Gordon—26
Top 10s	22	4th	Jeff Gordon—28
DNFs	3	32nd	Kenny Wallace—13
Poles	2	6th	Jeff Gordon—7
Front row starts	4	5th	Jeff Gordon—11
Laps led	812	5th	Mark Martin—1,730
Races led	22	3rd	Jeff Gordon—26
Times led	56	3rd	Jeff Gordon—76
Miles led	1,100	4th	Jeff Gordon—2,765
Times led most laps	2	4th	J. Gordon, Martin—8
Bonus points	120	3rd	Jeff Gordon—170
Laps completed	9,475	10th	Bobby Hamilton—9,840
Miles completed	12,361	9th	Jeff Gordon—12,785
Points per race	140.0	3rd	Jeff Gordon—161.5
Lead-lap finishes	25	3rd	Jeff Gordon—28

1998 Performance Chart

No. 88 Robert Yates Racing Ford

Career Race	Race No.	Date	Race	St.	Fin.	Total Laps	Laps Completed	Laps Led	Condition	Money	Pts.	Bonus Pts.	Current Standing	Behind Leader	Current Leader
323	1	Feb.15	Daytona—Daytona 500	5	34	200	196	0	Running	$111,505	61	0	34	-124	Earnhardt
324	2	Feb. 22	Rockingham—Goodwrench Service Plus 400	32	7	393	393	7	Running	42,500	151	5	20	-123	R. Wallace
325	3	Mar. 1	Las Vegas—Las Vegas 400	1	40	267	219	40	DNF– Engine	62,600	48	5	27	-245	R. Wallace
326	4	Mar. 9	Atlanta—Primestar 500	4	2	325	325	29	Running	72,600	175	5	15	-230	R. Wallace
327	5	Mar. 22	Darlington—TranSouth Financial 400	3	1	293	293	68	Running	110,035	180	5	10	-220	R. Wallace
328	6	Mar. 29	Bristol—Food City 500	6	3	500	500	18	Running	57,660	170	5	9	-124	R. Wallace
329	7	Apr. 5	Texas—Texas 500	13	11	334	334	51	Running	93,500	135	5	7	-116	R. Wallace
330	8	Apr. 19	Martinsville—Goody's Headache Powder 500	23	3	500	500	0	Running	58,525	165	0	5	-106	R. Wallace
331	9	Apr. 26	Talladega—Diehard 500	9	3	188	188	8	Running	82,370	170	5	4	-63	R. Wallace
332	10	May 3	California—California 500	36	41	250	86	0	DNF–Engine	44,275	40	0	6	-162	Mayfield
333	11	May 24	Charlotte—Coca-Cola 600	10	5	400	400	47	Running	78,700	160	5	6	-135	Gordon
334	12	May 31	Dover—MBNA Platinum 400	4	1	400	400	8	Running	89,950	180	5	5	-130	Gordon
335	13	June 6	Richmond—Pontiac Excitement 400	4	2	400	400	108	Running	75,625	180	10	4	-53	Mayfield
336	14	June 14	Michigan—Miller Lite 400	2	2	200	200	1	Running	76,125	175	5	4	-33	Mayfield
337	15	June 21	Pocono—Pocono 500	9	3	200	200	26	Running	62,220	170	5	3	-48	Mayfield
338	16	June 28	Sears Point—Save Mart/Kragen 350	3	15	112	112	5	Running	46,700	123	5	4	-74	Gordon
339	17	July 12	New Hampshire—Jiffy Lube 300	3	7	300	300	0	Running	55,825	146	0	3	-98	Gordon
340	18	July 26	Pocono—Pennsylvania 500	11	5	200	200	0	Running	63,815	155	0	3	-128	Gordon
341	19	Aug. 1	Indianapolis—Brickyard 400	2	16	160	160	27	Running	140,260	120	5	3	-193	Gordon
342	20	Aug. 9	Watkins Glen—Bud at the Glen	10	5	90	90	0	Running	52,980	155	0	3	-223	Gordon
343	21	Aug. 16	Michigan—Pepsi 400	4	3	200	200	6	Running	61,805	170	5	3	-233	Gordon
344	22	Aug. 22	Bristol—Goody's Headache Powder 500	9	4	500	500	35	Running	58,855	165	5	3	-223	Gordon
345	23	Aug. 30	New Hampshire—Farm Aid on CMT 300	7	4	300	300	2	Running	78,875	165	5	3	-238	Gordon
346	24	Sept. 6	Darlington—Mountain Dew Southern 500	1	3	367	367	15	Running	79,220	170	5	3	-248	Gordon
347	25	Sept. 12	Richmond—Exide Batteries 400	7	16	400	398	0	Running	39,630	115	0	3	-308	Gordon
348	26	Sept. 20	Dover—MBNA Gold 400	10	7	400	400	0	Running	43,590	146	0	3	-337	Gordon
349	27	Sept. 27	Martinsville—NAPA Autocare 500	10	42	500	299	0	DNF–Engine	32,350	37	0	3	-470	Gordon
350	28	Oct. 4	Charlotte—UAW-GM Quality 500	17	24	334	301	0	Running	33,850	91	0	3	-539	Gordon
351	29	Oct. 11	Talladega—Winston 500[1]	3	1	188	188	16	Running	1,110,125	180	5	3	-534	Gordon
352	30	Oct. 17	Daytona—Pepsi 400	3	23	160	159	38	Running	58,045	99	5	3	-620	Gordon
353	31	Oct. 25	Phoenix—Dura-Lube 500[2]	20	32	257	253	0	Running	34,595	67	0	3	-699	Gordon
354	32	Nov. 1	Rockingham—AC Delco 400	4	2	393	393	195	Running	80,625	180	10	3	-699	Gordon
355	33	Nov. 8	Atlanta—NAPA 500	3	2	221	221	62	Running	100,400	175	5	3	-709	Gordon

[1] —Won No Bull Million Bonus
[2] —Relieved by Michael Waltrip

Podium Finishes

Drivers with the most 1st-, 2nd-, and 3rd-place
finishes, 1996–99

Driver	No. of Podium Finishes
Jeff Gordon	70
Dale Jarrett	**58**
Mark Martin	47
Bobby Labonte	33
Jeff Burton	29

1999: That Championship Season

Dale Jarrett won the 1999 championship by assembling one of the steadiest, most consistent seasons in NASCAR history. Avoiding the slumps that had doomed his title hopes in previous seasons, Jarrett achieved the consistent strength that had propelled Gordon to three titles (and would ensure Bobby Labonte's championship run in 2000).

After an inauspicious start (Jarrett began the season with a DNF in the Daytona 500, thanks to a nudge from new teammate Kenny Irwin), he reeled off 20 Top-8 finishes in the next 21 races (the lone non-Top 10 was an 11th at Las Vegas). The streak produced the longest consecutive Top 5 (7) and Top 10 (19) streaks in Jarrett's career. His 29 Top 10s in 1999 are a modern era record.

Encased in that championship run were four victories at Richmond, Michigan, Daytona, and Indianapolis. At Michigan, a dominant Jarrett overpowered the field, building leads as great as 10 seconds and leading the final 148 laps. At Indy, he led 117 of 160 laps in another overwhelming performance. The win at Richmond gave Jarrett the points lead for the first time in 1999. He maintained his position atop the standings for the remaining 24 weeks of the season—the longest consecutive reign as points leader by a driver since Dale Earnhardt's great run in 1987 (when he led the final 28 weeks of the season).

When Jarrett's Top 10 streak ended in the Bristol night race, he held a commanding 314-point lead in the series standings. He would cruise to a 201-point margin of victory in the final series standings. His 5,262 championship points are the second highest total ever since the Winston Cup series adopted its current point system. Only Jeff Gordon in 1998 earned more points in a season.

By winning the Winston Cup title, Jarrett and his father, Ned (who won Grand National titles in 1961 and 1965), joined Lee and Richard Petty as the only father-son champions in NASCAR history. Jarrett also became the series' second oldest first-time champion, hoisting the Winston Cup champion's trophy at Homestead just 12 days before his 43rd birthday. By winning the title in his 13th season on the circuit, his championship came later in his career than any driver, except Bobby Allison, who won his lone title in 1983 in his 18th season.

The championship was equally important for Jarrett's car owner, Robert Yates. In 35 years of NASCAR racing, from mechanic to engine builder to crew chief to team owner, Yates was never a member of a title-winning team. He had won scores of races and poles and had come close to winning championships. His best hopes for titles during the early 1990s, with drivers Davey Allison and Ernie Irvan, were tragically cut short.

That Jarrett and the No. 88 car would win Yates' first championship was completely unforeseen in 1995 (when Jarrett joined Robert Yates Racing). Allison and Irvan were viewed as clearly superior drivers. Talented and hard-working, Jarrett and Yates were vindicated in 1999: Jarrett for his driving ability, Yates for his faith in Jarrett's driving ability.

As Jarrett said in one of the many commercials he would make following his title run, "It took a long time to become an overnight success."

Mr. Consistency

Most Top 10s in a season, Modern Era

Driver	Year	No. of Top 10s
Dale Jarrett	1999	29
Jeff Gordon	1998	28
Richard Petty	1972	28
Bobby Allison	1972	27
Richard Petty	1979	27
Cale Yarborough	1977	27

Jarrett in 1999

Category	Total	Rank	1999 Leader*
Money	$6,649,596	1st	(Jeff Gordon—5,858,633)
Total points	5,262	1st	(Bobby Labonte—5,061)
Avg. start	13.2	6th	Jeff Gordon—7.4
Avg. finish	6.8	1st	(Bobby Labonte—9.0)
Wins	4	4th	Jeff Gordon—7
Top 5s	24	1st	(Bobby Labonte—23)
Top 10s	29	1st	(B. Labonte, Martin—26)
DNFs	1	44th	Andretti, Craven, M. Waltrip—10
Poles	0	—	Jeff Gordon—7
Front row starts	4	5th	Jeff Gordon—9
Laps led	1,061	5th	Jeff Gordon—1,319
Races led	22	4th	Bobby Labonte—30
Times led	54	4th	Jeff Gordon—86
Miles led	1,812	2nd	Jeff Gordon—1,923
Times led most laps	4	5th	J. Burton, J. Gordon—6
Bonus points	130	3rd	Bobby Labonte—165
Laps completed	9,900	4th	Bobby Labonte—10,013
Miles completed	12,989	3rd	Bobby Labonte—13,135
Points per race	154.8	1st	(Bobby Labonte—148.9)
Lead-lap finishes	28	T-1st	(Bobby Labonte—28)

*—2nd-place driver listed if Jarrett is category leader

1999 Performance Chart

No. 88 Robert Yates Racing Ford

Career Race	Race No.	Date	Race	St.	Fin.	Total Laps	Laps Completed	Laps Led	Condition	Money	Pts.	Bonus Pts.	Point Standing	Behind Leader	Current Leader
356	1	Feb. 14	Daytona—Daytona 500	8	37	200	134	14	DNF–Crash	$121,379	57	5	36	-123	Gordon
357	2	Feb. 21	Rockingham—Dura-Lube/Big Kmart 400	11	2	393	393	0	Running	83,675	170	0	13	-88	Skinner
358	3	Mar. 7	Las Vegas—Las Vegas 400	9	11	267	266	0	Running	85,240	130	0	11	-118	Skinner
359	4	Mar. 14	Atlanta—Cracker Barrel Old Country Store 500	4	5	325	325	0	Running	53,675	155	0	6	-118	Skinner
360	5	Mar. 21	Darlington—TranSouth Financial 400	21	4	164	164	0	Running	60,305	160	0	6	-91	J. Burton
361	6	Mar. 28	Texas—Primestar 500	12	2	334	334	39	Running	250,100	175	5	3	-62	J. Burton
362	7	Apr. 11	Bristol—Food City 500	16	3	500	500	0	Running	68,650	165	0	2	-52	J. Burton
363	8	Apr. 18	Martinsville—Goody's Body Pain 500	31	8	500	500	0	Running	46,825	142	0	2	-85	J. Burton
364	9	Apr. 25	Talladega—Diehard 500	23	2	188	188	21	Running	104,955	175	5	2	-40	J. Burton
365	10	May 2	California—California 500	2	5	250	250	1	Running	71,140	160	5	2	-55	J. Burton
366	11	May 15	Richmond—Pontiac Excitement 400	21	1	400	400	32	Running	169,715	180	5	1	+63	(J. Burton)
367	12	May 30	Charlotte—Coca-Cola 600	28	5	400	400	0	Running	81,125	155	0	1	+33	(J. Burton)
368	13	June 6	Dover—MBNA Platinum 400	2	5	400	399	21	Running	67,745	160	5	1	+51	(J. Burton)
369	14	June 13	Michigan—Kmart 400	6	1	200	200	150	Running	151,240	185	10	1	+66	(J. Burton)
370	15	June 20	Pocono—Pocono 500	2	3	200	200	71	Running	86,670	175	10	1	+89	(B. Labonte)
371	16	June 27	Sears Point—Save Mart/Kragen 350k	29	6	112	112	0	Running	53,940	150	0	1	+157	(B. Labonte)
372	17	July 3	Daytona—Pepsi 400	12	1	160	160	40	Running	164,965	180	5	1	+177	(B. Labonte)
373	18	July 11	New Hampshire—Jiffy Lube 300	9	4	300	300	18	Running	75,550	165	5	1	+240	(J. Burton)
374	19	July 25	Pocono—Pennsylvania 500	15	2	200	200	41	Running	95,695	175	5	1	+254	(M. Martin)
375	20	Aug. 7	Indianapolis—Brickyard 400	4	1	160	160	117	Running	712,240	185	10	1	+274	(M. Martin)
376	21	Aug. 15	Watkins Glen—Frontier @ the Glen	9	4	90	90	0	Running	59,900	160	0	1	+300	(M. Martin)
377	22	Aug. 22	Michigan—Pepsi 400	3	4	200	200	27	Running	57,650	165	5	1	+314	(M. Martin)
378	23	Aug. 28	Bristol—Goody's Headache Powder 500	25	38	500	338	0	Running	43,425	49	0	1	+213	(M. Martin)
379	24	Sept. 5	Darlington—Pepsi Southern 500	36	16	270	270	23	Running	50,960	120	5	1	+168	(M. Martin)
380	25	Sept. 11	Richmond—Exide Batteries 400	13	3	400	400	0	Running	64,605	165	0	1	+270	(M. Martin)
381	26	Sept. 19	New Hampshire—Dura-Lube/Kmart 300	2	18	300	299	49	Running	66,500	114	5	1	+254	(B. Labonte)
382	27	Sept. 26	Dover—MBNA Gold 400	26	3	400	400	99	Running	74,935	170	5	1	+257	(M. Martin)
383	28	Oct. 3	Martinsville—NAPA AutoCare 500	14	10	500	499	0	Running	52,790	134	0	1	+251	(B. Labonte)
384	29	Oct. 10	Charlotte—UAW-GM Quality 500	9	7	334	334	33	Running	65,475	151	5	1	+222	(B. Labonte)
385	30	Oct. 17	Talladega—Winston 500	17	2	188	188	37	Running	85,345	175	5	1	+246	(B. Labonte)
386	31	Oct. 24	Rockingham—Pop Secret Popcorn 400	3	4	393	393	160	Running	61,175	170	10	1	+246	(B. Labonte)
387	32	Nov. 7	Phoenix—Checker Auto Parts/Dura-Lube 500K	5	6	312	312	50	Running	82,475	155	5	1	+231	(B. Labonte)
388	33	Nov. 14	Homestead—Pennzoil 400	12	5	267	267	1	Running	100,865	160	5	1	+211	(B. Labonte)
389	34	Nov. 21	Atlanta—NAPA 500	10	2	325	325	17	Running	94,400	175	5	1	+201	(B. Labonte)

Oldest Champs

The oldest Winston Cup champions when they won their first title

Driver	Year	Age
Bobby Allison	1983	45 years, 351 days
Dale Jarrett	**1999**	**42 years, 352 days**
Lee Petty	1954	40 years, 224 days
Joe Weatherly	1962	40 years, 152 days
Bobby Isaac	1970	38 years, 112 days

The 5,000 Club

Winston Cup drivers who have earned 5,000 or more championship points in a season

Driver	Year	Point Total	No. Races	Points per Race
Jeff Gordon	1998	5,328	33	161.5
Dale Jarrett	**1999**	**5,262**	**34**	**154.8**
Bobby Labonte	2000	5,130	34	150.9
Jeff Gordon	2001	5,112	36	142.0
Bobby Labonte	1999	5,061	34	148.9
Cale Yarborough	1977	5,000	30	166.7

2000: Title Defense Falters

No Winston Cup champion has ever opened his title defense quite like Dale Jarrett in 2000. The 1999 title winner so thoroughly dominated Speedweeks at Daytona, fans howled about the "Boring 500," and NASCAR changed its rules governing aerodynamics at restrictor-plate tracks. Has any champion ever caused such turmoil during a season's first eight days?

Inciting the tumult was Jarrett's nonstop excellence. In eight February days, he:
- won the pole for the Daytona 500
- won the qualifying race for the Bud Shootout all-star event
- won the Bud Shootout
- finished second in his Twin 125 qualifying event
- won the Daytona 500

Jarrett's performance is nearly unparalleled in Daytona history. Since the introduction of the Bud Shootout (formerly the Busch Clash) in 1979, only two other drivers have made such a determined run for Daytona's "Quadruple Crown." Elliott (in 1985 and 1987) and Cale Yarborough (1984) conducted similarly strong campaigns for the top four events of Speedweeks. Once again, Jarrett put himself in good company at Daytona.

The complaints that greeted Jarrett's supremacy left him in the awkward position of defending his dominant performance. For the 43-year-old veteran, it was a wonderful reversal of fortune. Just five years earlier, he had to defend against the perception that his performance wasn't good enough for a spot in Robert Yates' cars.

Making the complaints and ingratitude easier to handle was the Daytona 500's enormous winner's prize. Jarrett's take from the race was $2,277,975, the largest winner's check in American racing history. Included in the payday was his second No Bull Million bonus.

When Jarrett followed his Daytona success with a fifth-place finish at Rockingham, he seemed ready to mount a sturdy title defense. Then he stumbled. After starting from the pole at Atlanta in the season's fourth race, he fell to 36th in the finishing order thanks to engine failure, his first DNF in 36 races. Poor finishes in the following weeks at Bristol and Texas pushed Jarrett all the way to eighth place in the standings, 214 points behind eventual champ Bobby Labonte.

Jarrett climbed back into title contention with an impressive midseason string of 15 straight Top 10 finishes. With his fourth-place finish at Pocono in July, he was just 53 points behind Labonte. Stealing a page from Jarrett's 1999 championship run, however, Labonte kept pressure on the rest of the field with unfailing consistency. Jarrett could not muster the same. A wreck with Rusty Wallace at Charlotte resulted in a 40th-place finish and his second DNF of the year, slamming the door on any title hopes.

Despite missing a chance to win back-to-back championships, Jarrett's Daytona 500 win and, finally, his first-ever win at Rockingham highlighted a solid season. By finishing fourth in the final point standings, he earned his fifth consecutive Top 5 points finish.

Jarrett in 2000

Category	Total	Rank	2000 Leader*
Money	$5,984,475	3rd	Bobby Labonte—7,361,386
Total points	4,684	4th	Bobby Labonte—5,130
Avg. start	13.1	6th	Rusty Wallace—10.0
Avg. finish	11.1	4th	Bobby Labonte—7.4
Wins	2	6th	Tony Stewart—6
Top 5s	15	2nd	Bobby Labonte—19
Top 10s	24	T-1st	(D. Earnhardt, B. Labonte—24)
DNFs	2	42nd	J. Mayfield, S. Pruett—11
Poles	3	3rd	Rusty Wallace—9
Front row starts	5	4th	Rusty Wallace—11
Laps led	333	14th	Rusty Wallace—1,730
Races led	15	8th	J. Burton, B. Labonte—23
Times led	26	11th	Rusty Wallace—62
Miles led	691	6th	Rusty Wallace—1,869
Times led most laps	3	4th	Rusty Wallace—6
Bonus points	90	7th	Jeff Burton—140
Laps completed	9,749	8th	Bobby Labonte—10,158
Miles completed	12,712	8th	Bobby Labonte—13,268
Points per race	137.8	4th	Bobby Labonte—150.9
Lead-lap finishes	24	5th	D. Earnhardt, B. Labonte—28

*—2nd-place driver listed if Jarrett is category leader

2000 Performance Chart

No. 88 Robert Yates Racing Ford

Career Race	Race No.	Date	Race	St.	Fin.	Total Laps	Laps Completed	Laps Led	Condition	Money	Pts.	Bonus Pts.	Point Standing	Behind Leader	Current Leader*
390	1	Feb. 20	Daytona—Daytona 500	1	1	200	200	89	Running	$2,277,975	185	10	1	+15	(B. Elliott)
391	2	Feb. 27	Rockingham—Dura Lube/Kmart 400	23	5	393	392	0	Running	64,060	155	0	1	+5	(B. Labonte)
392	3	Mar. 5	Las Vegas—Carsdirect.com 400	6	7	148	148	0	Running	105,200	146	0	2	-4	B. Labonte
393	4	Mar. 12	Atlanta—Cracker Barrel Old Country Store 500	1	36	325	257	5	DNF–Engine	56,195	60	5	6	-119	B. Labonte
394	5	Mar. 19	Darlington—Mall.com 400	17	2	293	293	26	Running	90,905	175	5	5	-73	B. Labonte
395	6	Mar. 26	Bristol—Food City 500	20	21	500	499	7	Running	52,915	105	5	4	-118	B. Labonte
396	7	Apr. 2	Texas—DirecTV 500	5	33	334	285	18	Running	68,550	69	5	8	-219	B. Labonte
397	8	Apr. 9	Martinsville—Goody's Body Pain 500	28	5	500	500	0	Running	65,125	155	0	7	-196	B. Labonte
398	9	Apr. 16	Talladega—DieHard 500	3	17	188	187	4	Running	63,300	117	5	6	-203	Martin
399	10	Apr. 30	California—NAPA Auto Parts 500	33	9	250	250	0	Running	70,650	138	0	6	-211	B. Labonte
400	11	May 6	Richmond—Pontiac Excitement 400	18	3	400	400	0	Running	78,525	165	0	6	-131	B. Labonte
401	12	May 28	Charlotte—Coca-Cola 600	8	5	400	400	2	Running	95,000	160	5	6	-146	B. Labonte
402	13	June 4	Dover—MBNA Platinum 400	18	4	400	400	0	Running	95,755	160	0	6	-156	B. Labonte
403	14	June 11	Michigan—Kmart 400	26	4	194	194	3	Running	71,285	165	5	4	-161	B. Labonte
404	15	June 18	Pocono—Pocono 500	4	2	200	200	0	Running	131,520	170	0	3	-115	B. Labonte
405	16	June 25	Sears Point—Save Mart/Kragen 300	18	7	112	112	0	Running	69,665	146	0	3	-129	B. Labonte
406	17	July 1	Daytona—Pepsi 400	1	2	160	160	56	Running	126,350	180	10	3	-76	B. Labonte
407	18	July 9	New Hampshire—Jiffy Lube 300	10	7	273	273	1	Running	70,725	151	5	3	-68	B. Labonte
408	19	July 23	Pocono—Pennsylvania 500	11	4	200	200	73	Running	97,470	170	10	2	-53	B. Labonte
409	20	Aug. 5	Indianapolis—Brickyard 400	5	7	160	160	0	Running	155,710	146	0	2	-87	B. Labonte
410	21	Aug. 13	Watkins Glen—Global Crossing @ The Glen	2	7	90	90	0	Running	57,210	146	0	2	-101	B. Labonte
411	22	Aug. 20	Michigan—Pepsi 400	2	4	200	200	0	Running	70,275	160	0	2	-111	B. Labonte
412	23	Aug. 26	Bristol—Goracing.com 500	31	5	500	500	1	Running	56,715	143	5	2	-91	B. Labonte
413	24	Sept. 3	Darlington—Southern 500	9	5	328	328	3	Running	80,570	160	5	2	-111	B. Labonte
414	25	Sept. 9	Richmond—Chevrolet Monte Carlo 400	17	31	400	381	0	Running	48,840	70	0	3	-164	B. Labonte
415	26	Sept. 17	New Hampshire—New Hampshire 300	4	4	300	300	0	Running	93,400	160	0	3	-174	B. Labonte
416	27	Sept. 24	Dover—MBNA.com 400	8	32	400	301	0	Running	66,555	67	0	3	-267	B. Labonte
417	28	Oct. 1	Martinsville—NAPA AutoCare 500	31	6	500	500	0	Running	57,375	150	0	4	-251	B. Labonte
418	29	Oct. 8	Charlotte—UAW-GM Quality 500	5	40	334	158	0	DNF–Accident	48,175	43	0	4	-388	B. Labonte
419	30	Oct. 15	Talladega—Winston 500	12	15	188	188	0	Running	66,185	118	0	4	-402	B. Labonte
420	31	Oct.22	Rockingham—Pop Secret 400	21	1	393	393	43	Running	125,850	180	5	4	-330	B. Labonte
421	32	Nov. 5	Phoenix—Checker Auto Parts/DuraLube 500K	36	10	312	312	0	Running	86,000	134	0	4	-356	B. Labonte
422	33	Nov. 12	Homestead—Pennzoil 400	7	17	267	265	0	Running	63,300	112	0	4	-409	B. Labonte
423	34	Nov. 19	Atlanta—NAPA 500	3	15	325	323	2	Running	66,475	123	5	4	-446	B. Labonte

The Quadruple Crown

Since 1979, three drivers have nearly pulled off victories in the four main Winston Cup events—The Bud Shootout, the Daytona 500 pole, the Twin 125s, and the Daytona 500 itself—during Speedweeks at Daytona.

Driver	Year	Bud Shootout*	Daytona 500 Qualifying	Twin 125s	Daytona 500	Margin of Victory in Lost Event (Race Winner)
Dale Jarrett	2000	1st	Won pole	2nd	1st	2 car lengths (Bill Elliott)
Bill Elliott	1987	1st	Won pole	2nd	1st	12 inches (Ken Schrader)
Bill Elliott	1985	3rd	Won pole	1st	1st	1 second (Terry Labonte)
Cale Yarborough	1984	2nd	Won pole	1st	1st	2 car lengths (Neil Bonnett)

*—Originally called the Busch Clash when the event was introduced in 1979, it was renamed the Bud Shootout in 1998.

2001: The Big Brown Truck

Off-track activities seemed to draw more attention than on-track performance for Dale Jarrett in 2001. Not that his on-track exploits lacked impact: He won four races, contended seriously for the championship, and performed admirably through two painful injuries.

Still, a new primary sponsorship agreement with United Parcel Service defined Jarrett's year. The UPS deal guaranteed Jarrett's Robert Yates Racing team a reported $15 million per year for the right to change the No. 88 car's colors from red, white, and blue to brown and white. The move put Jarrett in line with the top sponsorship deals enjoyed by Jeff Gordon, Mark Martin, and the late Dale Earnhardt.

Jarrett nearly backed up his off-track attention with excellence on the track. Early in the season, he looked unstoppable. During one six-race stretch in March and April, he won two poles, three races (at Darlington, Texas, and Martinsville) and had five Top 5 finishes. Inspiring comparisons to golf's Tiger Woods, Jarrett's run helped him build what eventually became a 145-point lead over Gordon three months into the season. Of his early victories, Martinsville was the sweetest. Jarrett started his Winston Cup career at the .526-mile track in 1984 and had gone 30 races at the track without a victory.

Jarrett's invincibility faded quickly, however. After Martinsville, he finished 15 of the next 26 races outside of the Top 10 and won just one more race the rest of the season. He yielded the points lead to Jeff Gordon 14 races into the season, then fought back to create one of the most unusual championship points situations in NASCAR history. After the inaugural race at the new Chicagoland Speedway in July, Jarrett and Gordon were tied atop the standings. Such ties are rare, but not unusual. What was truly unique is what occurred the following week: They each scored 180 points at New Hampshire and remained tied for a second consecutive week. Mathematically improbable, maintaining a points tie after consecutive races has never happened since the introduction of the current point system in 1975.

After being deadlocked with Gordon for two weeks, Jarrett fell from the points lead when he finished 41st at Pocono, his worst finish in three seasons. Jarrett never again challenged Gordon's run for a fourth title. Making matters worse, hard crashes started taking a toll on his body. At Charlotte, while attempting to qualify for the Coca-Cola 600, he backed his car into the wall in Turn 4. Days later, a sharp pain developed in his side. Jarrett discovered that he had broken a rib in his earlier crash. Later, in the September inaugural event at the new Kansas Speedway, contact with Bobby Labonte spun his car and sent it driver's side first into Turn 1 wall. The heavy contact left Jarrett briefly unconscious. He suffered a concussion and a broken rib as a result of the crash.

Amazingly, despite his injuries, Jarrett didn't miss a race or even a lap during the season. In fact, only Bobby Hamilton (10,750) completed more laps in 2001 than Jarrett (10,744). Quantity of laps didn't translate into quality, however. For the first time since Jarrett and the No. 88 started racing together in 1996, he finished outside of the Top 20 10 times. The prolonged run of Top 10 finishes that Jarrett became known for never materialized. In many ways, Jarrett and his No. 88 team had their worst season. After five superlative seasons, Jarrett finished with fewer Top 5s, Top 10s, and championship points than any season since 1995. Meanwhile, his DNFs, average start, and average finish inched upward. His fifth-place finish in the point standings was his lowest since finishing 13th in 1995.

Perhaps in reaction to the slight slip, Jarrett's team was restructured during the off season. Todd Parrott, the team's successful crew chief, stepped aside to allow Jimmy Elledge to take over. Parrott assumed a new role as team manager.

Jarrett in 2001

Category	Total	Rank	2001 Leader
Money	$5,366,242	3rd	Jeff Gordon—10,436,757
Total points	4,612	5th	Jeff Gordon—5,112
Avg. start	14.8	5th	Jeff Gordon—9.5
Avg. finish	13.9	5th	Jeff Gordon—11.0
Wins	4	2nd	Jeff Gordon—6
Top 5s	12	4th	Jeff Gordon—18
Top 10s	19	6th	Jeff Gordon—24
DNFs	4	23rd	Todd Bodine—12
Poles	4	2nd	Jeff Gordon—8
Front row starts	6	2nd	Jeff Gordon—13
Laps led	511	6th	Jeff Gordon—2,320
Races led	17	4th	Jeff Gordon—25
Times led	39	4th	Jeff Gordon—88
Miles led	756	5th	Jeff Gordon—3,030
Times led most laps	1	8th	Jeff Gordon—11
Bonus points	90	5th	Jeff Gordon—180
Laps completed	10,744	2nd	Bobby Hamilton—10,750
Miles completed	14,050	3rd	Sterling Marlin—14,104
Points per race	128.1	5th	Jeff Gordon—142.0
Lead-lap finishes	27	3rd	Sterling Marlin—30

2001 Performance Chart
No. 88 Robert Yates Racing Ford

Career Race	Race No.	Date	Race	St.	Fin.	Total Laps	Laps Completed	Laps Led	Condition	Money	Pts.	Bonus Pts.	Point Standing	Behind Leader	Current Leader
424	1	Feb. 18	Daytona—Daytona 500	31	22	200	186	1	DNF–Crash	167,711	102	5	21	-78	M. Waltrip
425	2	Feb. 25	Rockingham—Dura Lube 400	18	10	393	393	0	Running	91,237	134	0	12	-75	R. Wallace
426	3	Mar. 4	Las Vegas—UAW-DaimlerChrysler 400	1	2	267	267	42	Running	257,977	175	5	4	-57	Marlin
427	4	Mar. 11	Atlanta—Cracker Barrel 500	1	4	325	325	44	Running	114,927	165	5	2	-37	Gordon
428	5	Mar. 18	Darlington—Carolina Dodge Dealers 400	2	1	293	293	16	Running	214,612	180	5	1	+65	(J. Benson)
429	6	Mar. 25	Bristol—Food City 500	19	16	500	500	0	Running	90,142	115	0	1	+45	(Gordon)
430	7	Apr. 1	Texas—Harrah's 500	3	1	334	334	122	Running	444,527	185	10	1	+75	(Gordon)
431	8	Apr. 8	Martinsville—Virginia 500	13	1	500	500	6	Running	170,027	180	5	1	+123	(Gordon)
432	9	Apr. 22	Talladega—Talladega 500	6	18	188	188	0	Running	92,012	109	0	1	+145	(Gordon)
433	10	Apr. 29	California—NAPA Auto Parts 500	5	24	250	250	2	Running	93,602	96	5	1	+66	(Gordon)
434	11	May 5	Richmond—Pontiac Excitement 400	20	15	400	400	0	Running	85,712	118	0	1	+14	(Gordon)
435	12	May 27	Charlotte—Coca-Cola 600	37	8	400	400	0	Running	108,552	142	0	1	+75	(Gordon)
436	13	June 3	Dover—MBNA Platinum 400	1	5	400	400	1	Running	115,007	160	5	1	+50	(Gordon)
437	14	June 10	Michigan—Kmart 400	21	18	200	199	0	Running	83,117	109	0	2	-26	(Gordon)
438	15	June 17	Pocono—Pocono 500	10	3	200	200	62	Running	119,947	170	5	2	-36	(Gordon)
439	16	June 24	Sears Point—Dodge/Save Mart 350	35	26	112	112	0	Running	85,702	85	0	2	-126	(Gordon)
440	17	July 7	Daytona—Pepsi 400	19	11	160	160	0	Running	99,052	130	0	2	-48	(Gordon)
441	18	July 15	Chicagoland—Tropicana 400	11	4	267	267	0	Running	101,300	160	0	2	0	Gordon
442	19	July 22	New Hampshire—New England 300	9	1	300	300	92	Running	238,027	180	5	1	0	(Gordon)
443	20	July 29	Pocono—Pennsylvania 500	37	41	200	152	1	DNF–Crash	75,027	45	5	3	-107	Gordon
444	21	Aug. 4	Indianapolis—Brickyard 400	6	12	160	160	0	Running	153,587	127	0	2	-160	Gordon
445	22	Aug. 12	Watkins Glen—Global Crossing @ The Glen	1	31	90	89	17	Running	82,962	75	5	3	-265	Gordon
446	23	Aug. 19	Michigan—Pepsi 400	17	37	162	160	2	Running	79,792	57	5	3	-354	Gordon
447	24	Aug. 25	Bristol—Sharpie 500	7	6	500	500	0	Running	115,492	150	5	3	-379	Gordon
448	25	Sept. 2	Darlington—Southern 500	27	34	367	356	53	Running	82,417	66	5	4	-493	Gordon
449	26	Sept. 8	Richmond—Chevrolet Monte Carlo 400	16	4	400	400	0	Running	107,107	160	0	3	-393	Gordon
450	27	Sept. 23	Dover—MBNA Cal Ripken Jr. 400	1	12	400	400	18	Running	98,142	132	5	4	-421	Gordon
451	28	Sept. 30	Kansas—Protection One 400	18	30	267	246	0	DNF–Crash	91,827	73	0	5	-528	Gordon
452	29	Oct. 7	Charlotte—UAW-GM Quality 500	25	6	334	334	0	Running	97,707	150	0	5	-493	Gordon
453	30	Oct. 14	Martinsville—Old Dominion 500	4	2	500	500	31	Running	114,252	175	5	4	-461	Gordon
454	31	Oct. 21	Talladega—EA Sports 500	10	25	188	187	1	DNF–Crash	86,532	93	5	5	-514	Gordon
455	32	Oct. 28	Phoenix—Checker Auto Parts 500	16	9	312	312	0	Running	96,452	138	0	4	-526	Gordon
456	33	Nov. 4	Rockingham—Pop Secret 400	31	4	393	393	0	Running	103,252	160	0	4	-454	Gordon
457	34	Nov. 11	Homestead—Pennzoil Freedom 400	18	41	267	256	0	Running	79,752	40	0	5	-493	Gordon
458	35	Nov. 18	Atlanta—NAPA 500	33	8	325	325	0	Running	103,702	142	0	5	-506	Gordon
459	36	Nov. 23	New Hampshire—New Hampshire 300	3	10	300	300	0	Running	96,452	134	0	5	-500	Gordon

Falling Down

Jarrett and the No. 88 team had 10 finishes outside of the Top 20 during the 2001 season, their highest total since the team was created in 1996.

Year	No. of Finishes Outside of the Top 20
2001	10
1998	7
1997	7
2000	6

Dale Jarrett's Career on Current and Former Winston Cup Tracks

The Winston Cup schedule includes a variety of tracks, from short tracks (less than 1 mile, such as Bristol) 1-mile ovals (Dover), speedways (less than 2 miles, such as Charlotte), superspeedways (2 miles or greater, such as Talladega), and road courses (Watkins Glen). Each track demands a different touch, a different set of skills. Over the course of a driver's career, patterns emerge that provide a glimpse into the style and skill of a driver. This section lays out in detail Jarrett's career on each Winston Cup track.

For each track on which Jarrett competed at least three times there is a statistical comparison to determine his place in the track's history. This comparison extends to 22 different statistical categories. Jarrett's total for each category is listed, along with his rank and that category's leader. If Jarrett is the leader in a category, the second-place driver is listed in parentheses with his total. For the older tracks, that is, tracks that have been part of the Winston Cup circuit for more than 35 years, the comparison is limited to the modern era (1972 to the present).

Accompanying the statistical comparison is a track summary that puts Jarrett's career at the track in context or details memorable moments. Perhaps most useful to understanding Jarrett's development at each track is the inclusion of a "performance chart" that lists in detail every race he started at the track. Listed for each race are the year, date, and race name, along with Jarrett's start, finish, total laps, laps completed, laps led, race-ending condition, money, points earned, and bonus points.

Each year, NASCAR impounds the Daytona 500 winner's car for display in the track's museum. Few drivers have signed away as many winning cars at Daytona as Jarrett.

For most of his career, Dover has been Jarrett's nightmare track. He failed to finish 12 of his first 21 Dover starts. In the 1994 SplitFire 500, he was involved in three wrecks, breaking his wrist in the third accident.

Jarrett's first career Winston Cup start came at Martinsville in 1984. He needed 17 years and 30 starts before getting his first victory at the .526-mile track.

Jarrett's first win for UPS came at Darlington in the spring of 2001. He went on to win three more races for his new sponsor that season.

Jarrett at Atlanta Motor Speedway

Qualify poorly, finish well. That has been the trend in Dale Jarrett's career at Atlanta Motor Speedway. Though he ranks 49th in average start on the 1.54-mile track, Jarrett ranks seventh in average finish. His ability to finish strongly at Atlanta is bettered only by some of the biggest names in NASCAR history, a short list consisting of Earnhardt, Yarborough, Pearson, Irvan, Bobby Labonte, and Gordon.

Even more interesting than Jarrett's starts and finishes is what has happened in between. Atlanta has been one of his most eventful tracks. Topping the list of memorable Atlanta races is Jarrett's only victory in the spring of 1997. Jarrett began the 1997 season in dominant fashion, leading 961 laps in the four races after the Daytona 500. One of those dominating performances came at Atlanta. Starting ninth, he quickly moved to the front of the field and led 253 of the race's 328 laps, the fifth highest number of laps led in a single race in track history.

That victory highlighted an amazing Atlanta run for Jarrett. Starting in the fall of 1996, he finished first or second in six of the next seven races at the Hampton, Georgia, track. During that stretch, Jarrett finished in second place five times. Only Dale Earnhardt, Atlanta's undisputed king, had more Atlanta runner-up finishes than Jarrett.

Another Atlanta performance, the Cracker Barrel 500 in the spring of 1999, trumpeted Jarrett and his team's championship capabilities. In a disastrous start, Jarrett fell a lap down early when a jack broke during a pit stop. Reacting to the amount of track position lost to the slow pit, Jarrett was caught speeding on pit road and penalized. In a later pit stop, lug nuts popped off a tire as it was being mounted on the car, causing another slow stop and more lost track position. Despite the trouble, Jarrett was able to regain his position on the lead lap and finish fifth. His team's ability to salvage a Top 5 finish gave the first indication of what was in store. Jarrett followed his Atlanta miracle with 18 consecutive Top 10 finishes (including 16 Top 5s) and marched to the 1999 Winston Cup title.

Of course, not all of Jarrett's memories at Atlanta are fond. His first three races there produced finishes of 36th, 29th, and 41st. In 1993, he raced while suffering from the effects of pneumonia, then finished 31st after getting spun. In 2000, a blown engine in the spring race dropped him to 36th place and gave an early jolt to his attempt to defend his Winston Cup title.

The news from Atlanta has been overwhelmingly positive, however, since he joined Robert Yates Racing in 1995. Jarrett has enjoyed a steady stream of solid finishes and has even seen improvement in his qualifying. In 2000 and 2001, he won consecutive poles for the spring Cracker Barrel 500.

Jarrett opened the 1997 season in dominating fashion, leading 961 laps in the first five races. Included in his impressive start was his first-ever victory at Atlanta.

Atlanta Record Book—Modern Era

Category	Jarrett's Total	Jarrett's Rank	Modern Era Track Leader
Money	$1,183,559	5th	Dale Earnhardt—1,796,225
Starts	28	24th	Darrell Waltrip—56
Total points[1]	3,543	17th	Dale Earnhardt—6,715
Avg. start	19.5	49th	David Pearson—4.7
Avg. finish	14.3	7th	Dale Earnhardt—9.6
Wins	1	15th	Dale Earnhardt—9
Winning pct.	3.6	19th	Bobby Labonte—27.8
Top 5s	10	10th	Dale Earnhardt—26
Top 10s	15	12h	Dale Earnhardt—30
DNFs	5	56th	Dave Marcis—19
Poles	2	10th	Buddy Baker—5
Front row starts	2	20th	Dale Earnhardt—10
Laps led	431	13th	Dale Earnhardt—2,647
Pct. laps led	4.8	20th	Cale Yarborough—21.2
Races led	10	19th	Dale Earnhardt—32
Times led	29	17th	Dale Earnhardt—125
Times led most laps	1	12th	Dale Earnhardt—9
Bonus points[1]	55	18th	Dale Earnhardt—205
Laps completed	8,014	22nd	Darrell Waltrip—14,818
Pct. laps completed	88.5	27th	Kenny Irwin—99.1
Points per race[1]	126.5	7th	Dale Earnhardt—146.0
Lead-lap finishes	12	4th	Dale Earnhardt—26

[1]—Since implementation of current point system in 1975

Jarrett Track Performance Chart

Atlanta Motor Speedway
Hampton, Georgia—1.54 miles—24° banking

Year	Date	Race	St.	Fin.	Total Laps	Laps Completed	Laps Led	Condition	Money	Pts.	Bonus Pts.
1987	Nov. 22	Atlanta Journal 500	33	36	328	84	0	DNF–Clutch	$4,065	55	0
1988	Mar. 20	Motorcraft Quality Parts 500	40	29	328	164	0	DNF–Brakes	2,175	76	0
	Nov. 20	Atlanta Journal 500	34	41	328	5	0	DNF–Crash	1,525	40	0
1989	Mar. 19	Motorcraft Quality Parts 500	10	9	328	324	0	Running	11,200	138	0
	Nov. 19	Atlanta Journal 500	37	16	328	324	0	Running	6,850	115	0
1990	Nov. 18	Atlanta Journal 500	21	4	328	328	0	Running	17,225	160	0
1991	Mar. 18	Motorcraft Quality Parts 500	22	20	328	325	0	Running	10,470	103	0
	Nov. 17	Hardee's 500	10	16	328	324	0	Running	8,750	115	0
1992	Mar. 15	Motorcraft Quality Parts 500	17	11	328	328	0	Running	7,670	130	0
	Nov. 15	Hooters 500	32	10	328	326	0	Running	16,950	134	0
1993	Mar. 20	Motorcraft Quality Parts 500	33	31	328	247	0	Running	15,145	70	0
	Nov. 14	Hooters 500	29	7	328	328	12	Running	23,380	151	5
1994	Mar. 13	Purolator 500	36	35	328	205	2	DNF–Engine	19,820	63	5
	Nov. 13	Hooters 500	23	9	328	326	0	Running	23,325	138	0
1995	Mar. 12	Purolator 500	18	5	328	327	0	Running	33,725	155	0
	Nov. 12	NAPA 500	38	31	328	316	0	Running	21,340	70	0
1996	Mar. 10	Purolator 500	36	11	328	326	0	Running	20,820	130	0
	Nov. 10	NAPA 500	5	2	328	328	0	Running	59,500	170	0
1997	Mar. 9	Primestar 500	9	1	328	328	253	Running	137,650	185	10
	Nov. 16	NAPA 500	3	2	325	325	5	Running	79,600	175	5
1998	Mar. 8	Primestar 500	4	2	325	325	29	Running	72,600	175	5
	Nov. 8	NAPA 500	3	2	221	221	62	Running	100,400	175	5
1999	Mar. 14	Cracker Barrel 500	4	5	325	325	0	Running	53,675	155	0
	Nov. 21	NAPA 500	10	2	325	325	17	Running	94,400	175	5
2000	Mar. 12	Cracker Barrel 500	1	36	325	257	5	DNF–Engine	56,195	60	5
	Nov. 19	NAPA 500	3	15	325	323	2	Running	66,475	123	5
2001	Mar. 11	Cracker Barrel 500	1	4	325	325	44	Running	114,927	165	5
	Nov. 18	NAPA 500	33	8	325	325	0	Running	103,702	142	0

Moving Forward

Jarrett's ability to improve his position at Atlanta is better than at any other track during his career (minimum five starts).

Track	Starts	Avg. Start	Avg. Finish	Improvement
Atlanta	28	19.5	14.3	5.2
Rockingham	29	18.5	13.5	5.0
Richmond	28	17.8	14.0	3.8
Charlotte	30	20.5	17.1	3.4
Bristol	31	17.8	14.8	3.0

Atlanta's Most Dominant

Most laps led in a single Atlanta race, modern era

Driver	Year	Laps Led
Dale Earnhardt	1988	270
Cale Yarborough	1980	269
Dale Earnhardt	1995	268
Bobby Allison	1978	261
Dale Jarrett	1997	253

Atlanta Runner-ups

Drivers with the most 2nd-place finishes at Atlanta (modern era)

Driver	No. of 2nds
Dale Earnhardt	7
Dale Jarrett	5
David Pearson	5
Richard Petty	4

Jarrett at Bristol Motor Speedway

Beginning with his first career victory at Michigan in 1991, Dale Jarrett's success on NASCAR's big tracks, particularly Daytona and Indianapolis, has distorted public perception about his ability on the short tracks. Before he became a monster on the superspeedways, he displayed muscle and dexterity on the bullrings. Even during his earliest days on the Winston Cup circuit, when he couldn't count on the best equipment, Jarrett revealed an ability to survive the 1/2-mile track's claustrophobic racing and has never gone more than three races outside of the Top 10.

Indeed, early in Jarrett's career, Bristol Motor Speedway was the stage on which he auditioned for Winston Cup jobs. In 1987 and 1990, his solid runs at Bristol went a long way toward helping him keep rides that appeared to be temporary. He extended his stay with Eric Freedlander's team with a 10th-place finish in the spring of 1987. In 1990, he led 38 laps and finished 11th at Bristol, earning another race with the Wood Brothers. Earning full-time rides with Freedlander and the Wood Brothers was invaluable in gaining the kind of experience that would eventually lead to his successful association with Robert Yates.

With Yates, Jarrett's success at Bristol increased markedly. Since 1995, Jarrett has been one of the Winston Cup series' best Bristol racers. His performance compares favorably to those of Jeff Gordon, Rusty Wallace, Terry Labonte, and Mark Martin, NASCAR's current short track specialists. Starting with the Food City 500 in 1995, Jarrett finished 14 consecutive Bristol races without a DNF, including 12 finishes on the lead lap, a feat matched only by Gordon. During that stretch, Jarrett has finished outside of the Top 6 just four times.

At the Bristol night race in 1997, Jarrett scored his first career short track win in 83 starts. As is typical at Bristol, he needed a little luck to win. Early in the race, he was involved in incidents with Geoffrey Bodine and Bobby Hamilton, but managed to keep his No. 88 Ford on the lead lap. Clear of trouble, he went on to lead a race-high 210 laps and took his final lead with 30 laps to go by passing Martin, one of Bristol's toughest competitors.

Of course, like all drivers, Jarrett has not escaped the psychological torture that Bristol's frenetic and close-quarter racing can have on a driver. In 1993, Jarrett reacted to getting wrecked by the lapped car of Bobby Hillin in the only sane way possible: He waited for Hillin to return to the scene of the crime and, with perfect aim, threw his helmet at Hillin's car. Perhaps because his aim was so good, NASCAR instructed Jarrett to park his car for the afternoon. In 1994, Jarrett endured more Bristol nightmares. In the spring race, he nailed the Turn 4 wall just 66 laps into the 500-lap event. Later that season, he followed with another wreck in the night race while battling for ninth place.

The last remaining hole on Jarrett's Bristol résumé is winning a pole. He has never started on the front row at Bristol. His best start came in a 1997 night race when he qualified third.

In 1997, Jarrett scored his first short-track victory in 83 tries at Bristol. He led 210 laps en route to a comfortable win in the .533-mile track's annual night race.

Bristol Record Book—Modern Era

Category	Jarrett's Total	Jarrett's Rank	Modern Era Track Leader
Money	$981,044	8th	Rusty Wallace—1,428,210
Starts	31	14th	Darrell Waltrip—52
Total points[1]	3,864	15th	Darrell Waltrip—7,205
Avg. start	17.8	47th	Cale Yarborough—2.5
Avg. finish	14.8	25th	Cale Yarborough—6.6
Wins	1	11th	Darrell Waltrip—12
Winning pct.	3.2	16th	Cale Yarborough—56.3
Top 5s	8	12th	Darrell Waltrip—26
Top 10s	16	10th	Terry Labonte—33
DNFs	8	13th	J. D. McDuffie—15
Poles	0	—	M. Martin, R. Wallace, C. Yarborough—7
Front row starts	0	—	Rusty Wallace—12
Laps led	543	13th	Cale Yarborough—3,872
Pct. laps led	3.5	18th	Cale Yarborough—50.3
Races led	12	13th	D. Earnhardt, D. Waltrip—30
Times led	17	14th	Darrell Waltrip—94
Times led most laps	2	8th	Darrell Waltrip—10
Bonus points[1]	70	13th	Darrell Waltrip—200
Laps completed	12,603	19th	Darrell Waltrip—22,964
Pct. laps completed	82.1	51st	Kevin Lepage—99.2
Points per race[1]	124.6	22nd	Cale Yarborough—158.1
Lead-lap finishes	14	7th	Darrell Waltrip—24

[1] —Since implementation of current point system in 1975

Jarrett Track Performance Chart

Bristol Motor Speedway

Bristol, Tennessee—.533 miles—36° banking

Year	Date	Race	St.	Fin.	Total Laps	Laps Completed	Laps Led	Condition	Money	Pts.	Bonus Pts.
1986	Aug. 23	Busch 500	28	29	500	69	0	DNF–Mechanical	$990	76	0
1987	Apr. 12	Valleydale Meats 500	24	10	500	497	0	Running	7,845	134	0
	Aug. 22	Busch 500	23	12	500	491	0	Running	5,810	127	0
1988	Apr. 10	Valleydale Meats 500	25	28	500	129	0	DNF–Mechanical	1,360	79	0
	Aug. 27	Busch 500	15	26	500	207	0	DNF–Crash	2,325	85	0
1989	Apr. 9	Valleydale Meats 500	20	22	500	440	0	Running	4,520	97	0
	Aug. 26	Busch 500	30	10	500	494	0	Running	10,975	134	0
1990	Apr. 8	Valleydale Meats 500	12	11	500	493	39	Running	8,300	135	5
	Aug. 25	Busch 500	9	7	500	499	29	Running	9,850	151	5
1991	Apr. 17	Valleydale Meats 500	18	7	500	500	0	Running	10,775	146	0
	Aug. 24	Bud 500	16	28	500	253	0	DNF–Crash	5,500	79	0
1992	Apr. 5	Food City 500	4	2	500	500	38	Running	29,835	175	5
	Aug. 29	Bud 500	14	17	500	492	0	Running	10,525	112	0
1993	Apr. 4	Food City 500	22	32	500	207	30	DNF–Crash	15,420	72	5
	Aug. 28	Bud 500	33	31	500	199	0	DNF–Rear End	15,600	70	0
1994	Apr. 10	Food City 500	36	36	500	66	0	DNF–Crash	12,025	55	0
	Aug. 27	Goody's 500	29	26	500	388	19	DNF–Crash	19,285	90	5
1995	Apr. 2	Food City 500	19	6	500	500	0	Running	27,660	150	0
	Aug. 26	Goody's 500	16	3	500	500	99	Running	39,390	175	10
1996	Mar. 31	Food City 500	7	6	342	342	0	Running	26,395	150	0
	Aug. 24	Goody's 500	9	4	500	500	18	Running	32,980	165	5
1997	Apr.13	Food City 500	6	4	500	500	0	Running	39,265	160	0
	Aug. 23	Goody's 500	3	1	500	500	210	Running	101,550	185	10
1998	Mar. 29	Food City 500	6	3	500	500	18	Running	57,660	170	5
	Aug. 22	Goody's 500	9	4	500	500	35	Running	58,855	165	5
1999	Apr. 11	Food City 500	16	3	500	500	0	Running	68,650	165	0
	Aug. 28	Goody's 500	25	38	500	338	0	Running	43,425	49	0
2000	Mar. 26	Food City 500	20	21	500	499	7	Running	52,915	105	5
	Aug. 26	Goracing.com 500	31	9	500	500	1	Running	56,715	143	5
2001	Mar. 25	Food City 500	19	16	500	500	0	Running	90,142	115	0
	Aug. 25	Sharpie 500	7	6	500	500	0	Running	115,492	150	0

Running with Bristol's Best

Since 1995, Dale Jarrett's performance at Bristol has been as solid as that of the acknowledged masters of the .533-mile, high-banked oval.

Driver	Avg. Start	Avg. Finish	Wins	Top 5s	Top 10s	Laps Led	Laps Completed	Lead Lap Finishes
Jeff Gordon	4.6	7.1	4	9	12	1,486	6,706	12
Dale Jarrett	13.8	8.9	1	7	11	388	6,679	12
Terry Labonte	14.1	7.0	1	6	11	339	6,838	10
Mark Martin	9.5	9.4	1	8	11	609	6,588	10
Rusty Wallace	5.1	8.0	4	9	10	1,947	6,738	10

Jarrett at California Speedway

Considering when California Speedway was introduced to the Winston Cup world and how the track is configured, the fact that Dale Jarrett has yet to make an impression on the 2-mile oval's record book is surprising. In a sense, Jarrett and California Speedway "arrived" at the same time. The Roger Penske–built track hosted its inaugural Winston Cup event in 1997, the same season Jarrett and his Yates team established themselves as true championship contenders.

Adding to the mystery is Jarrett's strong record on NASCAR's big tracks. Of his 28 career victories, 20 have come on tracks longer that 1 mile. Three of those wins came at Michigan, a track that mirrors California's configuration.

Given the timing and configuration, Jarrett's California struggles are confusing. Jarrett has won on every Winston Cup track measuring 2 miles or greater, except California. There, he has yet to finish better than fifth and his 17.4 average is 16th in track history.

Naturally, a good bit of racing luck is responsible for Jarrett's results. A blown engine in 1998 forced him to settle for a 41st-place finish, one of the worst finishes of his career. In 2001, a solid effort was undone when his engine dropped a cylinder near the end of the race. He ended in 24th place. In the 1997 inaugural race—Jarrett's best California performance—fuel mileage limitations dried up hopes for a top finish. After leading 49 laps and clinging to the fourth position, Jarrett had to pit for fuel with nine laps remaining. The extra stop knocked him back to eighth.

Even Jarrett's best finish at the track—fifth in 1999—was accompanied by difficult circumstances. He qualified second but got caught a lap down when the caution flag waved after a green-flag pit stop. After fighting to get his lap back, he was penalized for entering his pits when pit road was closed. Later in the race, he had a tire go down and lose its tread on the backstretch. Through all the turmoil, Jarrett stayed on the lead lap and finished with his only California Top 5.

Despite its similarity to Michigan – one of his best Winston Cup tracks – Jarrett has yet to conquer California Speedway. His best finish in Fontana was fifth in 1999.

California Record Book—All-Time (min. 2 starts)

Category	Jarrett's Total	Jarrett's Rank	All-Time California Leader
Money	$338,417	9th	Jeff Gordon—627,667
Starts	5	T-1st	21 others with 5 Starts
Total points	581	8th	Jeff Gordon—840
Avg. start	17.0	16th	Mark Martin—6.6
Avg. finish	17.4	15th	Jeff Gordon—3.8
Wins	0	—	Jeff Gordon—2
Winning pct.	0.0	—	Jeff Gordon—40.0
Top 5s	1	8th	Jeff Gordon—4
Top 10s	3	3rd	J. Gordon, J. Mayfield—4
DNFs	1	7th	Mark Martin—3
Poles	0	—	5 Tied with 1 Pole
Front row starts	1	1st	9 Others with 1 FRS
Laps led	52	8th	Jeff Gordon—329
Pct. laps led	4.2	8th	Jeff Gordon—26.3
Races led	3	5th	Mark Martin—5
Times led	4	6th	Jeff Gordon—24
Times led most laps	0	—	Jeff Gordon—2
Bonus points	15	5th	J. Gordon, M. Martin—30
Laps completed	1,086	19th	Jeff Gordon—1,250
Pct. laps completed	86.9	42nd	5 Tied at 100 percent
Points per race	116.2	15th	Jeff Gordon—168.0
Lead-lap finishes	4	2nd	Jeff Gordon—5

Jarrett Track Performance Chart

California Speedway
Fontana, California— 2.0 miles— 14° banking

Year	Date	Race	St.	Fin.	Total Laps	Laps Completed	Laps Led	Condition	Money	Pts.	Bonus Pts.
1997	June 22	California 500	9	8	250	250	49	Running	$58,750	147	5
1998	May 3	California 500	36	41	250	86	0	DNF–Engine	44,275	40	0
1999	May 2	California 500	2	5	250	250	1	Running	71,140	160	5
2000	Apr. 30	NAPA Auto Parts 500	33	9	250	250	0	Running	70,650	138	0
2001	Apr. 29	NAPA Auto Parts 500	5	24	250	250	2	Running	93,602	96	5

Michigan vs. California

Though similar in layout and identical in length, California and Michigan have not been equally friendly to Dale Jarrett. Below is a comparison of Jarrett's performance on each track since California joined the Winston Cup series in 1997.

Track	Starts	Avg. Start	Avg. Finish	Wins	Top 5s	Top 10s	Laps Led
California	5	17.0	17.4	0	1	3	52
Michigan	10	8.6	8.4	1	7	8	189

Jarrett at Darlington Raceway

Measured purely by victories and poles, venerable Darlington Raceway must be considered one of Jarrett's most successful tracks. Only Daytona has been as productive as the "Lady in Black" in Jarrett's career. Not surprisingly, much of that success has come since he joined the powerful Robert Yates Racing in 1995.

Most of the excitement started in 1996 when Jarrett made an improbable run at the Winston Million. Set up by R. J. Reynolds, the sponsoring company of Winston Cup racing, the Winston Million rewarded drivers who could win three of the series' four biggest races: the Daytona 500, the Winston 500 at Talladega, the Coca-Cola 600 at Charlotte, and the Southern 500 at Darlington. The program proved to be one of the most difficult challenges in NASCAR. In 1996, the 11-year-old bonus had been won just one time; Bill Elliott earned the bonus in 1985. Jarrett and his first-year Yates team threatened to win what even Dale Earnhardt and Darrell Waltrip couldn't win; it was inconceivable.

Threaten he did. Jarrett won the Daytona 500 by surviving a late-race duel with Earnhardt and then overwhelmed the field to take the Coca-Cola 600 in May. When he arrived at Darlington, the talk of the racing world centered on Jarrett's chances to win the Winston Million. Jarrett fueled excitement by winning the pole (his first ever at Darlington) and then by leading half of the race's first 46 laps. When an oil slick on Darlington's aging pavement sent Jarrett's car into the wall on lap 47, his chances at the Million withered.

But Jarrett's success at the track was just beginning. In the 1997 TranSouth Financial 400, he won his second straight Darlington pole and, for the first time in his Winston Cup career, won a race from the pole position. The win set off a nine-race streak at Darlington during which Jarrett finished fifth or better eight times. Included in the streak were two more wins in the spring race and another Southern 500 pole.

Despite this success, Darlington also has been a "what if" track for Jarrett. In the 1996 spring race, he took the lead from Jeff Gordon with seven laps to go, but then got squeezed into the Turn 4 wall by the lapped car of Dave Marcis. The lost momentum allowed Gordon to retake the lead. Moments later, Jarrett's car ran out of gas. Having passed his front-stretch pit stall, he jumped into his teammate Ernie Irvan's backstretch pit and got a push from Irvan's team to get the car started again. Because the white flag had been thrown, however, Jarrett had illegally received assistance on the final lap of a race. NASCAR stopped scoring Jarrett and he fell to 15th in the final finishing order.

Jarrett was also left to speculate on his fate after the spring race of his 1999 championship season. Starting 21st, he climbed into the Top 10 by lap 30 and appeared to be the car to beat. He moved into second place with 129 laps to go when rain stopped the race.

Jarrett was leading the Southern 500 in 1996 when oil on Darlington's aging pavement sent him into the wall. A victory in the 500 was all Jarrett needed to become just the second driver ever to win the Winston Million.

Darlington Record Book—Modern Era (min. 5 races)

Category	Jarrett's Total	Jarrett's Rank	Modern Era Darlington Leader
Money	$1,327,108	2nd	Dale Earnhardt—1,403,125
Starts	28	26th	Darrell Waltrip—55
Total points[1]	3,473	15th	Bill Elliott—6,781
Avg. start	15.4	32nd	David Pearson—4.8
Avg. finish	15.5	14th	Tony Stewart—8.5
Wins	3	9th	Dale Earnhardt—9
Winning pct.	10.7	9th	David Pearson—29.6
Top 5s	10	9th	Bill Elliott—20
Top 10s	12	19th	Bill Elliott—31
DNFs	6	46th	B. Baker, R. Petty—19
Poles	3	5th	David Pearson—10
Front row starts	4	9th	David Pearson—14
Laps led	479	14th	Dale Earnhardt—2,648
Pct. laps led	5.2	19th	Dale Earnhardt—17.7
Races led	16	9th	Darrell Waltrip—32
Times led	33	14th	Dale Earnhardt—116
Times led most laps	1	11th	Dale Earnhardt—10
Bonus points[1]	85	12th	Darrell Waltrip—190
Laps completed	8,009	24th	Darrell Waltrip—16,395
Pct. laps completed	87.3	25th	Tony Stewart—100.
Points per race[1]	124.0	12th	Jeff Burton—145.3
Lead-lap finishes	12	6th	Bill Elliott – 20

[1] —Since implementation of current point system in 1975

Jarrett Track Performance Chart

Darlington Raceway
Darlington, South Carolina—1.366 miles—25° banking

Year	Date	Race	St.	Fin.	Total Laps	Laps Completed	Laps Led	Condition	Money	Pts.	Bonus Pts.
1987	Sept. 6	Southern 500	38	15	202	200	0	Running	$9,110	118	0
1988	May 27	TranSouth 500	32	12	367	362	0	Running	3,520	127	0
	Sept. 4	Southern 500	18	34	367	239	0	DNF–Engine	2,850	61	0
1989	Apr. 2	TranSouth 500	9	40	367	83	0	DNF–Engine	3,645	43	0
	Sept. 3	Heinz Southern 500	26	20	367	361	0	Running	7,810	103	0
1990	Sept. 2	Heinz Southern 500	18	28	367	241	1	DNF–Crash	6,655	84	5
1991	Apr. 7	TranSouth 500	14	39	367	30	0	DNF–Crash	5,670	46	0
	Sept. 1	Heinz Southern 500	8	25	367	350	1	Running	7,545	93	5
1992	Mar. 29	TranSouth 500	9	21	367	328	0	Running	4,950	100	0
	Sept. 6	Mountain Dew Southern 500	17	6	298	298	21	Running	19,055	155	5
1993	Mar. 28	TranSouth 500	4	3	367	367	1	Running	30,685	170	5
	Sept. 5	Mountain Dew Southern 500	27	12	351	348	0	Running	16,510	127	0
1994	Mar. 27	TranSouth 500	14	4	293	293	9	Running	27,550	165	5
	Sept. 4	Southern 500	35	9	367	365	0	Running	23,370	138	0
1995	Mar. 26	TranSouth 500	26	38	293	133	0	DNF–Transmission	22,809	49	0
	Sept. 3	Southern 500	12	28	367	331	0	Running	24,870	79	0
1996	Mar. 24	TranSouth 500	3	15	293	291	10	DNF–Out of gas	22,950	123	5
	Sept. 1	Southern 500	1	14	367	365	23	Running	128,165	126	5
1997	Mar. 23	TranSouth Financial 400	1	1	293	293	171	Running	142,860	185	10
	Aug. 31	Mountain Dew Southern 500	3	3	367	367	38	Running	47,505	170	5
1998	Mar. 22	TranSouth Financial 400	3	1	293	293	68	Running	110,035	180	5
	Sept. 6	Southern 500	1	3	367	367	15	Running	79,220	170	5
1999	Mar. 21	TranSouth Financial 400	21	4	164	164	0	Running	60,305	160	0
	Sept. 5	Pepsi Southern 500	36	16	270	270	23	Running	50,960	120	5
2000	Mar. 19	Mall.com 400	17	2	293	293	26	Running	90,905	175	5
	Sept. 3	Southern 500	9	5	328	328	3	Running	80,570	160	5
2001	Mar. 18	Carolina Dodge Dealers 400	2	1	293	293	16	Running	214,612	180	5
	Sept. 2	Southern 500	27	34	367	356	53	Running	82,417	66	5

Most Wins, By Track
Measured by wins, Darlington is one of Jarrett's best tracks.

Daytona	4
Charlotte	3
Darlington	3
Michigan	3

Most Poles, By Track
Along with Daytona, Jarrett has won more poles at Darlington than any other track.

Darlington	3
Daytona	3
Atlanta	2
Las Vegas	2

Wins from the Pole
Jarrett has won two races after starting from the pole position, including at Darlington in 1997.

Track	Year	Race	Laps Led	Money Won
Darlington	1997	TranSouth Financial 400	171	$142,860
Daytona	2000	Daytona 500	89	2,277,975

Jarrett at Daytona International Speedway

Dale Earnhardt's death in the 2001 Daytona 500 affected fans and competitors in countless ways. For Dale Jarrett, it removed one of his most intense rivalries. On restrictor plate tracks the "Dale and Dale" show, a phrase coined by Ned Jarrett during the first Jarrett-Earnhardt clash in the 1993 Daytona 500, became a regular occurrence. Daytona gave rise to the rivalry, matching Jarrett's emerging big-track talent against Earnhardt's legendary drafting ability.

Though Earnhardt is rightly viewed as the undisputed master of restrictor-plate racing, Jarrett can proudly point to a simple fact: In head-to-head duels for victory at Daytona, Jarrett never lost to Earnhardt. Three times, the two drivers finished 1–2 in races at Daytona. Each time Jarrett emerged the winner. (At Talladega, the story was reversed. In their two duels on the 2.66-mile track—Earnhardt's best track—Jarrett couldn't prevent late-race passes by Earnhardt during Talladega's two 1999 races.)

The 1993 and 1996 Daytona 500s first established Jarrett as one of the best restrictor-plate racers (his domination of Speedweeks in 2000 solidified his place in track history). In 1993, with his father calling the action for CBS-TV, Jarrett pulled off the upset by passing rookie sensation Jeff Gordon with two laps to go, then making a dramatic last lap pass on Earnhardt.

Jarrett's move on Earnhardt started on lap 199 of the 200-lap race. Noticing Earnhardt's car was loose in Turn 3, Jarrett dipped under Earnhardt heading into Turn 4. The two cars raced side-by-side with Earnhardt leading by half a car length at the start-finish line. Still, side-by-side going into Turn 1, Jarrett got drafting help from Geoffrey Bodine. That push was enough for Jarrett to take the lead coming out of Turn 2. That's all he needed. Earnhardt could not mount a charge over the final 2 miles of the race, giving Jarrett his second career victory.

The Jarrett-Earnhardt rematch in the 1996 Daytona 500 ended the same way, with Jarrett winning, but the build up changed drastically. This time, Jarrett passed Earnhardt with 24 laps remaining … and waited. In a move he made famous in IROC races, Earnhardt simply hooked onto Jarrett's rear bumper and waited to spring a last-lap move on the Ford driver. Jarrett, however, was too strong. Earnhardt made four moves on Jarrett: entering Turn 1, down the backstretch, entering Turn 4, and coming off of Turn 4. Jarrett blocked each move and won the race by .12 seconds. Jarrett repeated his strategy in his win over Earnhardt in the 1999 Pepsi 400, though the race's ending, under yellow, was less exciting.

Bolstering Jarrett's claim to Daytona greatness, besides beating Earnhardt, is his record of strong finishes for multiple teams and car owners. At other tracks, Jarrett's success is often tied to his joining Joe Gibbs Racing or Robert Yates Racing. That pattern does not apply to Daytona. When he drove for the struggling Wood Brothers in 1990 and 1991, he revealed a knack for getting around the massive 2.5-mile track. In 1990, 10 races after taking over the No. 21 Citgo Ford, Jarrett finished eighth in the Pepsi 400—the team's best finish since Neil Bonnett had taken sixth place at Rockingham the previous season. Jarrett added a sixth-place finish for the Wood Brothers in the 1991 Daytona 500. A year later he took third place in the Pepsi 400 for Joe Gibbs. A year after that, he won the 1993 Daytona 500. In other words, Jarrett didn't seem to mind who was fielding his car at Daytona. With Jarrett, success at Daytona has been tied to the driver more than the car.

Daytona Record Book—Modern Era (min. 5 starts)

Category	Jarrett's Total	Jarrett's Rank	Modern Era Daytona Leader
Money	$3,314,947	2nd	Dale Earnhardt—4,441,856
Starts	29	23rd	Dave Marcis—56
Total points[1]	3,477	16th	Dale Earnhardt—6,507
Avg. start	16.7	28th	Bobby Isaac—4.2
Avg. finish	16.5	14th	Dale Earnhardt—10.7
Wins	4	5th	Richard Petty—7
Winning pct.	13.8	7th	Jeff Gordon—22.2
Top 5s	8	12th	Dale Earnhardt—22
Top 10s	12	15th	Dale Earnhardt—34
DNFs	6	41st	A.J. Foyt—23
Poles	3	5th	Cale Yarborough—8
Front row starts	4	10th	Cale Yarborough—13
Laps led	332	11th	Dale Earnhardt—1,286
Pct. laps led	6.5	13th	Dale Earnhardt Jr.—17.9
Races led	12	17th	Dale Earnhardt—36
Times led	27	18th	Dale Earnhardt—173
Times led most laps	2	9th	Dale Earnhardt—7
Bonus points[1]	70	16th	Dale Earnhardt—215
Laps completed	4,615	19th	Darrell Waltrip—8,482
Pct. laps completed	90.2	24th	Rick Mast—99.3
Points per race[1]	119.9	15th	Dale Earnhardt—141.5
Lead-lap finishes	16	9th	Dale Earnhardt—28

[1] —Since implementation of current point system in 1975

Jarrett vs. Earnhardt at Daytona

A look at the careers of two of the best drivers in Daytona history

Driver	Races	Wins	Top 5s	Top 10s	Poles	Avg. Start	Avg. Finish	Laps Led	Money
Dale Jarrett	29	4	8	12	3	16.7	16.5	332	3,314,947
Dale Earnhardt	46	3	22	34	3	9.4	10.7	1,286	4,441,856

Jarrett Track Performance Chart

Daytona International Speedway
Daytona Beach, Florida—2.5 miles—31° banking

Year	Date	Race	St.	Fin.	Total Laps	Laps Completed	Laps Led	Condition	Money	Pts.	Bonus Pts.
1984	July 4	Pepsi Firecracker 400	39	23	160	155	0	Running	$4,955	94	0
1987	July 4	Pepsi Firecracker 400	41	23	160	156	0	Running	6,110	94	0
1988	Feb. 14	Daytona 500	36	16	200	200	0	Running	18,845	115	0
	July 2	Pepsi Firecracker 400	17	14	160	159	0	Running	4,705	121	0
1989	Feb. 19	Daytona 500	20	32	200	131	0	Running	15,000	67	0
	July 1	Pepsi 400	30	31	160	108	0	DNF–Crash	5,510	70	0
1990	July 7	Pepsi 400	24	8	160	160	0	Running	13,500	142	0
1991	Feb. 17	Daytona 500 by STP	17	6	200	199	0	Running	74,900	150	0
	July 6	Pepsi 400	31	18	160	160	0	Running	9,810	109	0
1992	Feb. 16	Daytona 500 by STP	35	36	200	91	0	DNF–Crash	19,780	55	0
	July 4	Pepsi 400	10	3	160	160	26	Running	37,200	170	5
1993	Feb. 14	Daytona 500 by STP	2	1	200	200	8	Running	238,200	180	5
	July 3	Pepsi 400	13	8	160	160	3	Running	21,150	147	5
1994	Feb. 20	Daytona 500	41	35	200	146	3	DNF–Engine	38,325	63	5
	July 2	Pepsi 400	11	11	160	160	0	Running	24,265	130	0
1995	Feb. 19	Daytona 500	1	5	200	200	0	Running	119,855	155	0
	July 1	Pepsi 400	7	42	160	38	0	DNF–Engine	27,645	37	0
1996	Feb. 18	Daytona 500	7	1	200	200	40	Running	360,775	180	5
	July 6	Pepsi 400	3	6	117	117	14	Running	30,910	155	5
1997	Feb. 16	Daytona 500	3	23	200	200	0	Running	70,510	94	0
	July 5	Pepsi 400	16	5	160	160	0	Running	45,975	155	0
1998	Feb. 15	Daytona 500	5	34	200	196	0	Running	111,505	61	0
	Oct. 17	Pepsi 400	3	23	160	159	38	Running	58,045	99	5
1999	Feb. 14	Daytona 500	8	37	200	134	14	DNF–Crash	121,379	57	5
	July 3	Pepsi 400	12	1	160	160	40	Running	164,965	180	5
2000	Feb. 20	Daytona 500	1	1	200	200	89	Running	2,277,975	185	10
	July 1	Pepsi 400	1	2	160	160	56	Running	126,350	180	10
2001	Feb. 18	Daytona 500	31	22	200	186	1	DNF–Crash	167,711	102	5
	July 7	Pepsi 400	19	11	160	160	0	Running	99,052	130	0

Restrictor-Plate Rivalry
Dale Jarrett emerged as one of the few drivers who could keep up with the legendary Dale Earnhardt on NASCAR's two restrictor plate tracks, Daytona and Talladega. Here's a look at their 1–2 finishes.

Track/Race	Year	Winner	2nd-Place	Notes
Daytona 500	1993	Jarrett	Earnhardt	Last-lap pass propels Jarrett to his first Daytona 500 win
Daytona 500	1996	Jarrett	Earnhardt	Strong all day, Jarrett takes lead with 24 laps to go and fends off Earnhardt's every move to win second Daytona 500
Daytona/Pepsi 400	1999	Jarrett	Earnhardt	Jarrett uses a 2.2-second fuel stop to gain the lead, then holds off Earnhardt over final 10 laps; race ends under caution
Talladega/Diehard 500	1999	Earnhardt	Jarrett	Jarrett leads with 14 to go, but is passed by Earnhardt and cannot regain lead
Talladega/Winston 500	1999	Earnhardt	Jarrett	

Jarrett at Dover Downs International Speedway

Every driver has that one track where nothing seems to go right. Anything that can go wrong usually does. For Jarrett, that track is Dover Downs International Speedway. Except for the road courses, no track has caused more trouble in Jarrett's career than Delaware's 1-mile oval.

No track has forced more DNFs (Did Not Finish) from Jarrett than Dover. Among NASCAR's established oval tracks, none has been stingier with top finishes. His 18.8 average finish is his worst on an oval, and it ranks 48th in Dover history. In his first 19 starts at the track, he cracked the Top 5 just two times. Thanks to his 12 DNFs, he has completed just 76 percent of the laps he has attempted, a stunning 69th in track history.

Perhaps the best example of Jarrett's Dover jinx was the Miller 500 in 1997, a race in which he clearly had the best car. He quickly charged to the front of the field and led 255 of the first 463 laps. With victory in sight, his "Dover luck" struck. Slowing to avoid a wreck involving lapped cars, he was rear-ended by second-place driver Jeff Gordon, who didn't check up in time. The contact knocked Jarrett out of line but didn't prevent him from staying in the lead, at least for a few minutes. Seven laps after his contact with Gordon, his engine gave out and forced him behind the wall. He fell from 1st to 32nd, 37 laps off the pace.

Though that combination of events prevented a win, it doesn't begin to illustrate the extent of Jarrett's difficulty at Dover. During one dismal stretch from September 1993 through June 1996, he crashed out of four straight races, completing just 1,109 of 2,000 laps (including two laps in the 1995 Miller 500). Even worse, Dover became Jarrett's House of Pain. In the 1994 fall event, Jarrett was involved in *three* separate wrecks, the third of which caused a broken wrist after his No. 18 Joe Gibbs Chevy slammed into the Turn 3 wall. In the same event a year later, he broke a rib and had to be taken to the hospital after a flat tire caused a hard crash between Turns 3 and 4.

Given this history and its attendant medical bills, Jarrett's lone Dover win in 1998 was particularly satisfying. Gordon, who has been dominant at Dover throughout his career, led 376 of the 400 laps in the MBNA Platinum 400. Dooming Gordon's sure win, however, was fuel mileage. Unable to reach the finish, Gordon pitted on lap 295 for gas; Jarrett, meanwhile, waited until lap 298. The three-lap difference gave Jarrett all the advantage he needed. Gordon ducked into the pits on lap 392 for a final splash of gas while Jarrett stayed on the track and won the race. Besides easing some of the pain caused by Dover, the fuel mileage win also helped compensate for races Jarrett lost the previous season at California and Indianapolis due to poor mileage.

Though Jarrett's performance at Dover shows periodic glimmers of improvement, he cannot seem to escape nagging bad luck. After six straight Top 10 finishes, he was caught up in a Ward Burton spin on lap 27 of the fall race in 2000 and dropped 99 laps behind the leader (he finished in 32nd). In 2001, in the fall event, a late-race tap from Tony Stewart ruined what appeared to be a strong finish, dropping him from the Top 5 to 12th.

Dover Record Book—All-Time (min. 5 races)

Category	Jarrett's Total	Jarrett's Rank	All-Time Dover Leader
Money	$1,047,239	7th	Mark Martin—1,377,427
Starts	30	21st	Dave Marcis—54
Total points[1]	3,348	17th	Ricky Rudd—6,105
Avg. start	15.1	33rd	Bobby Isaac—2.2
Avg. finish	18.8	48th	Tony Stewart—3.3
Wins	1	16th	B. Allison, R. Petty—7
Winning pct.	3.3	20th	Tony Stewart—33.3
Top 5s	9	15th	Dale Earnhardt—19
Top 10s	11	22nd	R. Petty, R. Rudd—26
DNFs	12	8th	J. D. McDuffie—27
Poles	1	20th	David Pearson—6
Front row starts	3	19th	David Pearson—9
Laps led	516	20th	Bobby Allison—2,801
Pct. laps led	3.7	24th	David Pearson—26.9
Races led	10	19th	Dale Earnhardt—26
Times led	22	19th	Bobby Allison—84
Times led most laps	1	15th	Bobby Allison—7
Bonus points[1]	55	19th	Dale Earnhardt—150
Laps completed	10,840	24th	Darrell Waltrip—22,539
Pct. laps completed	76.9	69th	Tony Stewart—99.9
Points per race[1]	111.6	36th	Tony Stewart—171.0
Lead-lap finishes	9	8th	Mark Martin—14

[1] — Since implementation of current point system in 1975

Jarrett Track Performance Chart

Dover Downs International Speedway
Dover, Delaware—1.0 miles—24° banking

Year	Date	Race	St.	Fin.	Total Laps	Laps Completed	Laps Led	Condition	Money	Pts.	Bonus Pts.
1987	May 31	Budweiser 500	23	35	500	84	0	DNF–Transmission	$3,200	58	0
	Sept. 20	Delaware 500	17	38	500	45	0	DNF–Engine	3,175	49	0
1988	June 5	Budweiser 500	35	20	500	492	0	Running	3,700	103	0
	Sept. 18	Delaware 500	17	28	500	377	0	DNF–Crash	3,400	79	0
1989	June 4	Budweiser 500	14	11	500	494	0	Running	8,025	130	0
	Sept. 17	Peak Performance 500	28	23	500	472	0	DNF–Engine	5,400	94	0
1990	June 3	Budweiser 500	17	12	500	498	0	Running	8,425	127	0
	Sept. 16	Peak Antifreeze 500	11	6	500	499	0	Running	13,675	150	0
1991	June 2	Budweiser 500	20	35	500	18	0	DNF–Crash	5,600	58	0
	Sept. 15	Peak Antifreeze 500	8	34	500	68	0	DNF–Crash	5,800	61	0
1992	May 31	Budweiser 500	28	27	500	308	0	DNF–Engine	6,490	82	0
	Sept. 20	Peak Antifreeze 500	11	12	500	490	0	Running	12,505	127	0
1993	June 6	Budweiser 500	29	2	500	500	0	Running	42,435	170	0
	Sept. 19	SplitFire Spark Plug 500	26	4	500	500	2	Running	31,035	165	5
1994	June 5	Bud 500	13	29	500	424	0	Running	19,665	76	0
	Sept. 18	SplitFire 500	19	34	500	323	0	DNF–Crash	19,405	61	0
1995	June 4	Miller 500	18	40	500	2	0	DNF–Crash	26,680	43	0
	Sept. 17	MBNA 500	26	30	500	410	1	DNF–Crash	29,765	78	5
1996	June 2	Miller 500	6	36	500	374	82	DNF–Crash	22,055	60	5
	Sept. 16	MBNA 500	9	3	500	500	29	Running	40,880	170	5
1997	June 1	Miller 500	6	32	500	463	255	DNF–Engine	44,130	77	10
	Sept. 21	MBNA 400	3	5	400	399	0	Running	39,845	155	0
1998	May 31	MBNA Platinum 400	4	1	400	400	8	Running	89,950	180	5
	Sept. 20	MBNA Gold 400	10	7	400	400	0	Running	43,590	146	0
1999	June 6	MBNA Platinum 400	2	5	400	399	21	Running	67,745	160	5
	Sept. 26	MBNA Gold 400	26	3	400	400	99	Running	74,935	170	5
2000	June 4	MBNA Platinum 400	18	4	400	400	0	Running	95,755	160	0
	Sept. 24	MBNA.com 400	8	32	400	301	0	Running	66,555	67	0
2001	June 3	MBNA Platinum 400	1	5	400	400	1	Running	115,007	160	5
	Sept. 23	MBNA Cal Ripken Jr. 400	1	12	400	400	18	Running	98,142	132	5

Oval Madness
Oval tracks where Jarrett has trouble finishing

Track	Avg. Finish
Dover	18.8
Talladega	17.9
Charlotte	17.1
Daytona	16.5
North Wilkesboro	16.4

Dover Breakout Charts
Hard-Luck Tracks
Tracks where Jarrett has suffered the most DNFs during his Winston Cup career

Track	No. of DNFs
Dover	12
Charlotte	10
Bristol	8
Talladega	8
Darlington	6
Daytona	6

Jarrett at Homestead-Miami Speedway

As one of the newest tracks on the circuit, Homestead-Miami Speedway nonetheless holds a special place in Dale Jarrett's heart and career. In 1999, his fifth-place finish in the Florida track's inaugural *Winston* Cup event clinched Jarrett's championship over Bobby Labonte. Jarrett ended the race 211 points ahead of Labonte in the point standings, an insurmountable lead even if Jarrett had chosen not to start the season's final race at Atlanta.

In the warm, waning November sun of south Florida, Jarrett celebrated the pinnacle of his career, the culmination of a 13-year title quest that started accidentally in 1987. The title was also the first for Jarrett's legendary car owner, Robert Yates. Yates, a 35-year NASCAR veteran, had seen potential champions Davey Allison and Ernie Irvan succeed in his cars but never get to fulfill their promise. Allison died in a helicopter accident at Talladega in July 1993; Irvan was seriously injured in a practice crash at Michigan in August 1994.

Though Jarrett was solid in 1999, he was never much of a factor in the race. Homestead has shown a propensity for the "other" manufacturers in NASCAR racing; that is, Pontiacs and Dodges have been especially strong on the 1.5-mile flat oval. Chevy and Ford drivers have been forced to watch their less heralded competitors dominate. Jarrett has been no different. He was a nonfactor in 2000, falling two laps off the pace and finishing 17th. In 2001, a broken axle forced him off the track 187 laps into the race. His crew fixed the problem in record time, but Jarrett still dropped seven laps off the pace and fell to 41st in the final running order.

Though Homestead-Miami Speedway is a relatively nondescript track for Jarrett, it was the site of one of his greatest moments. In 1999, he clinched his Winston Cup championship at the track with a fifth-place finish.

Homestead Record Book—All-Time (min. 2 starts)

Category	Jarrett's Total	Jarrett's Rank	All-Time Homestead Leader
Money	$243,917	8th	Tony Stewart—628,940
Starts	3	T-1st	28 Others with 3 Starts
Total points	312	12th	Bobby Labonte—487
Avg. start	12.3	7th	Casey Atwood—3.5
Avg. finish	21.0	19th	Bobby Labonte—4.7
Wins	0	—	Tony Stewart—2
Winning pct.	0.0	—	Tony Stewart—66.7
Top 5s	1	5th	Four with 2 Top 5s
Top 10s	1	8th	Bobby Labonte— 3
DNFs	0	—	S. Compton, D. Waltrip—2
Poles	0	—	B. Elliott, D. Green, S. Park—1
Front row starts	0	—	Six with 1 Front Row Start
Laps led	1	17th	Tony Stewart—282
Pct. laps led	0.1	18th	Tony Stewart—35.2
Races led	1	5th	Tony Stewart—3
Times led	1	11th	Tony Stewart—14
Times led most laps	0	—	Tony Stewart—2
Bonus points	5	5th	Tony Stewart—25
Laps completed	788	20th	B. Labonte, M. Martin, T. Stewart —801
Pct. laps completed	98.4	32nd	Four with 100 percent Laps Completed
Points per race	104.0	19th	Bobby Labonte—162.3
Lead-lap finishes	1	8th	B. Labonte, M. Martin, T. Stewart —3

Jarrett Track Performance Chart

Homestead-Miami Speedway

Homestead, Florida— 1.5 miles— 6° banking

Year	Date	Race	St.	Fin.	Total Laps	Laps Completed	Laps Led	Condition	Money	Pts.	Bonus Pts.
1999	Nov. 14	Jiffy Lube Miami 400	12	5	267	267	1	Running	$100,865	160	5
2000	Nov. 12	Pennzoil 400	7	17	267	265	0	Running	63,300	112	0
2001	Nov. 11	Pennzoil Freedom 400	18	41	267	256	0	Running	79,752	40	0

Jarrett hoists the Winston Cup champion's trophy at Homestead-Miami Speedway. He clinched his 1999 title with a race still remaining on the schedule, winning by 201 points over Bobby Labonte.

Jarrett at Indianapolis Motor Speedway

Long after Dale Jarrett retires, he will be remembered most for three distinguishing features in his career: his 1999 championship, his multiple victories in the Daytona 500, and his performance at the Indianapolis Motor Speedway. Of the three, success at Indianapolis must be the most unexpected to Jarrett. When he allowed himself to dream, he probably saw himself hoisting a Winston Cup trophy or celebrating in Daytona's Victory Lane. Being a dominant force at the famed Brickyard, however, simply wasn't in the boyhood dreams of the kid from the Southeast.

Since NASCAR added Indianapolis to its schedule, few drivers have thrived on the 2.5-mile rectangular oval quite like Jarrett. Only the incomparable Jeff Gordon is a more accomplished stock car driver at Indy.

Making Jarrett so compelling in Indianapolis' brief NASCAR history is his ability to be part of the story even when he's not fighting for a victory. For instance, in the 1994 inaugural Brickyard 400, he was ensnared in the Bodines' famous family feud, the on-track fracas that gave texture to an already memorable race. Geoffrey and Brett Bodine were embroiled in a family dispute that spilled onto the track while they where fighting for position midway through the first Indy race. Finally, on the 100th lap, Brett, the victim of one too many bumps from his brother, tapped and spun Geoffrey. Among the victims as Geoffrey lost control was Jarrett, who suffered damage severe enough to prevent him from continuing. He finished the race in 40th. The wreck was one of six that affected the luckless Jarrett that season.

Another of Jarrett's memorable "no factor" Brickyard 400s came in 1998 (though, admittedly, he was the only factor during the first half of the race). On lap 80 of 160, Jarrett had a 2.5-second lead and appeared ready for a second Indy win. Then he ran out of gas. On the backstretch. Nearly 2 miles from his pit stall. The agonizing sight of Jarrett's incredibly fast car coasting around the track made an indelible impression on the 1998 race. When he finally got back to his pit and refueled, Jarrett was four laps off the pace and incensed by NASCAR's inaction. He felt the caution flag should have been waved to help get his car off the track more quickly.

His car still strong, Jarrett began an amazing comeback. Thanks to frequent on-track incidents, he was able to make up all four lost laps. When he got back on the lead lap, he jumped from 30th position to 16th during the final eight laps, essentially passing two cars per lap at a track on which passing is notoriously difficult.

Only Jarrett's two victories can overshadow his other 1994 and 1998 experiences. In 1999, driving the same car that had gone dry the year before, he started fourth and dusted the field. He led a Brickyard-record 117 laps. Only one other driver, Rusty Wallace in 2000, has ever reached 100 laps led in a Brickyard 400.

Though less dominant, Jarrett's first Brickyard victory in 1996 may have been more memorable. He hit the wall during qualifying and was forced to start in 24th position. After the race began, he reached the Top 10 on lap 60 and took his first lead on lap 135. On lap 154, he took the lead for good from his teammate Ernie Irvan and motored to the win. The victory gave Yates Racing a 1–2 finish in NASCAR's richest event and further solidified Jarrett's new "big race" reputation. In 1996, in overwhelming fashion, Jarrett won NASCAR's three biggest events: the Daytona 500, the Coca-Cola 600, and the Brickyard 400.

Jarrett earned $564,035 for his first Indy win that season, a then-career-high paycheck. After accepting the check, Jarrett commented that the paycheck from his first professional race, a Limited Sportsman event at Hickory (North Carolina) Speedway in 1979, was $25.

Indianapolis Record Book—All-Time (min. 3 starts)

Category	Jarrett's Total	Jarrett's Rank	All-Time Indianapolis Leader
Money	$2,186,157	2nd	Jeff Gordon—2,704,528
Starts	8	T-1st	15 Others with 8 Starts
Total points	1,136	5th	Bobby Labonte—1,162
Avg. start	10.5	2nd	Mike Skinner—9.3
Avg. finish	10.4	7th	Mike Skinner—8.5
Wins	2	2nd	Jeff Gordon—3
Winning pct.	25.0	2nd	Jeff Gordon—37.5
Top 5s	4	2nd	Jeff Gordon—5
Top 10s	5	4th	Rusty Wallace—7
DNFs	1	14th	C. Little, D. Marcis—3
Poles	0	—	Jeff Gordon—3
Front row starts	1	4th	Jeff Gordon—3
Laps led	186	2nd	Jeff Gordon—306
Pct. laps led	14.5	2nd	Jeff Gordon—23.9
Races led	4	2nd	Jeff Gordon—7
Times led	11	2nd	Jeff Gordon—23
Times led most laps	1	2nd	Jeff Gordon—2
Bonus points	25	2nd	Jeff Gordon—45
Laps completed	1,219	8th	B. Elliott, B. Labonte—1,279
Pct. laps completed	95.2	28th	M. Shepherd, M. Skinner, T. Stewart—100.0
Points per race	142.0	5th	Bobby Labonte—145.3
Lead-lap finishes	7	T-1st	B. Elliott, B. Labonte, R. Wallace—7

Jarrett Track Performance Chart

Indianapolis Motor Speedway
Speedway, Indiana—2.5 miles—9° banking

Year	Date	Race	St.	Fin.	Total Laps	Laps Completed	Laps Led	Condition	Money	Pts.	Bonus Pts.
1994	Aug. 6	Brickyard 400	14	40	160	99	0	DNF—Crash	$33,225	43	0
1995	Aug. 5	Brickyard 400	26	3	160	160	0	Running	203,200	165	0
1996	Aug. 3	Brickyard 400	24	1	160	160	11	Running	564,035	180	5
1997	Aug. 3	Brickyard 400	3	3	160	160	31	Running	223,900	170	5
1998	Aug. 1	Brickyard 400	2	16	160	160	27	Running	140,260	120	5
1999	Aug. 7	Brickyard 400	4	1	160	160	117	Running	712,240	185	10
2000	Aug. 5	Brickyard 400	5	7	160	160	0	Running	155,710	146	0
2001	Aug. 7	Brickyard 400	6	12	160	160	0	Running	153,587	127	0

Indianapolis Breakout Charts
Brickyard Frontrunners
Jarrett holds the Indianapolis record
for laps led in a single race.

Driver	Year	Laps Led
Dale Jarrett	1999	117
Rusty Wallace	2000	110
Jeff Gordon	1998	97
Jeff Gordon	1994	93
Johnny Benson	1996	70

Leading the field at Indianapolis is common for Jarrett, who owns the Brickyard 400's single-race record for laps led.

Of the "old time" NASCAR drivers, none has adapted to Indianapolis quite like Jarrett. Only Jeff Gordon can claim a better career at the Brickyard.

Jarrett at Las Vegas Motor Speedway

Shortly after winning the pole for the inaugural Las Vegas 400 at the new Las Vegas Motor Speedway, Dale Jarrett declared that, because of its wide, smooth surface, the track may produce one of the greatest races in NASCAR history. He envisioned five-wide racing and never-ending passing. The reality at Las Vegas has been less than spectacular single-file "action" that usually ends with a Roush rout. If, however, the theory is true that new tracks require years of racing before its "grooves" get worked in, NASCAR fans may yet enjoy the kind of competition foreseen by Jarrett.

The slow-to-develop theory also applies to Jarrett's performance at the 1.5-mile track. He won the pole for that inaugural race in 1998, but finished a disappointing 40th after engine troubles ended his day. Since then, Jarrett has seen steadily improving results at the Vegas venue. He finished 11th and a lap down in 1999, then followed with a seventh in 2000 and second in 2001 (after winning his second pole).

Las Vegas Record Book—All-Time (min. 2 starts)

Category	Jarrett's Total	Jarrett's Rank	All-Time Las Vegas Leader*
Money	$511,017	4th	Jeff Burton—966,615
Starts	4	T-1st	21 Others with 4 Starts
Total points	499	6th	Mark Martin—654
Avg. start	4.3	1st	(Bobby Labonte—5.8)
Avg. finish	15.0	8th	Mark Martin—5.0
Wins	0	—	Jeff Burton—2
Winning pct.	0.0	—	Jeff Burton—50.0
Top 5s	1	6th	Jeff Burton—3
Top 10s	2	5th	Mark Martin—4
DNFs	1	4th	R. Craven, H. Stricklin, K. Wallace—2
Poles	2	1st	(B. Labonte, R. Rudd—1)
Front row starts	2	1st	(Six with 1 Front Row Start)
Laps led	82	3rd	Jeff Burton204
Pct. laps led	8.6	5th	Jeff Burton—21.5
Races led	2	3rd	Mark Martin—4
Times led	6	4th	Mark Martin—13
Times led most laps	0	—	J. Burton, M. Martin—2
Bonus points	10	3rd	Mark Martin—30
Laps completed	900	12th	Mark Martin—949
Pct. laps completed	94.8	29th	D. Earnhardt, M. Martin—100.0
Points per race	124.8	7th	Mark Martin—163.5
Lead-lap finishes	2	7th	Mark Martin—4

* — 2nd-place driver(s) listed if Jarrett is category leader

Jarrett Track Performance Chart

Las Vegas Motor Speedway

Las Vegas, Nevada—1.5 miles—12° banking

Year	Date	Race	St.	Fin.	Total Laps	Laps Completed	Laps Led	Condition	Money	Pts.	Bonus Pts.
1998	Mar. 1	Las Vegas 400	1	40	267	219	40	DNF–Engine	$62,600	48	5
1999	Mar. 7	Las Vegas 400	9	11	267	266	0	Running	85240	130	0
2000	Mar. 5	Carsdirect.com 400	6	7	148	148	0	Running	105200	146	0
2001	Mar. 4	UAW–Daimler Chrysler 400	1	2	267	267	42	Running	257977	175	5

Since the Las Vegas Motor Speedway joined the Winston Cup circuit in 1998, Jarrett has seen a steady race-by-race improvement in his finishes. After a 40th-place finish in the inaugural race, he ended in 11th, seventh and second in the next three events.

Jarrett at Lowe's Motor Speedway at Charlotte

For Dale Jarrett, and most other NASCAR drivers, Lowe's Motor Speedway near Charlotte, North Carolina, is a quasi-home track. A longtime resident of nearby Conover, Jarrett started his serious professional racing at Hickory Speedway, just an hour's drive northwest of Charlotte. While growing up, young Dale saw some of the first races ever run at the 1.5-mile track, which opened in June 1960. His father, Ned, negotiated its high banks during Grand National races until his retirement in 1966.

Charlotte, in fact, feels like a home track for Jarrett in almost every respect, except one: He's not very good there. Trips to LMS have rarely felt like a homecoming. His first seven Charlotte starts resulted in a 33.4 average finish. In his first 30 starts, he never finished in the Top 5 more than twice in a row. The only thing more difficult than finishing at Charlotte for Jarrett over the years has been starting: He has yet to win a pole at LMS, or even start on the front row. His 20.5 starting average is the worst of his career on ovals and ranks 47th in the track's modern era.

Jarrett finally started to brighten his bleak history at Charlotte in 1993 when he raced to a strong third-place finish in the Coca-Cola 600. Though he had one prior strong Charlotte run, a fifth in 1991, he built momentum with his 1993 finish. In 1994, he found a groove while driving the No. 18 Interstate Batteries Chevy for Joe Gibbs, finishing fourth in the Coca-Cola 600 and winning the fall Mello Yello 500. In the 18 races following the 1993 600, he won three times, had 10 Top 5 finishes, and 13 Top 10s.

The victory in 1994 was significant for an unfortunate reason: The week before, Jarrett had failed to qualify at North Wilkesboro. After spending a Sunday on the couch watching racing for the first (and last) time in his Winston Cup career, he rebounded with his first Charlotte victory and the third win of his career. He led only the final four laps, passing Morgan Shepherd on the race's final restart.

If that first Charlotte win was less than dominant, his second victory in the 1996 Coca-Cola 600 was one of the most lopsided in track history. He led more laps in a Coca-Cola 600 than any driver has since Davey Allison in 1991 and beat second-place Dale Earnhardt to the finish line by a stunning 12 seconds.

When Jarrett added a third victory in the fall of 1997, by beating Charlotte master Bobby Labonte, he seemed to be on the verge of a Gordon-like run. With three wins in seven LMS races and a Yates race team that continued to excel, he looked like a sure bet whenever the Winston Cup series arrived in Concord. Instead, Jarrett settled into consistent, if not victorious, finishes. Since leading the 1998 Coca-Cola 600 by 2.1 seconds (before fading to fifth), he has had trouble getting back to the front. Of the 2,536 laps run at Charlotte from the fall of 1998 through 2001, Jarrett led just 35.

In 2001, Jarrett associated Charlotte with pain. He spun his car during qualifying for the Coca-Cola 600 and nailed the Turn 4 wall. The crash forced him to start the race in 37th with a provisional and resulted in a cracked rib. Driving in excruciating pain, he climbed all the way to third place before ending in eighth. Five months later, he raced at Charlotte with another rib injury. This time, he suffered a broken left rib after a vicious wreck at the new Kansas Speedway, an incident that left Jarrett momentarily unconscious. Like he had earlier in the season, Jarrett showed his toughness and completed the entire race. After starting 25th, he finished 6th.

Charlotte Record Book—Modern Era (min. 5 starts)

Category	Jarrett's Total	Jarrett's Rank	Modern Era Charlotte Leader
Money	$1,468,039	7th	Dale Earnhardt—1,934,793
Starts	30	23rd	Darrell Waltrip—55
Total points[1]	3,537	16th	Darrell Waltrip—6,379
Avg. start	20.5	47th	David Pearson—3.8
Avg. finish	17.1	29th	Tony Stewart—7.7
Wins	3	6th	Darrell Waltrip—6
Winning pct.	10.0	10th	Jeff Gordon—22.2
Top 5s	11	9th	Darrell Waltrip—19
Top 10s	15	12th	Darrell Waltrip—29
DNFs	10	23rd	Dave Marcis—30
Poles	0	—	David Pearson—13
Front row starts	0	—	David Pearson—16
Laps led	525	15th	Bobby Allison—1,844
Pct. laps led	4.8	22nd	Bobby Allison—16.3
Races led	12	18th	Dale Earnhardt—30
Times led	29	19th	Dale Earnhardt—120
Times led most laps	2	9th	Bobby Allison—8
Bonus points[1]	65	17th	Dale Earnhardt—175
Laps completed	9,184	23rd	Darrell Waltrip—18,239
Pct. laps completed	83.9	50th	Tony Stewart—99.8
Points per race[1]	117.9	23rd	Tony Stewart—150.3
Lead-lap finishes	14	3rd	Dale Earnhardt—18

[1] — Since implementation of current point system in 1975

Jarrett Track Performance Chart

Lowe's Motor Speedway

Concord, North Carolina—1.5 miles—24° banking

Year	Date	Race	St.	Fin.	Total Laps	Laps Completed	Laps Led	Condition	Money	Pts.	Bonus Pts.
1987	May 24	Coca-Cola 600	35	38	400	84	0	DNF–Engine	$4,310	49	0
	Oct. 11	Oakwood Homes 500	40	34	334	102	0	DNF–Engine	5,285	61	0
1988	May 29	Coca-Cola 600	39	41	400	27	0	DNF–Engine	4,200	40	0
	Oct. 9	Oakwood Homes 500	22	37	334	78	0	DNF–Engine	1,530	52	0
1989	May 28	Coca-Cola 600	24	28	400	331	0	DNF–Engine	5,200	79	0
	Oct. 8	All Pro Auto Parts 500	29	24	334	328	0	Running	5,450	91	0
1990	Apr. 8	Coca-Cola 600	19	32	400	241	4	DNF–Engine	7,120	72	5
	Oct. 7	Mello Yello 500	11	10	334	333	0	Running	14,625	134	0
1991	May 26	Coca-Cola 600	12	5	400	400	3	Running	27,400	160	5
	Oct. 6	Mello Yello 500	22	26	334	302	0	DNF–Valve	6,388	85	0
1992	May 24	Coca-Cola 600	23	12	400	397	1	Running	15,400	132	5
	Oct. 22	Mello Yello 500	7	24	334	324	0	DNF–Clutch	9,640	91	0
1993	May 30	Coca-Cola 600	32	3	400	400	114	Running	73,100	170	5
	Oct. 10	Mello Yello 500	38	26	334	325	0	Running	13,160	85	0
1994	May 29	Coca-Cola 600	16	4	400	400	9	Running	54,600	165	5
	Oct . 9	Mello Yello 500	22	1	334	334	4	Running	106,800	180	5
1995	May 28	Coca-Cola 600	22	32	400	317	0	DNF–Engine	21,050	67	0
	Oct. 8	UAW-GM 500	31	5	334	334	0	Running	51,400	155	0
1996	May 26	Coca-Cola 600	15	1	400	400	199	Running	165,250	185	10
	Oct. 6	UAW-GM 500	10	3	334	334	0	Running	58,300	165	0
1997	May 25	Coca-Cola 600	3	27	333	332	24	Running	40,875	87	5
	Oct. 5	UAW-GM Quality 500	5	1	334	334	85	Running	130,000	180	5
1998	May 24	Coca-Cola 600	10	5	400	400	47	Running	78,700	160	5
	Oct. 4	UAW-GM Quality 500	17	24	334	301	0	Running	33,850	91	0
1999	May 30	Coca-Cola 600	28	5	400	400	0	Running	81,125	155	0
	Oct. 10	UAW-GM Quality 500	9	7	334	334	33	Running	65,475	151	5
2000	May 28	Coca-Cola 600	8	5	400	400	2	Running	95,000	160	5
	Oct. 8	UAW-GM Quality 500	5	40	334	158	0	DNF–Accident	48,175	43	0
2001	May 27	Coca-Cola 600	37	8	400	400	0	Running	108,552	142	0
	Oct. 7	UAW-GM Quality 500	25	6	334	334	0	Running	97,707	150	0

Where to Start

Tracks where Dale Jarrett has had the most trouble qualifying (min. 5 starts)

Track	No. of Starts	Avg. Start
Sears Point	13	21.0
Charlotte	30	20.5
Atlanta	28	19.5
Rockingham	29	18.5

Lowe's Motor Speedway in Charlotte hasn't felt like much of a home track during Jarrett's career. Only Sears Point—a road course—has been a more difficult place to qualify.

Jarrett at Martinsville Speedway

Dale Jarrett's performance at Bristol Motor Speedway, especially since 1995, has gone a long way toward dispelling the notion that he can't handle Winston Cup short tracks. Unfortunately, Martinsville has had the opposite effect. His career at the tiny Virginia track is a curious mix of personal significance and historical indifference.

Certainly, from a personal standpoint, Martinsville is an important chapter in the story of Jarrett's racing career. The .526-mile track was the site of his first-ever Winston Cup start. At the time a dedicated Busch Grand National series driver, he hopped into Emanual Zervakis' No. 02 Chevy for the Sovran Bank 500 in April 1984. While he never contended for the lead, that first start was impressive nonetheless. Jarrett started 24th, ran the entire race, and picked up 10 spots en route to a 14th-place finish.

Five years later, Martinsville was the site of Jarrett's first truly strong Winston Cup performance and the first Top-5 finish of his career. In the fall Goody's 500, he marched to the front after starting 25th. He gained the race lead on lap 251 and stayed out front for 96 laps. Only Martinsville legends Rusty Wallace and Darrell Waltrip led more laps that day. That race still marks the most laps led by Jarrett in a Martinsville race.

When Jarrett finally won at Martinsville in 2001 in his 30th attempt, he called the victory one of the sweetest of his career. Finally winning at the track where his Winston Cup experience had started 17 years before was the successful end to yet another slowly developing quest in his career. Wins and championship have never come easily to Ned's son, and Martinsville epitomized his combination of patience and hard work better than any other track on the circuit.

Offsetting Jarrett's periodic personal achievements at Martinsville is his largely nondescript career record. While the tight-turned oval doesn't necessarily prove short-track inability, it does point out Jarrett's invisibility. After 15 years and 31 races, the 45-year-old barely registers in the track's record book. Of 22 major statistical categories, Jarrett ranks among the track's modern era leaders in just two ways: money (a false measure given today's increased purses) and lead-lap finishes. He has 12 finishes on the lead lap rank of fifth at Martinsville since the modern era began in 1972, a solid achievement on such a short track.

Still, the holes in Jarrett's Martinsville résumé are glaring. He has yet to win a pole, or even start on the front row. His best start in 31 tries is fourth (twice). Even more bizarre has been his inability to lead laps. Between 1990 and 2000—a 22-race stretch—he led 11 of 10,856 laps. During his career, he has led 144 of 15,356 possible laps, or 0.9 percent, his worst percentage on an oval (only the road course at Sears Point has been tougher on Jarrett).

Jarrett took a huge step toward erasing his irrelevance in Martinsville's annals in 2001. After winning the season's first race, he rebounded to take second in the fall race. The 1–2 finish gave him, by far, the best single-season Martinsville effort of his career.

Martinsville Record Book—Modern Era (min. 5 starts)

Category	Jarrett's Total	Jarrett's Rank	Modern Era Martinsville Leader
Money	$909,429	8th	Rusty Wallace—1,334,400
Starts	31	18th	Darrell Waltrip—52
Total points[1]	3,847	14th	Darrell Waltrip—7,317
Avg. start	16.1	39th	David Pearson—4.9
Avg. finish	14.2	24th	Cale Yarborough—6.3
Wins	1	11th	Darrell Waltrip—11
Winning pct.	3.2	20th	Cale Yarborough—29.4
Top 5s	8	14th	Darrell Waltrip—27
Top 10s	15	11th	Darrell Waltrip—31
DNFs	4	40th	Dave Marcis—16
Poles	0	—	Darrell Waltrip—8
Front row starts	0	—	Darrell Waltrip—12
Laps led	144	32nd	Darrell Waltrip—3,616
Pct. laps led	0.9	49th	Cale Yarborough—40.0
Races led	4	28th	Darrell Waltrip—32
Times led	4	37th	Darrell Waltrip—79
Times led most laps	0	—	R. Wallace, C. Yarborough—9
Bonus points[1]	20	28th	Darrell Waltrip—195
Laps completed	13,686	15th	Darrell Waltrip—23,727
Pct. laps completed	89.1	34th	Elliott Sadler—98.8
Points per race[1]	124.1	22nd	Cale Yarborough—156.8
Lead-lap finishes	12	5th	Darrell Waltrip—25

[1] — Since implementation of current point system in 1975

Jarrett Track Performance Chart

Martinsville Speedway

Martinsville, Virginia—.526 miles—12° banking

Year	Date	Race	St.	Fin.	Laps	Total Completed	Laps Led	Laps Condition	Money	Pts.	Bonus Pts.
1984	Apr. 29	Sovran Bank 500	24	14	500	492	0	Running	$1,515	121	0
1987	Apr. 26	Sovran Bank 500	14	29	500	113	0	DNF–Engine	4,135	76	0
	Sept. 27	Goody's 500	10	10	500	492	0	Running	8,345	134	0
1988	Apr. 24	Pannill Sweatshirts 500	13	13	500	491	0	Running	2,470	124	0
	Sept. 25	Goody's 500	25	32	500	14	0	DNF–Engine	1,310	67	0
1989	Apr. 23	Pannill Sweatshirts 500	23	15	500	495	0	Running	6,070	118	0
	Sept. 24	Goody's 500	25	5	500	500	96	Running	15,125	160	5
1990	Apr. 29	Hanes Activewear 500	5	30	500	171	0	DNF–Clutch	4,050	73	0
	Sept. 23	Goody's 500	6	10	500	497	0	Running	10,725	134	0
1991	Apr. 28	Hanes 500	7	12	500	495	0	Running	7,900	127	0
	Sept. 22	Goody's 500	20	18	500	496	0	Running	6,755	109	0
1992	Apr. 26	Hanes 500	21	28	500	351	0	Running	5,225	79	0
	Sept. 28	Goody's 500	13	23	500	477	0	Running	8,150	94	0
1993	Apr. 25	Hanes 500	11	3	500	500	0	Running	30,350	165	0
	Sept. 26	Goody's 500	17	5	500	499	0	Running	22,675	155	0
1994	Apr. 24	Hanes 500	20	21	500	494	0	Running	16,475	100	0
	Sept. 25	Goody's 500	8	5	500	500	0	Running	26,775	155	0
1995	Apr. 23	Hanes 500	10	7	356	356	0	Running	26,595	146	0
	Sept. 24	Goody's 500	14	10	500	500	11	Running	27,050	139	5
1996	Apr. 21	Goody's 500	12	29	500	458	0	Running	17,115	76	0
	Sept. 22	Hanes 500	4	16	500	498	0	Running	19,500	115	0
1997	Apr. 20	Goody's 500	23	16	500	499	0	Running	28,265	115	0
	Sept. 28	Hanes 500	21	12	500	500	0	Running	28,800	127	0
1998	Apr. 19	Goody's 500	23	3	500	500	0	Running	58,525	165	0
	Sept. 27	NAPA Autocare 500	10	42	500	299	0	DNF–Engine	32,350	37	0
1999	Apr. 18	Goody's Body Pain 500	31	8	500	500	0	Running	46,825	142	0
	Oct. 3	NAPA AutoCare 500	14	10	500	499	0	Running	52,790	134	0
2000	Apr. 9	Goody's Body Pain 500	28	5	500	500	0	Running	65,125	155	0
	Oct. 1	NAPA AutoCare 500	31	6	500	500	0	Running	57,375	150	0
2001	Apr. 8	Virginia 500	13	1	500	500	6	Running	170,027	180	5
	Oct. 14	Old Dominion 500	4	2	500	500	31	Running	114,252	175	5

Waiting to Win*

Most starts needed by Jarrett before getting his first win

Track	No. of Starts
Martinsville	30
Rockingham	27
Talladega	24
Bristol	23
Dover	23
Richmond	20

* — Never won at North Wilkesboro (19 starts), Watkins Glen (15), or Sears Point (13).

Back in the Pack

Tracks where Jarrett has had the most difficulty leading laps (min. 5 starts)

Track	Starts	Possible Laps	Laps Led	Pct. Led
Sears Point	13	1,114	8	.12
Martinsville	31	15,356	144	.94
North Wilkesboro	19	7,600	111	1.46
Watkins Glen	15	1,311	31	2.36
Richmond	28	11,200	385	3.44

Best Martinsville Seasons

Jarrett's best two-race efforts at Martinsville, as measured by average finish

Year	Avg. Finish
2001	1.5
1993	4.0
2000	5.5
1995	8.5
1999	9.0

Jarrett at Michigan International Speedway

Dale Jarrett's 1999 championship and his performances at Daytona and Indianapolis have cemented his place in NASCAR history. Michigan International Speedway, however, may play a larger role in establishing Jarrett's credibility in the minds of fans and insiders. The reason is simple, and probably unfair: He won there in 1992.

Starting that year, Jarrett began associating with Joe Gibbs and Robert Yates, two of the most powerful car owners in the Winston Cup series. Though Gibbs was a rookie owner when Jarrett signed to drive his cars in 1992, Gibbs' history of success as a coach in the National Football League and his broad appeal among sports fans helped him land a competitive and resourceful sponsorship, Interstate Batteries, immediately. Yates, meanwhile, owned one of the most coveted rides in motorsports, the No. 28 Havoline Ford. For much of Jarrett's career, skeptics and naysayers pointed to the car owner, not the driver, to explain Jarrett's later success.

The most compelling fact that dispels this notion is the 1991 Champion Spark Plug 400. On that hot August day in Brooklyn, Michigan, Jarrett stunned the racing world by winning his first Winston Cup race, and by beating Davey Allison and his Yates-powered Ford. The victory came while Jarrett was driving the Wood Brothers' No. 21 Citgo Ford. Though certainly one of the most storied teams in NASCAR history, the WB team had long since fallen out of championship contention. In fact, even contending for Top 5 race finishes proved difficult for the No. 21 team. Prior to Jarrett's Michigan win, the last Wood Brothers winner was Kyle Petty in 1987.

Besides winning for a generally uncompetitive team, Jarrett's victory was a breakthrough for another reason: He was the *only* first-time winner in the Winston Cup series in 1991. The other 11 winners that season were the usual suspects: Allison, Dale Earnhardt, Darrell Waltrip, Harry Gant, Rusty Wallace, and Ricky Rudd. The fact that Jarrett bested Allison, the winningest driver in 1991, is another indication that the driver, not his owner or his car, was responsible for the victory at Michigan.

Of course, augmenting Jarrett's talents with Yates power didn't hurt. Since he took over Yates' new No. 88 team in 1996, Michigan has been one of the most giving tracks on the circuit for Jarrett. During a five-year, 10-race span beginning in 1996, Jarrett never finished worse than 10th. That string included two more wins on the 2-mile oval and six straight finishes of fourth or better.

Jarrett's third Michigan win was one of the most dominant in track history. In the 1999 Kmart 400, he took the lead on lap 53 and maintained his advantage over the final 148 consecutive laps, the most consecutive laps led in a single race in Michigan history. Building leads as great as 10 seconds over second-place running Gordon, Jarrett crossed the finish line nearly 30 seconds ahead of the fifth-place finisher, Bobby Labonte. Jarrett spent much of his postrace Victory Lane celebration fending off charges that he made the race boring. He pointed out a curious phenomenon: When Gordon or Earnhardt dominate a race, their talent is credited; when Jarrett dominates, NASCAR racing suddenly becomes boring.

Thanks to his Michigan win in 1991, Jarrett proved that he, too, is a talented driver.

Michigan Record Book—All-Time (min. 5 starts)

Category	Jarrett's Total	Jarrett's Rank	All-Time Michigan Leader
Money	$1,182,047	5th	Bill Elliott—1,392,149
Starts	30	25th	Dave Marcis—56
Total points[1]	3,711	15th	Bill Elliott—6,323
Avg. start	18.0	46th	Bobby Isaac—3.1
Avg. finish	15.3	22nd	Jeff Gordon—6.7
Wins	3	8th	David Pearson—9
Winning pct.	10.0	12th	David Pearson—31.0
Top 5s	11	11h	Cale Yarborough—21
Top 10s	16	14th	Bill Elliott—29
DNFs	5	44th	Dave Marcis—21
Poles	1	16th	David Pearson—10
Front row starts	3	14th	Bill Elliott—12
Laps led	262	17th	Cale Yarborough—1,308
Pct. laps led	4.4	21st	Jeff Gordon—18.5
Races led	12	18th	Darrell Waltrip—33
Times led	20	23rd	Cale Yarborough—152
Times led most laps	1	14th	Cale Yarborough—8
Bonus points[1]	65	18th	Darrell Waltrip—190
Laps completed	5,248	23rd	Dave Marcis—8,974
Pct. laps completed	88.1	50th	Matt Kenseth—99.9
Points per race[1]	123.7	17th	Jeff Gordon—156.5
Lead-lap finishes	16	10th	Bill Elliott—26

[1] — Since implementation of current point system in 1975

Jarrett Track Performance Chart

Michigan International Speedway
Brooklyn, Michigan—2.0 miles—18° banking

Year	Date	Race	St.	Fin.	Total Laps	Laps Completed	Laps Led	Condition	Money	Pts.	Bonus Pts.
1987	June 28	Miller American 400	37	20	200	197	0	Running	$7,060	103	0
	Aug. 16	Champion Spark Plug 400	37	39	200	25	0	DNF–Engine	4,400	46	0
1988	June 26	Miller High Life 400	33	25	200	183	0	Running	3,255	88	0
	Aug. 21	Champion Spark Plug 400	11	41	200	50	0	DNF–Mechanical	2,210	40	0
1989	June 25	Miller High Life 400	18	22	200	197	0	Running	6,785	97	0
	Aug. 20	Champion Spark Plug 400	27	38	200	119	0	DNF–Mechanical	5,350	49	0
1990	June 24	Miller Genuine Draft 400	26	34	200	101	0	DNF–Transmission	7,010	61	0
	Aug. 19	Champion Spark Plug 400	16	10	200	200	0	Running	14,825	134	0
1991	June 23	Miller Genuine Draft 400	14	12	200	199	0	Running	12,825	127	0
	Aug. 18	Champion Spark Plug 400	11	1	200	200	12	Running	74,150	180	5
1992	June 21	Miller Genuine Draft 400	13	24	200	191	0	Running	11,425	91	0
	Aug. 16	Champion Spark Plug 400	14	8	200	200	4	Running	18,265	147	5
1993	June 20	Miller Genuine Draft 400	17	4	200	200	0	Running	29,590	160	0
	Aug. 15	Champion Spark Plug 400	27	4	200	200	0	Running	29,045	160	0
1994	June 19	Miller 400	35	14	200	199	0	Running	22,675	121	0
	Aug. 21	Goodwrench 400	31	30	200	133	0	Running	19,965	73	0
1995	June 18	Miller 400	29	6	200	200	8	Running	33,500	155	5
	Aug. 20	Goodwrench 400	17	33	200	101	36	DNF–Engine	35,465	69	5
1996	June 23	Miller 400	30	10	200	200	5	Running	27,850	139	5
	Aug. 18	Goodwrench 400	11	1	200	200	8	Running	83,195	180	5
1997	June 15	Miller 400	1	6	200	200	0	Running	46,525	150	0
	Aug. 17	DeVilbiss 400	4	5	200	200	0	Running	46,848	155	0
1998	June 14	Miller Lite 400	2	2	200	200	1	Running	76,125	175	5
	Aug. 16	Pepsi 400	4	3	200	200	6	Running	61,805	170	5
1999	June 13	Kmart 400	6	1	200	200	150	Running	151,240	185	10
	Aug. 22	Pepsi 400	3	4	200	200	27	Running	57,650	165	5
2000	June 11	Kmart 400	26	4	194	194	3	Running	71,285	165	5
	Aug. 20	Pepsi 400	2	4	200	200	0	Running	70,275	160	0
2001	June 10	Kmart 400	21	18	200	199	0	Running	83,117	109	0
	Aug. 19	Pepsi 400	17	37	162	160	2	Running	79,792	57	5

Most Laps Led at Michigan
Drivers who have led the most laps in a single race at Michigan, all-time

Driver	Race	Laps Led
Rusty Wallace	1989 Champion Spark Plug 400	162
Geoffrey Bodine	1994 GM Goodwrench Dealer 400	160
Davey Allison	1992 Miller Genuine Draft 400	158
David Pearson	1972 Motor State 400	155
Bobby Allison	1971 Yankee 400	155
Dale Earnhardt	1987 Miller American 400	152
Dale Jarrett	1999 Kmart 400	150

Consecutive Laps Led
Jarrett's 148 consecutive laps led in 1999's Kmart 400 was the most in a single race in Michigan history

Driver	Race	Laps Led
Dale Jarrett	1999 Kmart 400	148
Rusty Wallace	1989 Champion Spark Plug 400	127
Terry Labonte	1984 Champion Spark Plug 400	117
David Pearson	1972 Yankee 400	97
Mark Martin	1996 GM Goodwrench Dealer 400	88

Jarrett at New Hampshire International Speedway

A funny thing happened to Dale Jarrett on the way to his first New Hampshire victory: The nice guy suddenly became the bad guy. Making a strong final charge as the New England 300 ended in July 2001, he caught and passed his teammate Ricky Rudd, who had been leading and appeared headed to his second New Hampshire win. Instead, thanks to a late caution, Rudd was forced to restart on cooled tires, which caused him problems throughout the race.

When Jarrett, who was much stronger on restarts, got inside of Rudd coming out of Turn 4 with four laps to go, the two appeared to make contact. Rudd slid up the race track but avoided hitting the wall. That momentary slip, however, allowed Jarrett and third-place runner Jeff Gordon to pass. After the race, Rudd fans accused Jarrett of taking out his own teammate. Though no contact occurred, as even Rudd pointed out, Jarrett found himself the proud owner of a new reputation: a hyper-competitive bully only out for wins, points, and his own good.

Those charges point out one of the most amazing accomplishments of Jarrett's career: his transformation of Robert Yates Racing from an organization centered on the powerful toughness of No. 28 team to one dominated by his nice-guy personality and the No. 88 team. When Jarrett arrived at Yates Racing in 1995, the black Havoline Ford was the series' second-most intimidating force, revered for its hard-headed, anything-to-win drivers. Davey Allison and Ernie Irvan gained popularity as much for toughness as talent. That Jarrett, driving cheerful red-white-and-blue cars or acting funny in UPS commercials could so thoroughly change the character of Yates Racing is remarkable.

A more immediate, but no less remarkable, outcome of Jarrett's 2001 win at New Hampshire was his points tie with Jeff Gordon atop the Winston cup standings. Jarrett and Gordon finished the race with the same number of points, 180, thanks to Gordon leading the most laps. As a result, the two drivers remained tied as points leaders for a second consecutive week, a mathematical improbability that has never occurred before in NASCAR history.

The week before Jarrett's New Hampshire victory, Gordon's poor finish at the new Chicagoland Speedway allowed Jarrett to pull even in the point standings. Technically, via NASCAR's tie-breaking system, Gordon maintained his points lead because he had the same number of wins (three) but more second-place finishes at that point in the season. After Jarrett's New Hampshire win, the two remained tied, points-wise, but Jarrett assumed the lead because he now had more victories than Gordon (4–3). Though historic, Jarrett's points lead was his last of the season. Gordon took over the following week at Pocono and went on to win his fourth Winston Cup title.

Jarrett's career at New Hampshire has not always been as eventful as his 2001 experience, but it has been consistently excellent. He is the track's all-time leader in laps completed, running all but 12 of 4,172 laps ever run there. He is also among the track's Top 5 in 17 of 22 statistical categories. Only 3 of his 14 starts at the flat 1-mile oval have resulted in finishes outside of the Top 10. Though he has yet to win a pole and can claim just 1 front row start, his average starting position at New Hampshire is better than at any other track where he has at least 10 starts.

New Hampshire Record Book—All-Time (min. 5 starts)

Category	Jarrett's Total	Jarrett's Rank	All-Time New Hampshire Leader
Money	$1,023,654	3rd	Jeff Gordon—1,367,044
Starts	14	T-1st	15 Others with 14 Starts
Total points	1,953	3rd	Mark Martin—2,043
Avg. start	9.6	2nd	Ken Schrader—7.8
Avg. finish	10.6	4th	Tony Stewart—7.7
Wins	1	3rd	Jeff Burton—4
Winning pct.	7.1	5th	Jeff Burton—28.6
Top 5s	6	4th	Jeff Gordon—8
Top 10s	10	2nd	Mark Martin—11
DNFs	0	—	J. Andretti, T. Labonte—5
Poles	0	—	Jeff Gordon—4
Front row starts	1	8th	Jeff Gordon—6
Laps led	263	5th	Jeff Gordon—912
Pct. laps led	6.3	7th	Jeff Gordon—21.9
Races led	8	2nd	Jeff Gordon—10
Times led	11	3rd	Jeff Gordon—30
Times led most laps	0	—	Jeff Gordon—5
Bonus points	40	3rd	Jeff Gordon—75
Laps completed	4,161	1st	(Mark Martin—4,156)
Pct. laps completed	99.7	3rd	Tony Stewart—99.8
Points per race	139.5	4th	Tony Stewart—151.3
Lead-lap finishes	11	2nd	Mark Martin—12

Jarrett Track Performance Chart

New Hampshire International Speedway

Loudon, New Hampshire—1.058 miles—12° banking

Year	Date	Race	St.	Fin.	Total Laps	Laps Completed	Laps Led	Condition	Money	Pts.	Bonus Pts.
1993	July 11	Slick 50 300	9	4	300	300	1	Running	$33,850	165	5
1994	July 10	Slick 50 300	31	14	300	300	0	Running	23,775	121	0
1995	July 9	Slick 50 300	14	30	300	296	0	Running	26,925	73	0
1996	July 14	Jiffy Lube 300	10	2	300	300	2	Running	59,725	175	5
1997	July 13	Jiffy Lube 300	5	38	300	293	98	Running	51,900	54	5
	Sept. 14	CMT 300	19	6	300	300	0	Running	52,125	150	0
1998	July 12	Jiffy Lube 300	3	7	300	300	0	Running	55,825	146	0
	Aug. 30	New Hampshire 300	7	4	300	300	2	Running	78,875	165	5
1999	July 11	Jiffy Lube 300	9	4	300	300	18	Running	75,550	165	5
	Sept. 19	Dura-Lube/Kmart 300	2	18	300	299	49	Running	66,500	114	5
2000	July 9	Jiffy Lube 300	10	7	273	273	1	Running	70,725	151	5
	Sept. 17	New Hampshire 300	4	4	300	300	0	Running	93,400	160	0
2001	July 22	New England 300	9	1	300	300	92	Running	238,027	180	5
	Nov. 23	New Hampshire 300	3	10	300	300	0	Running	96,452	134	0

Getting Started

Jarrett's best qualifying tracks (min. 10 starts)

Track	No. of Starts	Avg. Finish
New Hampshire	14	9.6
Watkins Glen	15	11.1
Dover	30	15.1
Darlington	28	15.4

Jarrett angered Ricky Rudd fans at New Hampshire when he appeared to make contact with the No. 28 car in a late-race pass that prevented what seemed to be a sure Rudd victory. Though no contact had occurred, it was the second time during the 2001 season that Jarrett had "stolen" a win from his teammate.

Jarrett at North Carolina Speedway

Is it the driver (Dale Jarrett), the crew chief (Todd Parrott), or the owner (Robert Yates)? Or, as is far more likely, is it the perfect combination of all three? In other words, what force explains Dale Jarrett's unconscious performance at North Carolina Motor Speedway, a.k.a. Rockingham, since 1996? Even more perplexing, what countervailing force can possibly explain his inability to win?

At The Rock, Jarrett morphed from a questionable driver into the track's unquestioned master beginning in 1996. Since the formation of Yates' No. 88 team, Jarrett has been Rockingham's best driver. Indeed, no other driver even approaches his effort, save Jeff Gordon, who has more victories during that span.

About the only thing Jarrett has *not* been able to do at Rockingham is win consistently, though certainly not for a lack of trying. Between 1996 and 2001, he finished 10 of 12 races in the Top 5, seven of which were second-place finishes. During one mind-boggling stretch, Jarrett finished in second place six times in seven races. The most heart-breaking of his runner-up finishes was his overpowering effort in the spring of 1997. Dominant throughout, he led 323 of the race's first 343 laps. With 50 circuits to go, however, Gordon slipped by and wrested away what appeared to be a sure Jarrett win. In 1996, after leading 207 laps, a bad set of tires tarnished another promising day.

Another of Jarrett's unusual second-place runs came in October 1998 when he was hospitalized for gallstones, a painful condition that had forced him out of the Phoenix race and into an Arizona hospital a week earlier. Bedridden for five days in a hospital across the country, he arrived at Rockingham on the day of qualifications. With a 1-inch stone still lodged in his body, he nevertheless qualified fourth, led a race-high 195 laps, and finished second.

The ability to lead laps at Rockingham, while sick or healthy, is one of the highlights of Jarrett's career. No other Winston Cup track has been as friendly. His 1,016 laps led since 1996 is more than twice as many as the next closest driver. Four times he has paced the field for 160 or more laps. Dominance, unfortunately, has not translated into victories. On each of those four occasions, he failed to win the race (finishing second three times).

When Jarrett finally won at Rockingham, in the fall of 2000, he led just one time. He passed Bobby Labonte with 43 laps to go and never relinquished his lead. By beating nemesis Gordon to the finish line by 2.2 seconds, Jarrett ended a 27-race winless streak at the track. Only Martinsville was more difficult for Jarrett to conquer (requiring 30 races before his first win in 2001).

Jarrett vs. The Rock

Since 1996, no driver has dominated at Rockingham quite like Dale Jarrett.

Driver	Wins	Top 5s	Top 10s	Avg. Finish	Laps Led	Laps Completed
Dale Jarrett	1	10	12	3.6	1,016	4,715
Jeff Gordon	3	6	7	12.4	458	4,368
Bobby Labonte	1	4	6	12.5	317	4,530
Mark Martin	1	3	7	14.5	208	4,344
Jeff Burton	1	6	6	14.8	453	4,663

Rockingham Record Book—All-Time (min. 5 starts)

Category	Jarrett's Total	Jarrett's Rank	All-Time Rockingham Leader
Money	$1,106,829	4th	Rusty Wallace—1,167,735
Starts	29	25th	Dave Marcis—61
Total points[1]	3,756	15th	Darrell Waltrip—6,443
Avg. start	18.5	47th	Jeff Gordon—6.1
Avg. finish	13.5	8th	Tony Stewart—7.7
Wins	1	15th	Richard Petty—11
Winning pct.	3.4	28th	Jeff Gordon—22.2
Top 5s	11	11th	B. Allison, R. Petty—23
Top 10s	14	14th	Darrell Waltrip—29
DNFs	5	64th	Buddy Baker—25
Poles	1	21st	M. Martin, K. Petty, D. Pearson, C. Yarborough—5
Front row starts	2	23rd	Richard Petty—11
Laps led	1,019	13th	Cale Yarborough—3,733
Pct. laps led	7.8	12th	Cale Yarborough—18.9
Races led	10	19th	Richard Petty—32
Times led	35	16th	Cale Yarborough—131
Times led most laps	4	5th	Cale Yarborough—11
Bonus points[1]	70	17th	R. Petty, C. Yarborough—200
Laps completed	11,474	24th	Darrell Waltrip—24,031
Pct. laps completed	88.4	39th	Tony Stewart—99.9
Points per race[1]	129.5	6th	Tony Stewart—145.2
Lead-lap finishes	12	6th	D. Earnhardt, R. Petty—16

[1] — Since implementation of current point system in 1975

Jarrett Track Performance Chart

North Carolina Speedway

Rockingham, North Carolina.—1.017 miles—25° banking

Year	Date	Race	St.	Fin.	Total Laps	Laps Completed	Laps Led	Condition	Money	Pts.	Bonus Pts.
1984	Oct. 21	Warner W. Hodgdon American 500	27	37	492	149	0	DNF–Engine	$835	52	0
1987	Oct. 25	AC-Delco 500	20	16	492	486	0	Running	7,460	115	0
1988	Mar. 6	Goodwrench 500	7	16	492	488	0	Running	3,370	115	0
	Oct. 23	AC-Delco 500	22	32	492	255	0	DNF–Engine	2,450	67	0
1989	Mar. 5	Goodwrench 500	21	11	492	489	2	Running	8,525	135	5
	Oct. 22	AC-Delco 500	32	39	492	74	0	DNF–Clutch	4,450	46	0
1990	Oct. 21	AC-Delco 500	10	16	492	489	0	Running	8,525	115	0
1991	Mar. 3	GM Goodwrench 500	18	11	492	488	0	Running	11,100	130	0
	Oct. 20	AC-Delco 500	8	25	492	479	0	Running	7,275	88	0
1992	Mar. 1	GM Goodwrench 500	18	37	492	73	0	DNF–Cam Shaft	4,075	52	0
	Oct. 25	AC-Delco 500	27	15	492	488	0	Running	12,550	118	0
1993	Feb. 28	GM Goodwrench 500	22	6	492	492	0	Running	21,885	150	0
	Oct. 24	AC-Delco 500	21	30	492	454	1	DNF–Rear End	15,675	78	5
1994	Feb. 27	Goodwrench 500	41	18	492	485	0	Running	20,635	109	0
	Oct. 23	AC-Delco 500	27	12	492	489	0	Running	21,850	127	0
1995	Feb. 26	Goodwrench 500	26	5	492	491	0	Running	34,075	155	0
	Oct. 22	AC-Delco 400	27	23	393	390	0	Running	24,700	94	0
1996	Feb. 25	Goodwrench 400	13	2	393	393	8	Running	48,960	175	5
	Oct. 20	AC-Delco 400	1	2	393	393	207	Running	62,125	180	10
1997	Feb. 23	Goodwrench Service 400	3	2	393	393	323	Running	68,760	180	10
	Oct. 27	AC-Delco 400	2	2	393	393	73	Running	65,175	175	5
1998	Feb. 22	Goodwrench Service Plus 400	32	7	393	393	7	Running	42,500	151	5
	Nov. 1	AC-Delco 400	4	2	393	393	195	Running	80,625	180	10
1999	Feb. 21	Dura-Lube/Big Kmart 400	11	2	393	393	0	Running	83,675	170	0
	Oct. 24	Pop Secret Popcorn 400	3	4	393	393	160	Running	61,175	170	10
2000	Feb. 27	Dura-Lube/Kmart 400	23	5	393	392	0	Running	64,060	155	0
	Oct. 22	Pop Secret Popcorn 400	21	1	393	393	43	Running	125,850	180	5
2001	Feb. 25	Dura-Lube 400	18	10	393	393	0	Running	91,237	134	0
	Nov. 4	Pop Secret 400	31	4	393	393	0	Running	103,252	160	0

Rockingham Runner-up

Jarrett has the second most second-place finishes in Rockingham history.

Driver	No. of Rockingham Starts	No. of Second-Place Finishes
Bobby Allison	44	7
Cale Yarborough	40	7
Dale Jarrett	29	6
David Pearson	26	5
Harry Gant	32	5

Friendly Confines

Jarrett has led more laps at Rockingham than any other Winston Cup track during his career.

Track	Laps Led
Rockingham	1,019
Bristol	543
Charlotte	525
Dover	516
Darlington	479

Front Runners

Since races at Rockingham were shortened to 393 laps (from 492) in 1995, Jarrett holds the record for leading the most laps in a single race.

Driver	Year/Race	Laps Led
Dale Jarrett	1997 Goodwrench Service 400	323
Jeff Burton	1999 Dura-Lube/Kmart 400	228
Dale Jarrett	1996 AC-Delco 400	207
Terry Labonte	1996 Goodwrench 400	198
Joe Nemechek	2001 Pop Secret Popcorn 400	196

Jarrett at North Wilkesboro Speedway

Dale Jarrett's career at North Wilkesboro Speedway inexorably focuses on one race, the Tyson Holly Farms 400 in September 1994. Fans may remember the race thanks to Geoffrey Bodine, who lapped the entire field on his way to victory (the last NASCAR race to be won by a full lap). For Jarrett, the race was unforgettable for a different reason: He didn't race.

The 1994 season was supposed to be different for Jarrett. Things like not qualifying for a race were not supposed to happen. In his third season with Joe Gibbs Racing and a year removed from the most successful year of his career, Jarrett should have been contending for a title in 1994 as the series invaded Wilkes County. Instead, he was talking to Robert Yates behind the scenes about taking over the No. 28 Havoline Ford and thinking about cutting out on Gibbs with two more years left on his contract.

When Jarrett and his Interstate Batteries team arrive at North Wilkesboro, they were a dismal 18th in the point standings. In 1993, Jarrett never fell lower than eight in the standings and finished fourth. Besides not being competitive in 1994, his effort was hampered by an unceasing string of bad luck. If an accident occurred in a race, you could bet that the green No. 18 car was somehow involved.

Qualifying, like all other aspects, had been suspect. Jarrett's average start in 1994 was his worst in five years. In the 26 events leading up to North Wilkesboro, he started in the Top 10 just twice. Interestingly, the week before his DNQ at Martinsville (another Winston Cup short track), Jarrett started eighth, his best qualifying effort at that point in the season. That success didn't carry over to Wilkesboro, however. He failed to make the field on speed in either round of qualifying. When he reached for a provisional, two other drivers in better standing, Morgan Shepherd and Lake Speed, locked Jarrett out of the race by using their own free passes. The DNQ broke Jarrett's streak of 219 consecutive starts (he finally matched that string in 2001 by starting his 219th straight race at Pocono in July).

A month after missing North Wilkesboro, Jarrett signed with Yates to take over for the injured Ernie Irvan in the No. 28 Ford. Jarrett's life would never be the same once he switched to Robert Yates Racing, including at North Wilkesboro. One year after his DNQ, he returned with one of his strongest efforts at the .625-mile track. Jarrett led 108 laps in the 1995 Tyson 400 and was in the lead on lap 340 when a scuffle with a lapped car knocked him from the top position. Later, while in third place, he was spun out by Hut Stricklin and ended the race in seventh.

Irvan finished one spot ahead of Jarrett in the fall 1995 race. Capping a remarkable comeback from severe injuries suffered in a crash during a practice at Michigan in August 1994, Irvan climbed into the No. 88 Havoline car (Jarrett stayed in the No. 28), led 31 laps, and finished an impressive sixth. Two months prior to Irvan's comeback, Jarrett and Yates had informally agreed on forming a second RYR team. At the end of the 1995 season, Jarrett and Irvan simply switched cars, Irvan returning to his No. 28 ride, while Jarrett took on the new No. 88.

Though Jarrett never won a race at North Wilkesboro before it was eliminated from the Winston Cup schedule in 1996, he did make peace with the track. In the 1996 Tyson Holly Farms 400, the track's final Winston Cup race, he scored his best North Wilkesboro finish, taking third place behind winner Jeff Gordon and second-place Dale Earnhardt.

North Wilkesboro Record Book—Modern Era (min. 5 starts)

Category	Jarrett's Total	Jarrett's Rank	Modern Era North Wilkesboro Leader
Money	$205,515	22nd	Dale Earnhardt—853,685
Starts	19	26	Dave Marcis—46
Total points[1]	2,196	23	Darrell Waltrip—6,375
Avg. start	17.9	44	Cale Yarborough—3.9
Avg. finish	16.4	37	Cale Yarborough—5.7
Wins	0	—	Darrell Waltrip—10
Winning pct.	0.0	—	Cale Yarborough—31.3
Top 5s	1	27	Dale Earnhardt—21
Top 10s	5	29	Dale Earnhardt—32
DNFs	3	27	J. D. McDuffie—16
Poles	0	—	Darrell Waltrip—9
Front row starts	0	—	Darrell Waltrip—13
Laps led	111	24	Darrell Waltrip—2,923
Pct. laps led	1.5	25	Cale Yarborough—25.2
Races led	3	22	D. Earnhardt, D. Waltrip—24
Times led	8	19	Darrell Waltrip—65
Times led most laps	0	—	Darrell Waltrip—8
Bonus points[1]	15	25	Darrell Waltrip—160
Laps completed	7,239	25	Darrell Waltrip—17,370
Pct. laps completed	95.3	19	Ken Schrader—99.2
Points per race[1]	115.6	35	Cale Yarborough—158.3
Lead-lap finishes	3	24	Dale Earnhardt—22

[1] —Since implementation of current point system in 1975

Jarrett Track Performance Chart

North Wilkesboro Speedway

Wilkesboro, North Carolina—.625 miles—14° banking

Year	Date	Race	St.	Fin.	Total Laps	Laps Completed	Laps Led	Condition	Money	Pts.	Bonus Pts.
1987	Apr. 5	First Union 400	14	12	400	398	0	Running	$4,725	127	0
	Oct. 4	Holly Farms 400	14	18	400	394	0	Running	4,995	109	0
1988	Apr. 17	First Union 400	21	21	400	393	0	Running	1,510	100	0
	Oct. 16	Holly Farms 400	19	23	400	395	0	Running	2,250	94	0
1989	Apr. 16	First Union 400	18	19	400	383	0	Running	4,745	106	0
	Oct. 15	Holly Farms 400	25	27	400	218	0	DNF–Overheating	3,830	82	0
1990	Apr. 22	First Union 400	16	14	400	399	0	Running	5,975	121	0
	Sept. 30	Tyson/Holly Farms 400	4	19	400	396	0	Running	5,150	106	0
1991	Apr. 21	First Union 400	6	25	400	369	0	DNF–Crash	5,500	88	0
	Sept. 29	Tyson/Holly Farms 400	5	9	400	400	0	Running	7,975	138	0
1992	Apr. 12	First Union 400	24	17	400	399	0	Running	3,885	112	0
	Oct. 5	Tyson/Holly Farms 400	10	10	400	397	0	Running	12,755	134	0
1993	Apr. 18	First Union 400	11	32	400	311	1	DNF–Engine	12,155	72	5
	Oct. 3	Tyson/Holly Farms 400	24	9	400	397	2	Running	14,455	143	5
1994	Apr. 17	First Union 400	31	25	400	394	0	Running	16,275	88	0
	Oct. 2	Tyson 400	Did Not Qualify								
1995	Apr. 9	First Union 400	33	11	400	398	0	Running	22,140	130	0
	Oct. 1	Tyson 400	6	7	400	400	108	Running	24,790	151	5
1996	Apr. 14	First Union 400	29	11	400	398	0	Running	16,615	130	0
	Sept. 29	Tyson 400	30	3	400	400	0	Running	35,790	165	0

Before and After

A comparison of Jarrett's performance during his 219-consecutive race streaks before and after failing to qualify at North Wilkesboro in 1994

Period	Wins	Top 5s	Top 10s	Poles	Laps Led	Money
Before (1987–94)	2	24	55	0	637	$3,420,845
After (1994–2001)	26	114	148	14	5,756	27,264,958

The low point in Jarrett's career came at North Wilkesboro, where he failed to qualify for the 1994 Tyson 400. Two years later in the track's final Winston Cup race, he finished third – his best North Wilkesboro finish.

Jarrett at Phoenix International Raceway

The most important Phoenix race in Dale Jarrett's career was the 1995 Dura Lube 500, though not for any apparent reason. Starting 26th and finishing 11th, the race was neither his best nor worst on the oddly shaped 1-mile oval. Rather, the importance of the event lay in the presence of a second Robert Yates Racing car—the No. 88 Ford—and its new crew chief, Todd Parrott.

The 1995 Phoenix race was Parrott's first as a crew chief for Yates. A former member of Penske Racing, he had accepted a job with RYR after Yates decided to add a second team to accommodate Ernie Irvan and Jarrett. Phoenix was the second stop in Irvan's three-race comeback in 1995. With Parrott at the helm, Irvan led 111 laps at Phoenix before engine trouble ended his day (he finished 40th).

Parrott followed his terrific debut at Phoenix with a more amazing opening act as Jarrett's crew chief at Daytona in 1996. Parrott and Jarrett won their first race together (the Busch Clash), then won their first points race (the Daytona 500). Though generally overlooked, much like his driver, Parrott's record as a crew chief is remarkable. In six seasons with the No. 88, he engineered 24 wins, 13 poles, 5,546 laps led, and a Winston Cup championship. In 2001, he stepped down as Jarrett's crew chief, taking on a new team manager role with RYR.

Jarrett and Parrott won their second Phoenix race together in 1997. The last of Jarrett's career-high seven victories that season, it was won in typical, workman style. Caught on pit road when the yellow flag came out, he nearly fell a lap off of the pace. Forced to restart the race at the tail end of the lead lap just ahead of the leader, Jarrett took off and nearly worked his way back to the front of the field under green. Finally, on lap 340, he passed Rusty Wallace and motored to a two-second win.

Though an important track in Jarrett's career, highlights at Phoenix have been generally few and far between. The win in 1997 was one of just two Top 5 finishes in 14 starts. Of course, one of those poor finishes was understandable. In 1998, suffering from severe abdominal pain, Jarrett was forced to get out of his car and accept relief from Michael Waltrip. Jarrett was taken from the track to a Phoenix hospital and diagnosed with gallstones. He was hospitalized for five days, but still raced the following weekend at Rockingham with a 1-inch stone still lodged in his body. Waltrip finished the race for Jarrett in 32nd place, four laps behind the leader.

Though otherwise unremarkable, the 1995 Phoenix race proved to be one of the most important in Jarrett's career. The race marked the debut of Todd Parrott, who acted as crew chief for Ernie Irvan (who was in the midst of his amazing comeback). A month later Robert Yates paired Jarrett and Parrott together, forming one of the most successful tandems in NASCAR.

Phoenix Record Book—All-Time (min. 5 starts)

Category	Jarrett's Total	Jarrett's Rank	All-Time Phoenix Leader
Money	$532,309	5th	Mark Martin—688,636
Starts	14	T-1st	Eight Others with 14 Starts
Total points	1,673	5th	Mark Martin—2,088
Avg. start	18.1	20th	Rusty Wallace—4.9
Avg. finish	15.9	12th	Alan Kulwicki—5.2
Wins	1	3rd	D. Allison, J. Burton—2
Winning pct.	7.1	7th	Davey Allison—40.0
Top 5s	2	13th	Mark Martin—7
Top 10s	7	3rd	Mark Martin—11
DNFs	3	3rd	Dick Trickle—5
Poles	0	—	Rusty Wallace—3
Front row starts	0	—	Rusty Wallace—5
Laps led	175	9th	Rusty Wallace—868
Pct. laps led	4.1	11th	Rusty Wallace—20.1
Races led	5	3rd	Rusty Wallace—10
Times led	7	9th	Rusty Wallace—24
Times led most laps	0	—	Rusty Wallace—3
Bonus points	25	7th	Rusty Wallace—65
Laps completed	4,032	7th	Terry Labonte—4,307
Pct. laps completed	93.5	23rd	Alan Kulwicki—100.0
Points per race	119.5	12th	Alan Kulwicki—160.0
Lead-lap finishes	7	4th	Mark Martin—12

Jarrett Track Performance Chart

Phoenix International Raceway

Phoenix, Arizona— .0 mile—11° banking

Year	Date	Race	St.	Fin.	Total Laps	Laps Completed	Laps Led	Condition	Money	Pts.	Bonus Pts.
1988	Nov. 6	Checker 500	32	31	312	215	0	DNF–Engine	$2,600	70	0
1989	Nov. 5	Autoworks 500	31	5	312	312	0	Running	22,112	155	0
1990	Nov. 4	Checker 500	21	30	312	299	0	DNF–Accident	6,395	73	0
1991	Nov. 3	Pyroil 500	17	35	312	151	19	DNF–Engine	6,000	63	5
1992	Nov. 1	Pyroil 500K	17	20	312	309	0	Running	10,485	103	0
1993	Oct. 31	Slick 50 500	14	16	312	311	0	Running	15,320	115	0
1994	Oct. 30	Slick 50 300	5	9	312	310	4	Running	21,920	143	5
1995	Oct. 29	Dura-Lube 500	26	11	312	312	0	Running	26,070	130	0
1996	Oct. 27	Dura-Lube 500	5	8	312	312	29	Running	22,055	147	5
1997	Nov. 2	Dura-Lube 500	9	1	312	312	73	Running	99,830	180	5
1998	Oct. 25	Dura-Lube 500	20	32	257	253	0	Running	34,595	67	0
1999	Nov. 7	Checker/Dura-Lube 500	5	6	312	312	50	Running	82,475	155	5
2000	Nov. 5	Checker/Dura-Lube 500	36	10	312	312	0	Running	86,000	134	0
2001	Oct. 28	Checker Auto Parts 500	16	9	312	312	0	Running	96,452	138	0

In 1997, Jarrett picked up his only Phoenix victory. In his first 14 starts, he finished in the Top 5 just two times.

Jarrett at Pocono Raceway

Calling Pocono Raceway the birthplace of Dale Jarrett's Winston Cup career is a slight reach. But it's impossible to ignore just how important his victory at the Pennsylvania track in 1995 meant to his career, or how extraordinary events seemed to develop after it. Jarrett was a marked man when he arrived at Pocono on that hot July day; he left the track a wanted man.

Before he won the Miller 500, Jarrett was the favorite target of critics attempting to explain the sudden fall of the No. 28 Havoline team. Occupying one of the best rides in NASCAR, Jarrett was 16th in the championship point standings and the focus of intense criticism. After winning the Miller 500, the pieces began to fall into place. He followed Pocono with a stronger second half of the season, and more important, solidified his future with his car owner Robert Yates. A month after his Pocono win, Yates offered Jarrett the keys to the new No. 88 RYR car. That deal led to one of the Winston Cup series' most successful teams in the late 1990s.

Since 1995, Jarrett seemed to celebrate his reversal of fortune every time NASCAR returned to Pocono. The 2.5-mile track became one of his most consistent Winston Cup circuits. He finished third in the 1996 Miller 500, sparking a remarkable 10-race streak in which his average finish was 2.9. His worst finish during the streak was fifth place in the 1998 Pennsylvania 500, though circumstances suggest it was one of his best efforts. He dropped from the Top 5 to deep in the field after debris knocked a hole in his oil pan. Thanks to quick work by his crew, he was able to get the problem fixed without losing a lap. He repaid the good service by fighting his way back to fifth. Jarrett needed no such miracles in 1997 when he won the 1997 Pennsylvania 500. The best Pocono race of his career, he dominated throughout the event, leading 108 laps and charging to an easy victory.

Jarrett's luck at Pocono finally ran out in 2001. Forced to use a provisional to make the field, he was involved in a wreck on lap 150 between Jeff and Ward Burton. Though he got back into the race, he hit the wall eight laps later and was forced to retire. The resulting 41st-place finish was his worst ever at the track and ended his run of 10 consecutive Pocono races on the lead lap.

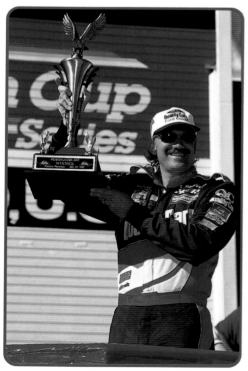

Victories at Pocono have been special for Jarrett. His 1995 win helped salvage his career with Robert Yates. His victory in 1997 was part of a breakthrough season that included a career-high seven wins.

Pocono Record Book—All-Time (min. 5 starts)

Category	Jarrett's Total	Jarrett's Rank	All-Time Pocono Leader
Money	$1,220,014	2nd	Jeff Gordon—1,297,649
Starts	30	13th	Ricky Rudd—45
Total points	3,861	11th	Ricky Rudd—5,319
Avg. start	16.1	25th	David Pearson—4.7
Avg. finish	14.0	10th	Tony Stewart—8.7
Wins	2	9th	B. Elliott, T. Richmond, R. Wallace, D. Waltrip—4
Winning pct.	6.7	14th	Tim Richmond—28.6
Top 5s	11	5th	Mark Martin—15
Top 10s	16	6th	D. Earnhardt, M. Martin—22
DNFs	4	49th	Dave Marcis—15
Poles	0	—	Ken Schrader—5
Front row starts	2	16th	Ken Schrader—8
Laps led	472	6th	Geoffrey Bodine—809
Pct. laps led	7.9	9th	David Pearson—27.8
Races led	15	8th	Dale Earnhardt—24
Times led	39	15th	Darrell Waltrip—106
Times led most laps	3	4th	Geoffrey Bodine—6
Bonus points	90	9th	Geoffrey Bodine—145
Laps completed	5,528	13th	Terry Labonte—7,889
Pct. laps completed	92.5	23rd	Tony Stewart—99.9
Points per race	128.7	10th	Jeff Gordon—148.3
Lead-lap finishes	16	10th	Mark Martin—24

Jarrett Track Performance Chart

Pocono Raceway

Long Pond, Pennsylvania—2.5 miles—14° banking

Year	Date	Race	St.	Fin.	Total Laps	Laps Completed	Laps Led	Condition	Money	Pts.	Bonus Pts.
1987	June 14	Miller High Life 500	24	35	200	103	0	DNF–Ignition	$3,700	58	0
	July 19	Summer 500	28	12	200	198	0	Running	7,670	127	0
1988	June 19	Miller High Life 500	20	13	200	199	0	Running	5,950	124	0
	July 24	AC Spark Plug 500	21	25	200	188	0	Running	3,425	88	0
1989	June 18	Miller High Life 500	14	7	200	200	1	Running	11,150	151	5
	July 23	AC Spark Plug 500	17	18	200	198	0	Running	7,550	109	0
1990	June 17	Miller Genuine Draft 500	13	31	200	171	0	DNF–Crash	6,425	70	0
	July 22	AC Spark Plug 500	18	18	200	198	0	Running	7,950	109	0
1991	June 16	Champion Spark Plug 500	25	19	200	200	0	Running	8,250	106	0
	July 21	Miller Genuine Draft 500	12	6	179	179	3	Running	13,700	155	5
1992	June 14	Champion Spark Plug 500	7	22	200	187	0	Running	10,150	97	0
	July 19	Miller Genuine Draft 500	18	10	200	200	0	Running	15,190	134	0
1993	June 13	Champion Spark Plug 500	21	19	200	195	1	Running	15,815	111	5
	July 18	Miller Genuine Draft 500	23	8	200	200	47	Running	19,915	147	5
1994	June 12	UAW-GM 500	22	20	200	198	5	Running	20,860	108	5
	July 17	Miller 500	17	10	200	199	0	Running	24,510	134	0
1995	June 11	UAW-GM 500	14	38	200	126	0	Running	22,610	49	0
	July 16	Miller 500	15	1	200	200	26	Running	72,970	180	5
1996	June 16	UAW-GM 500	28	38	200	37	0	DNF–Engine	16,520	49	0
	July 21	Miller 500	20	3	200	200	2	Running	35,705	170	5
1997	June 8	Pocono 500	2	3	200	200	5	Running	53,245	170	5
	July 20	Pennsylvania 500	4	1	200	200	108	Running	104,570	185	10
1998	June 21	Pocono 500	9	3	200	200	26	Running	62,220	170	5
	July 26	Pennsylvania 500	11	5	200	200	0	Running	63,815	155	0
1999	June 20	Pocono 500	2	3	200	200	71	Running	86,670	175	10
	July 25	Pennsylvania 500	15	2	200	200	41	Running	95,695	175	5
2000	June 18	Pocono 500	4	2	200	200	0	Running	131,520	170	0
	July 23	Pennsylvania 500	11	4	200	200	73	Running	97,470	170	10
2001	June 17	Pocono 500	10	3	200	200	62	Running	119,947	170	5
	July 29	Pennsylvania 500	37	41	200	152	1	DNF–Crash	75,027	45	5

Jarrett served notice at Pocono in 1998 that his team was championship-ready. In the Pennsylvania 500, he nearly went a lap down after debris knocked a hole in his oil pan. Instead, his crew fixed the problem quickly and Jarrett recovered to finish an impressive fifth.

Jarrett at Richmond International Raceway

Only a cynic, or a close friend, would point out that Dale Jarrett's success at Richmond International Raceway derives from the fact that the track acts more like a speedway than a true short track. Short tracks have generally frustrated Jarrett throughout his career. Richmond, however, has been friendlier than the others. Its length (3/4 mile versus 1/2 mile), shape (D-shaped versus oval), and smooth, wide track have suited Jarrett's style. The proof is in the results: He has more wins and Top 5s, a better average finish, and a larger wallet at the Virginia track than at Bristol, Martinsville, or the now defunct North Wilkesboro.

His success at Richmond began in earnest in 1995. In the spring race that year, he was running in the Top 5 when a tangle with Robert Pressley dropped him to 25th in the final order. Though not a quality finish, the effort behind it signaled a shift in Jarrett's performance. In the 10 races that followed, he finished fourth or better nine times. The streak included three victories, well, two if you go by official NASCAR results. One of his "wins" was nullified by a controversial red flag that got even the mild-mannered Jarrett angry.

NASCAR provoked Jarrett's ire at the end of the 1998 Pontiac Excitement 400. While leading with six laps to go, Winston Cup officials halted the race after a debris-laden four-car wreck threatened a yellow-flag finish. Though NASCAR's use of red flags to guarantee green-flag finishes has become common, it was a rarely seen tactic in 1998. Naturally, Jarrett, an 11-year veteran with 334 starts under his belt, protested the call. When the race resumed, his fears were realized. A tap from Terry Labonte got Jarrett out of shape going into Turn 3 with just over one lap to go. The slide was enough to allow Labonte into the lead. The final insult for Jarrett: just after losing the lead, the caution flag came out (due to an unrelated accident) with Labonte in front. The race ended under yellow, just as NASCAR had hoped it would not. At 45 miles per hour, Jarrett followed Labonte to the finish line in second place.

Jarrett's two official victories at Richmond were far more satisfying and much less controversial. In 1997, he claimed his first Richmond win in the Exide Batteries 400, passing local hero Jeff Burton with 39 laps to go. The win was Jarrett's second career short-track victory, coming just two weeks after he won his first at Bristol. In 1999, his championship season, Jarrett added a second win at Richmond, leading the final 32 laps and beating Mark Martin. The 1999 victory was redemption for the red-flag induced loss he suffered the year before.

Jarrett's victory in the 1997 Exide Batteries 400 was sweet revenge for his travails in 1996. A year after a NASCAR-mandated red flag cost him a win, Jarrett bounced back with his 1997 victory.

Richmond Record Book—Modern Era (min. 5 starts)

Category	Jarrett's Leader	Jarrett's Rank	Modern Era Richmond Leader
Money	$1,083,199	5th	Rusty Wallace—1,279,150
Starts	28	21	Darrell Waltrip—51
Total points[1]	3,554	15	Darrell Waltrip—7,011
Avg. start	17.8	45	Benny Parsons—5.2
Avg. finish	14.0	23	Tony Stewart—6.3
Wins	2	8	B. Allison, R. Petty, R. Wallace, D. Waltrip—6
Winning pct.	7.1	15	Tony Stewart—33.3
Top 5s	11	8	Dale Earnhardt—25
Top 10s	12	15	D. Earnhardt, D. Waltrip—33
DNFs	4	31	J. D. McDuffie—2
Poles	0	—	Bobby Allison—8
Front row starts	0	—	Darrell Waltrip—14
Laps led	385	20	Rusty Wallace—3,024
Pct. laps led	3.4	22	Rusty Wallace—21.
Races led	6	19	Darrell Waltrip—27
Times led	17	18	Rusty Wallace—76
Times led most laps	2	7	Rusty Wallace—9
Bonus points[1]	40	18	R. Wallace, D. Waltrip—165
Laps completed	10,269	18	Darrell Waltrip—18,741
Pct. laps completed	91.7	34	Tony Stewart—100.0
Points per race[1]	126.9	21	Tony Stewart—155.2
Lead-lap finishes	12	9	D. Earnhardt, R. Wallace—25

[1] —Since implementation of current point system in 1975

Jarrett Track Performance Chart

Richmond International Raceway

Richmond, Virginia—.75 miles—14° banking

Year	Date	Race	St.	Fin.	Total Laps	Laps Completed	Laps Led	Condition	Money	Pts.	Bonus Pts.
1987	Sept. 13	Wrangler Jeans Indigo 400	18	27	400	109	0	DNF–Crash	$2,430	82	0
1988	Feb. 21	Pontiac Excitement 400	32	26	400	337	0	DNF–Crash	1,510	85	0
	Sept. 11	Miller High Life 400	33	15	400	395	0	Running	4,430	118	0
1989	Mar. 26	Pontiac Excitement 400	32	23	400	390	0	Running	4,025	94	0
	Sept. 10	Miller High Life 400	26	35	400	17	0	DNF–Crash	3,675	58	0
1990	Sept. 9	Miller Genuine Draft 400	13	29	400	272	0	DNF–Crash	4,355	76	0
1991	Feb. 24	Pontiac Excitement 400	13	21	400	392	0	Running	5,825	100	0
	Sept. 7	Miller Genuine Draft 400	25	20	400	396	0	Running	6,925	103	0
1992	Mar. 8	Pontiac Excitement 400	21	13	400	398	0	Running	4,800	124	0
	Sept. 12	Miller Genuine Draft 400	16	25	400	397	0	Running	8,855	88	0
1993	Mar. 7	Pontiac Excitement 400	9	4	400	400	0	Running	29,050	160	0
	Sept. 11	Miller Genuine Draft 400	13	14	400	398	0	Running	14,955	121	0
1994	Mar. 6	Pontiac Excitement 400	22	10	400	399	0	Running	21,825	134	0
	Sept. 10	Miller 400	25	16	400	397	0	Running	18,830	115	0
1995	Mar. 5	Pontiac Excitement 400	13	25	400	393	0	Running	24,375	88	0
	Sept. 9	Miller 400	27	4	400	400	0	Running	40,605	160	0
1996	Mar. 3	Pontiac Excitement 400	11	2	400	400	23	Running	44,225	175	5
	Sept. 7	Miller 400	8	4	400	400	11	Running	30,505	165	5
1997	Mar. 26	Pontiac Excitement 400	3	3	400	400	172	Running	50,750	175	10
	Sept. 6	Exide Batteries 400	23	1	400	400	39	Running	91,490	180	5
1998	June 6	Pontiac Excitement 400	4	2	400	400	108	Running	75,625	180	10
	Sept. 12	Exide Batteries 400	7	16	400	398	0	Running	39,630	115	0
1999	May 15	Pontiac Excitement 400	21	1	400	400	32	Running	169,715	180	5
	Sept. 11	Exide Batteries 400	13	3	400	400	0	Running	64,605	165	0
2000	May 6	Pontiac Excitement 400	18	3	400	400	0	Running	78,525	165	0
	Sept. 9	Chevrolet Monte Carlo 400	17	31	400	381	0	Running	48,840	70	0
2001	May 5	Pontiac Excitement 400	20	15	400	400	0	Running	85,712	118	0
	Sept. 8	Chevrolet Monte Carlo 400	16	4	400	400	0	Running	107,107	160	0

Jarrett at Sears Point Raceway

Just throw out those first few races. Forget they ever happened. After all, Sears Point is a road course and Dale Jarrett is the product of Hickory Speedway, the tight little North Carolina oval that measures less than half a mile. Throw out his first race at the California track, the one where he smoked his transmission just eight laps into the event (and finished dead last in 42nd place). And toss out the 1991 race where his ignition system failed (and dropped him to 41st). And don't forget about the 1992 race, in which he tore up another transmission and ended up 39th.

OK, if you get rid of those early debacles … Jarrett isn't that bad at Sears Point. Between 1993 and 2001, he completed all 818 laps run at the track and finished outside of the Top 20 just two times. Sure, it's not spectacular, but it's a start.

Of course, the bad finishes tend to be more interesting. In 1995, for instance, while trying to impress his new boss (Robert Yates), he ended up on his side after an on-track scuffle with Rusty Wallace. With less than 14 laps to go in the race, Jarrett was suspended helplessly in his driver's seat as track safety officials rocked his car back and forth until it tipped back onto its wheels. He ended the race in 23rd. In 2001, again running pretty well while recovering from a broken rib suffered a month before in Charlotte, Jarrett was spun out after contact with Johnny Benson on the second-to-last lap. The incident left Jarrett fighting for 26th place.

Unfortunately for Jarrett, there isn't much to offset the bad memories from California's wine country. His best Sears Point race was in 1997 when he led two laps and finished fourth. He added Top 10s in 1999 and 2000. Otherwise, his other 10 starts at the 1.99-mile track have ended in 12th place worse.

Sears Point Record Book—All-Time (min. 5 starts)

Category	Jarrett's Total	Jarrett's Rank	All-Time Sears Point Leader
Money	$409,042	7th	Jeff Gordon—736,742
Starts	13	T-1st	8 Others with 13 Starts
Total points	1,390	10th	Mark Martin—1,892
Avg. start	20.1	20th	Jeff Gordon—4.8
Avg. finish	19.5	20th	Jeff Gordon—7.2
Wins	0	—	Jeff Gordon—3
Winning pct.	0.0	—	Jeff Gordon—33.3
Top 5s	1	14th	R. Rudd, R. Wallace—8
Top 10s	3	13th	Mark Martin—11
DNFs	3	2nd	Hershel McGriff—4
Poles	0	—	Ricky Rudd—4
Front row starts	0	—	Ricky Rudd—6
Laps led	8	18th	Jeff Gordon—238
Pct. laps led	0.7	16th	Jeff Gordon—29.1
Races led	3	8th	Rusty Wallace—8
Times led	3	9th	Rusty Wallace—15
Times led most laps	0	—	Jeff Gordon—4
Bonus points	15	7th	Rusty Wallace—55
Laps completed	998	10th	Michael Waltrip—1,108
Pct. laps completed	89.6	39th	Johnny Benson Jr.—100.0
Points per race	106.9	19th	Jeff Gordon—155.8
Lead-lap finishes	10	6th	D. Earnhardt, M. Martin, R. Rudd, R. Wallace, M. Waltrip—11

Jarrett Track Performance Chart

Sears Point Raceway
Sonoma, California—1.99 miles—Road Course

Year	Date	Race	St.	Fin.	Total Laps	Laps Completed	Laps Led	Condition	Money	Pts.	Bonus Pts.
1989	June 11	Banquet Frozen Foods 300	33	42	74	8	0	DNF–Transmission	$4,250	37	0
1990	June 10	Banquet Frozen Foods 300	10	14	74	74	0	Running	5,800	121	0
1991	June 9	Banquet Frozen Foods 300	21	41	74	46	1	DNF–Ignition	5,475	45	5
1992	June 7	Save Mart 300K	23	39	74	52	0	DNF–Transmission	4,750	46	0
1993	May 16	Save Mart Supermarkets 300K	32	13	74	74	0	Running	16,610	124	0
1994	May 15	Save Mart 300	20	12	74	74	0	Running	20,755	127	0
1995	May 7	Save Mart 300	9	23	74	74	0	Running	24,730	94	0
1996	May 5	Save Mart 300	20	12	74	74	0	Running	20,530	127	0
1997	May 5	Save Mart Supermarkets 300	8	4	74	74	2	Running	50,135	165	5
1998	June 28	Save Mart/Kragen 300K	3	15	112	112	5	Running	46,700	123	5
1999	June 27	Save Mart/Kragen 350K	29	6	112	112	0	Running	53,940	150	0
2000	June 25	Save Mart/Kragen 300K	18	7	112	112	0	Running	69,665	146	0
2001	June 24	Dodge/Save Mart 350	35	26	112	112	0	Running	85,702	85	0

Since 1993, Jarrett has completed every lap run at Sears Point. Unfortunately, durability failed to result in quality finishes. He had only three Top-10 finishes in that span.

Jarrett at Talladega Superspeedway

Unhappy with the state of restrictor-plate racing, Dale Jarrett has embarked on a strategy in recent years that may tarnish his well-earned superspeedway reputation. Especially at Talladega, his approach has been unusual, but simple: Don't participate until the end of the race. Particularly in 2001, he studiously dropped to the back of the field, bided time, and, when the time was right, attempted a late points-saving charge to the front. Joined by Tony Stewart and Bobby Labonte from his former Joe Gibbs racing team, Jarrett's move has become a regular part of Talladega races.

Though controversial (in 2001, fans began to voice displeasure with Jarrett and others who choose not to give a full effort on the restrictor plate tracks), the "wait-and-see" strategy cannot be called irrational. Starting in 1999, thanks to master draftsman Dale Earnhardt, Talladega became a three-lane track. But unlike Charlotte or Atlanta or other multigroove ovals, Talladega's three lanes are packed with side-by-side, nose-to-tail traffic for 500 miles. Even the best cars are stuck in the draft, unable to break away with the current aerodynamic rules imposed by NASCAR.

Jarrett, like many other drivers, doesn't have to think for very long to remember some of the horrific crashes in Talladega history. In Jarrett's first-ever Talladega race in 1987, Bobby Allison's car got airborne and flew into the catch fence near the grandstand. The wreck injured several fans, red-flagged the event for nearly three hours and ushered in the restrictor-plate era (which started with the 1988 Daytona 500). Other, more recent crashes are also fresh in Jarrett's memory: Dale Earnhardt's rolling wrecks in 1996 and 1998, Ricky Craven's catch fence fiasco in 1995, Rusty Wallace's tumbling finish in 1993, and Mark Martin's guard-rail scare in 1994, to name a few.

While safe and smart, Jarrett's strategy has a cost. His results at Talladega have declined. Despite having one of the series' best cars, he led just 5 of 752 laps and failed to finish better than 15th in the four 2000 and 2001 races. Though he obviously cares about his performance on every track, it's just as clear that, in Jarrett's mind, Talladega is a track to survive, not thrive. His comment after every Talladega race since 1999 has been the same: "That's not racing."

Before 2000, Jarrett was a consistent Talladega threat. Even before joining the horse-powerhouse at Robert Yates Racing, Jarrett circled Talladega as well as any driver (save Earnhardt) in the Winston Cup series. In 1991, during a generally unspectacular year with the Wood Brothers, he led with less than 30 laps to go before taking eighth. In 1993, he finished the two Alabama races in third and fifth. With Yates, his success only increased. He finished second three straight times in 1995 and 1996, then claimed his first Talladega win (and his first "No Bull Million" bonus check) in the fall of 1998. In fact, in 1998 and 1999, he finished all four races in the Top 3.

If NASCAR's constant aerodynamic rules tinkering ever satisfies Jarrett's safety concerns and he decides to re-enter the fray, Winston Cup racing will regain one of its best practitioners of superspeedway racing.

Talladega Record Book—All-Time (min. 5 starts)

Category	Jarrett's Total	Jarrett's Rank	All-Time Talladega Leader
Money	$1,170,824	7th	Dale Earnhardt—2,081,045
Starts	30	23rd	Dave Marcis—61
Total points[1]	3,473	17th	Bill Elliott—6,259
Avg. start	16.5	30th	Bobby Isaac—3.6
Avg. finish	17.9	28th	Pete Hamilton—5.6
Wins	1	17th	Dale Earnhardt—10
Winning pct.	3.3	26th	Dale Earnhardt—22.7
Top 5s	9	12th	Dale Earnhardt—23
Top 10s	11	17th	Dale Earnhardt—27
DNFs	8	36th	Darrell Waltrip—23
Poles	0	—	Bill Elliott—8
Front row starts	1	28th	Bill Elliott—13
Laps led	222	18th	Dale Earnhardt—1,377
Pct. laps led	4.0	28th	Pete Hamilton—22.9
Races led	15	16th	Dale Earnhardt—38
Times led	38	17th	Buddy Baker—228
Times led most laps	0	—	Dale Earnhardt—11
Bonus points[1]	75	19th	Dale Earnhardt—245
Laps completed	4,777	20th	Dave Marcis—9,777
Pct. laps completed	85.7	41st	Buckshot Jones—99.7
Points per race[1]	115.8	20th	Dale Earnhardt—138.3
Lead-lap finishes	15	11th	Dale Earnhardt—27

[1] —Since implementation of current point system in 1975

Jarrett Track Performance Chart

Talladega Superspeedway
Talladega, Alabama—2.66 miles—33° banking

Year	Date	Race	St.	Fin.	Total Laps	Laps Completed	Laps Led	Condition	Money	Pts.	Bonus Pts.
1987	May 3	Winston 500	38	28	178	96	0	DNF–Engine	$6,200	79	0
	July 26	Talladega 500	37	21	188	183	0	Running	7,210	100	0
1988	May 1	Winston 500	28	11	188	188	0	Running	9,790	130	0
	July 31	Talladega DieHard 500	26	37	188	141	1	DNF–Engine	2,795	57	5
1989	May 7	Winston 500	28	40	188	37	0	DNF–Crash	5,375	43	0
	July 30	Talladega DieHard 500	41	23	188	184	0	Running	7,235	94	0
1990	May 6	Winston 500	16	34	188	103	0	DNF–Crash	7,230	61	0
	July 19	DieHard 500	22	39	188	51	0	DNF–Engine	7,005	46	0
1991	May 6	Winston 500	22	35	188	70	0	DNF–Crash	7,850	58	0
	July 28	DieHard 500	40	8	188	188	8	Running	14,400	147	5
1992	May 3	Winston 500	15	7	188	188	0	Running	19,215	146	0
	July 26	DieHard 500	8	21	188	186	13	Running	12,270	105	5
1993	May 2	Winston 500	3	3	188	188	35	Running	44,870	170	5
	July 25	DieHard 500	15	5	188	188	5	Running	30,390	160	5
1994	May 1	Winston 500	9	21	188	186	0	Running	20,860	100	0
	July 24	DieHard 500	13	39	188	34	0	DNF–Mechanical	20,690	46	0
1995	Apr. 30	Winston 500	5	19	188	188	35	Running	27,240	111	5
	July 23	DieHard 500	13	2	188	188	0	Running	65,895	170	0
1996	Apr. 28	Winston Select 500	2	2	188	188	20	Running	64,145	175	5
	July 28	DieHard 500	3	2	129	129	5	Running	55,070	175	5
1997	May 10	Winston 500	9	35	188	184	0	Running	31,365	58	0
	Oct. 12	DieHard 500	18	21	188	187	13	Running	39,930	105	5
1998	Apr. 26	DieHard 500	9	3	188	188	8	Running	82,370	170	5
	Oct. 11	Winston 500	3	1	188	188	16	Running	1,110,125	180	5
1999	Apr. 25	DieHard 500	23	2	188	188	21	Running	104,955	175	5
	Oct. 17	Winston 500	17	2	188	188	37	Running	85,345	175	5
2000	Apr. 16	DieHard 500	3	17	188	187	4	Running	63,300	117	5
	Oct. 15	Winston 500	12	15	188	188	0	Running	66,185	118	0
2001	Apr. 22	Talladega 500	6	18	188	188	0	Running	92,012	109	0
	Oct. 21	EA Sports 500	10	25	188	187	1	DNF–Crash	86,532	93	5

The Restrictor Plate Races

A look at Jarrett's performance at Daytona and Talladega since the implementation of restrictor plates in 1988

Category	Jarrett's Total	Jarrett's Rank	Category Leader
Avg. start	14.9	11th	Davey Allison—5.7
Avg. finish	16.7	13th	Dale Earnhardt—9.4
Poles	3	5th	Sterling Marlin—7
Wins	5	3rd	Dale Earnhardt—11
Top 5s	17	3rd	Dale Earnhardt—32
Top 10s	23	6th	Dale Earnhardt—40
Laps led	554	5th	Dale Earnhardt—2,135

Jarrett at Texas Motor Speedway

With a track configuration to his liking, Texas Motor Speedway entered the Winston Cup world at the just right time for Dale Jarrett. A high-banked, high-speed oval, Texas first appeared on NASCAR's schedule in 1997, shortly after Jarrett had settled in with his high-powered Robert Yates Racing team. Unlike other, more established NASCAR tracks, Jarrett's career performance at Texas isn't sullied by years of poor finishes with uncompetitive race teams.

The results have been impressive. In Texas' five-race history, Jarrett is either first or second in nearly all statistical categories. No other Winston Cup driver has more wins, Top 5s, or laps led. His victory in 2001 marked the third time he finished first or second at the track. Strong throughout the 2001 race (leading 122 of 334 laps), Jarrett earned the victory by passing Johnny Benson with just five laps remaining. (Benson was also Jarrett's late-pass victim in the Daytona 500 in 2000.)

Texas hasn't always been kind to Jarrett, however. In 2000, after leading 18 laps, he slammed into the wall between Turns 1 and 2, causing heavy car damage and a severely banged-up knee. He was able to finish the race, but 49 laps down in 33rd place, by far his worst Texas finish. Jarrett's only other finish outside of the Top 2 came in 1998, when a lost cylinder late in the race stole any chances of victory. He finished 11th.

Since being added to the Winston Cup schedule in 1997, Texas Motor Speedway has been one of Jarrett's best tracks. He ranks first or second in nearly every statistical category in the track's brief history.

Texas Record Book—All-Time (min. 2 starts)

Category	Jarrett's Total	Jarrett's Rank	All-Time Texas Leader
Money	$1,089,477	1st	(Jeff Burton—898,421)
Starts	5	T-1st	21 Others with 5 Starts
Total points	739	2nd	Terry Labonte—776
Avg. start	6.8	4th	Dale Earnhardt Jr.—2.5
Avg. finish	9.8	3rd	Dale Earnhardt Jr.—4.5
Wins	1	T-1st	J. Burton, D. Earnhardt Jr., T. Labonte, M. Martin—1
Winning pct.	20.0	2nd	Dale Earnhardt Jr.—50.0
Top 5s	3	T-1st	(Bobby Labonte—3)
Top 10s	3	3rd	B. Labonte, T. Labonte—4
DNFs	0	—	E. Irvan, J. Nemechek, J. Spencer—3
Poles	0[1]	—	D. Earnhardt Jr., K. Irwin, T. Labonte, J. Mayfield—1
Front row starts	1	2nd	Bobby Labonte—2
Laps led	272	1st	(Terry Labonte—231)
Pct. laps led	16.3	2nd	Dale Earnhardt Jr.—31.9
Races led	5	1st	(B. Labonte, M. Martin—4)
Times led	18	1st	(Mark Martin—14)
Times led most laps	1	2nd	Terry Labonte—2
Bonus points	30	1st	(Terry Labonte—25)
Laps completed	1,621	7th	Terry Labonte—1,670
Pct. laps completed	97.1	16th	D. Earnhardt Jr., T. Labonte—100.0
Points per race	147.8	3rd	Dale Earnhardt Jr.—166.0
Lead-lap finishes	4	2nd	Terry Labonte—5

[1] – Field for inaugural 1997 race set by points after qualifying rained out; Jarrett started on pole as points leader

Jarrett Track Performance Chart

Texas Motor Speedway

Ft. Worth, Texas—1.5 miles—24° banking

Year	Date	Race	St.	Fin.	Total Laps	Laps Completed	Laps Led	Condition	Money	Pts.	Bonus Pts.
1997	Apr. 6	Interstate Batteries 500	1	2	334	334	42	Running	$232,800	175	5
1998	Apr. 5	Texas 500	13	11	334	334	51	Running	93,500	135	5
1999	Mar. 28	Primestar 500	12	2	334	334	39	Running	250,100	175	5
2000	Apr. 2	DirecTV 500	5	33	334	285	18	Running	68,550	69	5
2001	Apr. 1	Harrah's 500	3	1	334	334	122	Running	444,527	185	10

Jarrett's only disappointing Texas race came in 2000 when he finished 33rd. Here he makes a move on Scott Pruett on the 1.5-mile oval's frontstretch.

Jarrett at Watkins Glen International

Entering the 2001 season, Dale Jarrett had already begun reshaping his woeful reputation on NASCAR's road courses. Strong finishes at Sears Point and Watkins Glen hinted at the emergence of a new road warrior among Winston Cup ranks. Then Jarrett took a very public step backwards. He struggled to a 26th-place finish at Sears Point, and two months later, suffered through a disastrous weekend at Watkins Glen.

Jarrett's effort at Watkins Glen started promisingly enough. He set a new track qualifying record with an amazing lap of 122.698 miles per hour, his first and only road course pole. In the race two days later, he charged to a two-second lead while pacing the field through the first 17 laps. Suddenly, Jarrett's world began to unravel. With the car to beat and a new reputation to cultivate, he, well, went off the road … by himself … and got stuck in the gravel area just off of Turn 1.

Unable to get the car out himself, Jarrett was forced to sit in the sand while the track safety crew towed his car back onto the pavement. He watched as the rest of the field, the same cars that couldn't chase him down moments earlier, passed him not once, but twice under caution.

Dropping from a two-second lead to a lap back in 40th place, Jarrett set out to prove his road course abilities once again. He fought through the field and, thanks to a well-timed caution, got back on the lead lap. Back up to 17th midway through the race, Jarrett looked poised for a miraculous comeback. Then he, well, got stuck in the Turn 1 sand again. This time the result of contact with Mark Martin, Jarrett spun off the course and was forced to watch again as the field passed him at 45 miles per hour. He finished the race in 31st place, one lap behind winner Jeff Gordon.

Visibly disappointed after the race, Jarrett blamed himself for running a first-place car off the road twice. The odd turn of events added even more nuance to his career at Watkins Glen. Though not very successful on NASCAR's non-ovals, Jarrett isn't easily painted a traditional "left-turn only" stock car racer. Besides his 2001 pole, Jarrett shares the all-time Watkins Glen record for most front row starts (four). His 11.1 starting average is seventh in track history.

Some of Jarrett's poor Watkins Glen finishes are not his doing. In one of his earliest run-ins with NASCAR, the 1997 race turned on a controversial call that may have cost him a chance at the Winston Cup title. After the race in the early laps, Jarrett experienced transmission troubles (his car lost third gear) and began to fade. Detecting smoke coming from the rear of his car, Winston Cup officials black-flagged Jarrett with just five laps remaining. When he stopped, NASCAR couldn't find anything wrong with his car. The inadvertent penalty dropped Jarrett a lap down and into 32nd place in the running order. When Gordon won the race, Jarrett lost 113 points in the standings. Gordon eventually won the 1997 crown by 14 points over Jarrett.

Watkins Glen Record Book—All-Time (min. 5 starts)

Category	Jarrett's Total	Jarrett's Rank	All-Time Watkins Glen Leader
Money	$411,892	6th	Mark Martin—816,311
Starts	15	5th	R. Rudd, K. Schrader, R. Wallace, M. Waltrip—16
Total points	1,663	12th	Mark Martin—2,211
Avg. start	11.1	7th	Rusty Wallace—6.6
Avg. finish	18.2	19th	Mark Martin—5.9
Wins	0	—	Jeff Gordon—4
Winning pct.	0.0	—	Jeff Gordon—44.4
Top 5s	3	5th	Mark Martin—11
Top 10s	4	11th	Mark Martin—12
DNFs	3	9th	Derrike Cope—6
Poles	1	4th	D. Earnhardt, M. Martin—3
Front row starts	4	T-1st	(Mark Martin—4)
Laps led	31	13th	Mark Martin—204
Pct. laps led	2.4	14th	Jeff Gordon—19.8
Races led	2	13th	Rusty Wallace—9
Times led	2	21st	M. Martin, R. Wallace—16
Times led most laps	0	—	J. Gordon, M. Martin—3
Bonus points	10	16th	Rusty Wallace—55
Laps completed	1,228	9th	Michael Waltrip—1,360
Pct. laps completed	93.7	21st	Darrell Waltrip—100.0
Points per race	110.9	19th	Mark Martin—157.9
Lead-lap finishes	9	10th	D. Earnhardt, D. Waltrip—14

Jarrett Track Performance Chart

Watkins Glen International

Watkins Glen, New York—2.45 miles—Road Course

Year	Date	Race	St.	Fin.	Total Laps	Laps Completed	Laps Led	Condition	Money	Pts.	Bonus Pts.
1987	Aug. 10	The Budweiser at the Glen	20	36	90	42	0	DNF–Transmission	$4,280	55	0
1988	Aug. 14	The Budweiser at the Glen	18	11	90	90	0	Running	6,180	130	0
1989	Aug. 13	The Budweiser at the Glen	14	23	90	87	0	DNF–Engine	5,480	94	0
1990	Aug. 12	The Budweiser at the Glen	26	20	90	89	0	Running	7,445	103	0
1991	Aug. 11	The Budweiser at the Glen	14	5	90	90	0	Running	18,565	155	0
1992	Aug. 9	The Budweiser at the Glen	7	15	51	51	0	Running	11,420	118	0
1993	Aug. 8	The Budweiser at the Glen	14	32	90	61	0	DNF–Clutch	13,650	67	0
1994	Aug. 14	The Bud at the Glen	14	11	90	90	0	Running	20,250	130	0
1995	Aug. 13	The Bud at the Glen	13	17	90	90	0	Running	25,100	112	0
1996	Aug. 11	The Bud at the Glen	2	24	90	90	0	Running	28,365	72	5
1997	Aug. 10	The Bud at the Glen	2	32	90	89	14	Running	52,980	155	0
1998	Aug. 9	The Bud at the Glen	10	5	90	90	0	Running	59,900	160	0
1999	Aug. 15	Frontier at the Glen	9	4	90	90	0	Running	57,210	146	0
2000	Aug. 13	Global Crossing at the Glen	2	7	90	90	0	Running	82,962	75	5
2001	Aug. 12	Global Crossing at the Glen	1	31	90	89	17	Running			

In Good Company

Though not a great qualifier throughout his career, Jarrett is one of the best in Watkins Glen history. Only NASCAR's road course greats have better average starting positions.

Rank	Driver	Avg. Start
1	Rusty Wallace	6.6
2	Jeff Gordon	6.7
3	Mark Martin	6.8
4	Dale Earnhardt	8.2
5	Terry Labonte	9.1
6	Ricky Rudd	10.1
7	Bill Elliott	11.1
7	Dale Jarrett	11.1

Jarrett led a lap at Watkins Glen for the first time in 1997. The next time he led at the upstate New York road course, in 2001, he suffered one of the most discouraging races of his Winston Cup career.

Major Races

Dale Jarrett's Performance in the Winston Cup Series' Biggest Events: Daytona 500, Coca-Cola 600, and Southern 500

On the Winston Cup schedule, there are races, and then there are events. In the NASCAR world, the biggest events are the season-opening Daytona 500, the Memorial Day Coca-Cola 600, and the Labor Day Southern 500. While other races are popular or important to the Winston Cup schedule—races such as the Brickyard 400, the Bristol night race, and the Talladega races—none has yet reached the prestige of the Big Three.

This section details Jarrett's career in the Major Races, listing career statistics, season-by-season totals, and individual race performances.

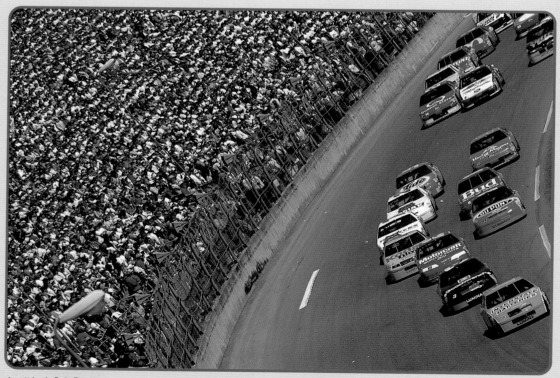

Jarrett leads Dale Earnhardt to the start-finish line during the early laps of the 1993 Daytona 500. A dramatic last-lap pass on Earnhardt secured Jarrett's first victory in the 500.

Jarrett in the Daytona 500

Next to his 1999 Winston Cup championship, nothing distinguishes Dale Jarrett's career quite like his performance in the Daytona 500. In the event's 42-year history, only three drivers, Richard Petty (seven wins), Cale Yarborough (four), and Bobby Allison (three), have equaled or bettered Jarrett's three Daytona 500 victories. In no other significant aspect of his career is Jarrett in such historic company.

What makes Jarrett's record in the Great American Race so impressive is the manner in which it was achieved. In each of his first two 500 victories, he defeated the best driver in Daytona history, Dale Earnhardt, and he did so in a manner suggesting that neither win was a fluke. In 1993, he passed Earnhardt in Turn 2 of the final lap. In 1996, he held off Earnhardt over the final 24 laps, nearly 60 miles, countering every move the master of drafting could throw at him. Beating Earnhardt at his own game (twice, in radically different ways) put Jarrett in exclusive company as one of just seven drivers with more than one Daytona 500 victory.

Jarrett's third Daytona 500 trophy in 2000 was just as notable, if for different reasons. Winning the race capped off a magical Speedweek, during which Jarrett won the pole for the Daytona 500, the Bud Shootout qualifying race, the Bud Shootout itself, and the 500. The only Winston Cup event he failed to win during the week was the Twin 125 qualifying race, which he lost by two-tenths of a second to Bill Elliott.

Jarrett's dominance in 2000 concealed the amount of effort exerted by his team in the hours leading up to the Daytona 500. While trying to avoid a slower car in practice the day before the event, Jarrett was accidentally tapped and spun around by Jeff Gordon. Though not severe, the damage to the No. 88 car was extensive. Fabricators from Robert Yates Racing's Charlotte shop were flown in to fix the car overnight. Their fixes were good enough to put Jarrett among the leaders throughout the race.

Thanks to the repairs, Jarrett was able to pull off another late-race pass for victory. With three laps remaining, Jarrett faked a pass high on race leader Johnny Benson entering Turn 1, then dipped low coming out of Turn 2. He took the lead on the backstretch and never looked back. His nifty drafting ploy, taken straight out of Earnhardt's playbook, illustrated Jarrett's deft touch in Daytona's turbulent draft. It also earned him the largest purse ($2,277,975) in American racing history.

Daytona 500 Breakout Charts
All-Time Daytona 500 Victories
Since the first Daytona 500 in 1959, only two other drivers have more wins in the event.

Driver	No. of Daytona 500 Wins
Richard Petty	7
Cale Yarborough	4
Dale Jarrett	3
Bobby Allison	3
Bill Elliott	2
Sterling Marlin	2
Jeff Gordon	2

Daytona 500 Performance Chart
Daytona 500
Daytona International Speedway

Year	Date	St.	Fin.	Total Laps	Laps Completed	Laps Led	Condtition	Money	Pts.	Bonus Pts.
1993	Feb 14	3	5	200	200	2	Running	$111,150	160	5
1994	Feb 20	6	4	200	200	7	Running	112,525	165	5
1995	Feb 19	4	22	200	199	61	Running	67,915	102	5
1996	Feb 18	8	42	200	13	0	DNF—Handling	59,052	37	0
1997	Feb 16	6	1	200	200	40	Running	456,999	180	5
1998	Feb 15	29	16	200	200	56	Running	114,730	120	5
1999	Feb 14	1	1	200	200	17	Running	2,172,246	180	5
2000	Feb 20	11	34	200	195	0	Running	106,100	61	0

Coca-Cola 600 Summary

Early in his career, Dale Jarrett must have wondered what all of the fuss was about when the Winston Cup series set up in Charlotte for its longest race of the season, the Coca-Cola 600. One hundred miles longer than the next longest race, the annual Veterans' Day race is considered a grueling test of man and machinery. A test, that is, if you're around for all 600 miles.

For young Jarrett, the race never seemed very long. His first four Coca-Cola 600s ended before 500 miles had elapsed, and usually much less. His first 600 in 1987 ended on mile 126. The following year, Jarrett ran the Coca-Cola 40.5, dropping out of the race just 27 laps after the green flag fell (thanks to engine trouble). Not until 1991 did he complete all 600 miles.

Once Jarrett got a chance to race a full season with an established team (the Wood Brothers), he began to flourish in NASCAR's marathon. In the 11 Coca-Cola 600s between 1991 and 2001, no driver completed more laps than Jarrett. His eight lead-lap finishes are second only to Dale Earnhardt in Modern Era Coca-Cola 600 history.

Not surprisingly, endurance has translated into success. In those 11 races, Jarrett has seven Top 5 finishes. Since his inauspicious debut, he has become one of the 400-lap race's perennial favorites. Highlighting his efforts was his 1996 win, a truly dominant performance that saw him cross the finish line 12 seconds ahead of second-place Earnhardt. Jarrett led 199 laps during the race, the most since Davey Allison's 263 in 1991.

The 2001 race was nearly as impressive, though not for where he finished. Jarrett broke a rib (following a hard wreck during qualifying) and was forced to start the race with a provisional in 37th place. In extreme pain throughout the four-hour race, he climbed all the way to 2nd place before settling for 8th in the final running order.

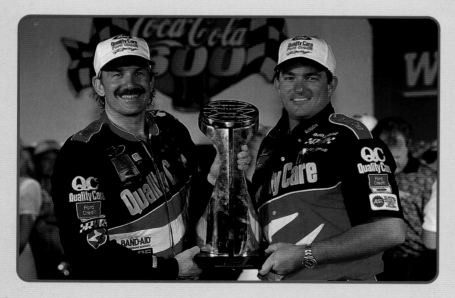

Jarrett and crew chief Todd Parrott celebrate their 1996 Coca-Cola 600 victory. Jarrett led 199 of the race's 400 laps, one of the most dominating performances in the race's history.

Though a major accomplishment, Jarrett's Coca-Cola 600 win took a backseat in 1996 to two other feats: his victories in the Daytona 500 and Brickyard 400.

Coca-Cola 600 Breakout Charts
Being There at the End

Between 1991 and 2001, no driver endured the Coca-Cola 600 better than Jarrett. He has completed more of the event's 4,333 laps in that span than any other driver.

Driver	Laps Competed
Dale Jarrett	4,246
Michael Waltrip	4,207
Ricky Rudd	4,079
Sterling Marlin	4,070
Ken Schrader	4,054

Coca-Cola 600 Stats Chart
Coca-Cola 600 Record Book—Modern Era (min. 5 starts)

Category	Jarrett's Total	Jarrett's Rank	Modern Era Coca-Cola 600 Leader
Starts	15	22nd	Darrell Waltrip—28
Total points[1]	1,823	17th	Darrell Waltrip—3,370
Avg. start	21.5	47th	David Pearson—2.8
Avg. finish	16.4	17th	Bobby Labonte—9.9
Wins	1	10th	Darrell Waltrip—5
Winning pct.	6.7	12th	Jeff Gordon—33.3
Top 5s	7	6th	Darrell Waltrip—11
Top 10s	8	9th	Darrell Waltrip—15
DNFs	5	18th	Dave Marcis—15
Poles	0	—	David Pearson—6
Front row starts	0	—	David Pearson—9
Laps led	403	10th	Dale Earnhardt—975
Pct. laps led	6.8	15th	Davey Allison—15.2
Races led	9	7th	Dale Earnhardt—16
Times led	21	14th	Dale Earnhardt—72
Times led most laps	1	9th	Bobby Allison—4
Bonus points[1]	50	8th	Dale Earnhardt—95
Laps completed	4,929	23rd	Darrell Waltrip—10,317
Pct. laps completed	83.1	43rd	Mike Skinner—97.7
Points per race[1]	121.5	12th	Bobby Labonte—145.2
Lead-lap finishes	8	2nd	Dale Earnhardt – 10

[1] —Since implementation of current point system in 1975

Coca-Cola 600 Performance Chart
Coca-Cola 600
Charlotte Motor Speedway

Year	Date	St.	Fin.	Total Laps	Laps Completed	Laps Led	Condition	Money	Pts.	Bonus Pts.
1987	May 24	35	38	400	84	0	DNF–Engine	$4,310	49	0
1988	May 29	39	41	400	27	0	DNF–Engine	4,200	40	0
1989	May 28	24	28	400	331	0	DNF–Engine	5,200	79	0
1990	May 27	19	32	400	241	4	DNF–Engine	7,120	72	5
1991	May 26	12	5	400	400	3	Running	27,400	160	5
1992	May 24	23	12	400	397	1	Running	15,400	132	5
1993	May 30	32	3	400	400	114	Running	73,100	170	5
1994	May 29	16	4	400	400	9	Running	54,600	165	5
1995	May 28	22	32	400	317	0	DNF–Engine	21,050	67	0
1996	May 26	15	1	400	400	199	Running	165,250	185	10
1997	May 25	3	27	333	332	24	Running	40,875	87	5
1998	May 24	10	5	400	400	47	Running	78,700	160	5
1999	May 30	28	5	400	400	0	Running	81,125	155	0
2000	May 28	8	5	400	400	2	Running	95,000	160	5
2001	May 27	37	8	400	400	0	Running	108,552	142	0

Southern 500 Summary

The major remaining holes in Dale Jarrett's career record are a road course victory and a Southern 500 crown. For stock car racers, it's easy to choose which is more important.

The oldest continuous event in NASCAR history, the Southern 500 is one of the few races that allow comparison across eras. Since 1950, the nation's best stock car driver congregated at the oddly shaped 1.366-mile track on Labor Day weekend and competed for 500 miles. Like Wrigley Field or Yankee Stadium, it's where all the greats have played.

Though his first really strong Southern 500 run came in 1992 (his first season with Joe Gibbs Racing), Jarrett's best efforts have come since joining Robert Yates Racing in 1995. His most famous chance at winning Darlington's fall race was in 1996 while chasing the Winston Million bonus. Enjoying a breakthrough season with the new No. 88 team, he had won the Daytona 500 and the Coca-Cola 600 that season. He even won the pole for the Southern 500 and looked strong early.

Jarrett's hopes faded, however, with his famous "I'm in the wall" radio communication back to his pits. Oil from Ed Berrier's back-of-the-field car caused Jarrett's car to smack the Turn 4 wall on lap 46. The contact with the wall broke a shock, bent the lower control arm, loosened ball joints, damaged crush panels on the right side, and played havoc with his alignment. Though his team performed admirably to get the car back on the track quickly, he finished two laps down in 14th.

The following season, Jarrett nearly played the spoiler in Jeff Gordon's successful Winston Million run. He fought Gordon for 60 laps at the end of the race, but eventually gave way and finished third. Jarrett added Top 5s in 1998 (third) and 2000 (fifth). Perhaps his best effort came in 2001, when he led a career Southern 500-best 53 laps. Problems with his left rear wheel forced him off the track, however, and dropped him to 34th.

The No. 88 crew works on Jarrett's car following contact with the wall in Turn 4 during the early stages of the 1996 Southern 500.

Southern 500 Performance Chart

Southern 500 — Darlington Raceway

Year	Date	St.	Fin.	Total Laps	Laps Completed	Laps Led	Condition	Money	Pts.	Bonus Pts.
1987	Sept. 6	38	15	202	200	0	Running	$9,110	118	0
1988	Sept. 4	18	34	367	239	0	DNF–Engine	2,850	61	0
1989	Sept. 3	26	20	367	361	0	Running	7,810	103	0
1990	Sept. 2	18	28	367	241	1	DNF–Crash	6,655	84	5
1991	Sept. 1	8	25	367	350	1	Running	7,545	93	5
1992	Sept. 6	17	6	298	298	21	Running	19,055	155	5
1993	Sept. 5	27	12	351	348	0	Running	16,510	127	0
1994	Sept. 4	35	9	367	365	0	Running	23,370	138	0
1995	Sept. 3	12	28	367	331	0	Running	24,870	79	0
1996	Sept. 1	1	14	367	365	23	Running	128,165	126	5
1997	Aug. 31	3	3	367	367	38	Running	47,505	170	5
1998	Sept. 6	1	3	367	367	15	Running	79,220	170	5
1999	Sept. 5	36	16	270	270	23	Running	50,960	120	5
2000	Sept. 3	9	5	328	328	3	Running	80,570	160	5
2001	Sept. 2	27	34	367	356	53	Running	82,417	66	5

Southern 500 Record Book—Modern Era (min. 5 starts)

Category	Jarrett's Total	Jarrett's Rank	Modern Era Southern 500 Leader
Starts	15	21st	Darrell Waltrip—27
Total points[1]	1,770	15th	Bill Elliott—3,481
Avg. start	18.4	38th	David Pearson—4.7
Avg. finish	16.8	23rd	Jeff Gordon—5.7
Wins	0	—	J. Gordon, C. Yarborough—4
Winning pct.	0.0	—	Jeff Gordon—44.4
Top 5s	3	17th	Bill Elliott—11
Top 10s	5	22nd	Bill Elliott—17
DNFs	2	61st	H.B. Bailey, B. Baker—9
Poles	2	2nd	David Pearson—5
Front row starts	2	7th	B. Elliott, D. Pearson—6
Laps led	178	19th	Dale Earnhardt—1,138
Pct. laps led	3.5	20th	Cale Yarborough—17.0
Races led	9	8th	Bill Elliott—17
Times led	16	13th	Darrell Waltrip—56
Times led most laps	0	—	Dale Earnhardt—9
Bonus points[1]	45	10th	B. Elliott, D. Waltrip—95
Laps completed	4,786	16th	Darrell Waltrip—8,252
Pct. laps completed	93.5	11th	Jeff Gordon—99.8
Points per race[1]	118.0	31st	Jeff Gordon—160.7
Lead-lap finishes	5	10th	Bill Elliott—13

[1] —Since implementation of current point system in 1975

Earnhardt and Jarrett share a laugh before the beginning of the 2000 Southern 500. Earnhardt won the Southern 500 three times during his illustrious career. Jarrett is still searching for his first Labor Day victory.

Chapter 6

Dale Jarrett's Performance in All-Star Events:
The Bud Shootout and the Winston

Adding spice to the Winston Cup schedule are two high-stakes shootouts that, despite having no direct effect on the championship, are run with an unbridled urgency sometimes missing from regular events. To race in these two all-star events—the Bud Shootout and the Winston—a driver must perform at a top level. The field for the Bud Shootout at Daytona is dependent on winning a pole during the previous season. The Winston at Charlotte is reserved for race winners over the previous season.

This section details Jarrett's career performance in these races.

Jarrett in the Bud Shootout

A history of poor qualifying prevented Dale Jarrett from getting into the Bud Shootout for nearly 10 years. An invitation-only event that is limited to pole winners from the previous season, he didn't win his first pole until 1995. When Jarrett finally got a chance, however, he made an immediate impact.

Even when not invited, Jarrett won the Bud Shootout. After going pole-less in 1999, he earned a spot in the 2000 Shootout by winning the qualifier. He then went on to win the main event.

The winner of the 1995 Daytona 500 pole, Jarrett eagerly took his spot in the 1996 Busch Clash line-up. The 25-lap event offered the first test of his new team and rookie crew chief. Needless to say, the new No. 88 Quality Care Ford passed with flying red-white-and-blue colors. Jarrett outran a gaggle of Chevrolets to win his first Clash. He and Jeff Gordon are the only drivers to win their first Bud Shootout starts.

In 2000, Jarrett proved that even when he's not invited, he's still a threat. As part of the race's new format, a qualifying race was created to allow one nonpole winner to earn the right to compete in the Bud Shootout. Jarrett used the qualifying race as a springboard to one of the most dominating Speedweeks in Daytona history. He won the qualifier, and then won the Bud Shootout itself. Already holding the 2000 Daytona 500 pole, he went on to win the 500 for the third time in his career.

With his two victories, Jarrett is second among winners in the event's 23-year history. Only Dale Earnhardt, with six victories, has won more often.

Bud Shootout Stats Chart

Bud Shootout Record Book—All Time

Category	Jarrett's Total	Jarrett's Rank	All-Time Bud Shootout Leader
Money	$296,604	7th	Dale Earnhardt—601,222
Starts	6	17th	Bill Elliott—16
Avg. finish	5.3	6th	Dale Earnhardt—2.8
Wins	2	2nd	Dale Earnhardt—6
Winning pct.	33.3	2nd	Dale Earnhardt—50.0
Top 5s	3	15th	Dale Earnhardt—11
Top 10s	5	14th	Bill Elliott—14
DNFs	0	—	Ricky Rudd—6
Laps led	8	16th	Dale Earnhardt—98
Pct. laps led	4.3	19th	Tony Stewart—37.9
Races led	2	12th	Dale Earnhardt—9
Times led	2	15th	Dale Earnhardt—15
Times led most laps	0	—	Dale Earnhardt—6
Laps completed	185	12th	Bill Elliott—375
Pct. laps completed	100.0	T-1st	15 Others with 100 percent
Lead-lap finishes	6	15th	Bill Elliott—16

Bud Shootout Performance Chart

Busch Clash & Bud Shootout

Daytona International Speedway

Year	Date	Race	St.	Fin.	Total Laps	Laps Completed	Laps Led	Condition	Money
1996	Feb 11	Busch Clash	12	1	20	20	7	Running	$62,500
1997	Feb 9	Busch Clash	4	7	20	20	0	Running	25,000
1998	Feb 8	Bud Shootout	16	11	25	25	0	Running	22,382
1999	Feb 7	Bud Shootout	14	8	25	25	0	Running	25,500
2000	Feb 13	Bud Shootout	15	1	25	25	1	Running	115,000
2001	Feb 11	Bud Shootout	3	4	70	70	0	Running	45,722

The Winston all-star race at Charlotte has escaped Jarrett's victory quest. His best finish is second (in 2000 and 2001).

Jarrett in the Winston

Dale Jarrett has yet to make much of an impression on the Winston, NASCAR's midseason all-star race. A mainstay in the event since his first career win at Michigan in 1991, he endured an early string of bad luck before seeing his performance improve. Three of his first four starts in the Winston ended at or near the bottom of the finishing order due to crashes.

Starting in 1996, however, his outlook improved. He led a career-high 24 laps in the 1996 event and before finishing ninth. Except for a crash in 1999 that dropped him to a 19th-place finish, Jarrett has steadily gotten closer to his first victory. He ended the 1998 race in third and finished second in 2000 and 2001. Given his solid career at Lowe's Motor Speedway, where he has won three times, Jarrett figures to be a Winston winner soon.

The Winston Stats Chart

The Winston Record Book—All Time

Category	Jarrett's Total	Jarrett's Rank	The Winston All-Time Leader
Money	$296,604	7th	Dale Earnhardt—601,222
Starts	6	17th	Bill Elliott—16
Avg. finish	5.3	6th	Dale Earnhardt—2.8
Wins	2	2nd	Dale Earnhardt—6
Winning pct.	33.3	2nd	Dale Earnhardt—50.0
Top 5s	3	15th	Dale Earnhardt—11
Top 10s	5	14th	Bill Elliott—14
DNFs	0	—	Ricky Rudd—6
Laps led	8	16th	Dale Earnhardt—98
Pct. laps led	4.3	19th	Tony Stewart—37.9
Races led	2	12th	Dale Earnhardt—9
Times led	2	15th	Dale Earnhardt—15
Times led most laps	0	—	Dale Earnhardt—6
Laps completed	185	12th	Bill Elliott—375
Pct. laps completed	100.0	T-1st	15 Others with 100 percent
Lead-lap finishes	6	15th	Bill Elliott—16

The Winston Performance Chart

The Winston

Lowe's Motor Speedway

Year	Date	Race	St.	Fin.	Total Laps	Laps Completed	Laps Led	Condition	Money
1992	May 16	The Winston	10	18	70	11	0	DNF–Crash	$18,000
1993	May 2	The Winston	7	19	70	31	0	DNF–Crash	18,000
1994	May 22	The Winston	3	7	70	70	0	Running	35,500
1995	May 20	The Winston	3	19	70	39	0	DNF–Crash	23,000
1996	May 18	The Winston	4	9	70	70	24	Running	70,500
1997	May 17	The Winston	6	7	70	70	11	Running	73,000
1998	May 16	The Winston	7	3	70	70	0	Running	57,500
1999	May 22	The Winston	6	19	70	11	0	DNF–Crash	18,000
2000	May 20	The Winston	7	2	70	70	8	Running	141,410
2001	May 19	The Winston	11	2	70	70	0	Running	125,000

IROC

Chapter 7

Dale Jarrett's Performance in the International Race of Champions Series

For 26 years, the International Race of Champions (IROC) has been staged as an exhibition series. Designed to pit the champions of various series together in identically prepared cars, the series attempts to isolate driver talent by removing any mechanical advantage and thereby determine which driver from which series is truly the best. This section details Jarrett's IROC career, listing career statistics, season-by-season totals, and individual race performances.

IROC Summary

One of the benefits of Dale Jarrett's rise in the Winston Cup series has been a steady invitation to compete in the annual four-race International Race of Champions (IROC) series. His breakthrough Winston Cup season in 1993, during which he finished fourth in the final standings, prompted an IROC invite in 1994. After a two-year hiatus in 1995 and 1996, he has become a fixture in the all-star series, competing every year since 1997.

Jarrett's NASCAR success has not transferred to the IROC series, however. In his first six seasons, he finished no better than fifth in the final standings. His first five years of IROC competition were unremarkable, winless efforts that produced either eighth-, ninth-, or tenth-place finishes in the 12-driver standings. Jarrett can't be faulted too much, of course. Mark Martin and the late Dale Earnhardt turned IROC into a personal playground, winning the series a combined seven straight years.

In 2001, Jarrett enjoyed an IROC breakthrough. At Daytona, he won for the first time in 22 starts. Jarrett's victory wasn't the story that day, however. Earnhardt and Eddie Cheever stole the spotlight with a back-and-forth battle that resulted in Earnhardt's spectacular drive through the grass below the apron in Turn 1. The race was Earnhardt's last IROC start; he died the next day in the last turn of the Daytona 500.

Jarrett's Position in the Final Standings During His First Six IROC Seasons

Year	Final Standing	Total Points	Money	Season Champion (Point Total)
1994	8th	34	$40,000	Mark Martin (66)
1997	8th	34	40,000	Mark Martin (72)
1998	10th	29	40,000	Mark Martin (86)
1999	8th	30	40,000	Dale Earnhardt (75)
2000	9th	41	40,000	Dale Earnhardt (74)
2001	5th	47	70,000	Bobby Labonte (68)

IROC Record Book—All Time (min. 8 starts)

Category	Jarrett's Total	Jarrett's Rank	All-Time IROC Shootout Leader
Championships	0	—	D. Earnhardt, M. Martin—4
Money	$270,000	16th	Dale Earnhardt—1,286,960
Starts	24	11th	Dale Earnhardt—59
Wins	1	20th	D. Earnhardt, A. Unser Jr.—11
Winning pct.	4.2	30th	Neil Bonnett—37.5
Total points	196	16th	Dale Earnhardt—693
Avg. finish	7.4	38th	Mark Martin—3.7
Top 5s	6	26th	Al Unser Jr.—38
Top 10s	20	13th	Dale Earnhardt—53
DNFs	3	8th	Al Unser Jr.—8
Laps led	38	29th	Mark Martin—426
Pct. led	3.6	32nd	Mark Martin—28.5
Races led	10	6th	Dale Earnhardt—26
Times led	16	6th	Dale Earnhardt—70
Laps completed	968	11th	Dale Earnhardt—2,321
Pct. completed	90.6	31st	B. Labonte, K. Brack—100.0

Career IROC Results

Year	Date	Track	St.	Fin.	Laps	Laps Completed	Laps Led	Condition
1994	Feb. 20	Daytona International Speedway	9	3	40	40	2	Running
	Mar. 28	Darlington Raceway	10	12	60	9	0	DNF–Crash
	May 2	Talladega SuperSpeedway	6	3	38	38	0	Running
	Aug. 1	Michigan International Speedway	6	12	50	3	0	DNF–Crash
1996	Aug. 19	Michigan International Speedway[1]	2	9	50	50	0	Running
1997	Feb. 16	Daytona International Speedway	9	7	40	40	2	Running
	May 18	Charlotte Motor Speedway	5	10	67	67	0	Running
	June 23	California Speedway	3	8	50	50	1	Running
	July 29	Michigan International Speedway	3	3	50	50	0	Running
1998	Feb. 15	Daytona International Speedway	2	6	30	30	1	Running
	May 4	California Speedway	7	8	50	50	0	Running
	June 15	Michigan International Speedway	6	10	50	50	0	Running
	Aug. 2	Indianapolis Motor Speedway	3	7	40	40	0	Running
1999	Feb. 14	Daytona International Speedway	1	8	40	40	2	Running
	May 1	Talladega SuperSpeedway	5	10	38	38	16	Running
	June 13	Michigan International Speedway	5	11	50	50	0	Running
	Aug. 8	Indianapolis Motor Speedway	3	6	40	40	0	Running
2000	Feb. 20	Daytona International Speedway	10	8	40	40	4	Running
	Apr. 17	Talladega SuperSpeedway	5	8	38	38	2	Running
	June 12	Michigan International Speedway	3	5	50	50	0	Running
	Aug. 6	Indianapolis Motor Speedway	6	8	40	40	0	Running
2001	Feb. 17	Daytona International Speedway	7	1	40	40	7	Running
	Apr. 23	Talladega SuperSpeedway	11	11	38	35	1	DNF–Crash
	June 9	Michigan International Speedway[2]	Did Not Start					
	Aug. 6	Indianapolis Motor Speedway	6	4	40	40	0	Running

[1] —Drove for Steve Kinser

[2] —Dave Marcis drove for Jarrett, who was injured in qualifying at Charlotte

Photo Gallery

Each year, NASCAR impounds the Daytona 500 winner's car for display in the track's museum. Few drivers have signed away as many winning cars at Daytona as Jarrett.

Jarrett got a chance to work with one of the most respected Winston Cup crew chiefs, Larry McReynolds, in 1995. McReynolds was the crew chief for Davey Allison and Ernie Irvan at Robert Yates Racing, and later was Dale Earnhardt's crew chief when he won the 1998 Daytona 500.

Jarrett is congratulated by his brother-in-law and former crew chief Jimmy Makar after clinching the Winston Cup title in 1999. Makar, who is married to Jarrett's sister Patti, was Jarrett's crew chief at Joe Gibbs Racing.

Before joining Robert Yates Racing in 1995, Jarrett had three victories in 228 starts. In his first 228 starts with Yates, he won 25 times.

Due to his friendly manner and willingness to speak his mind, Jarrett is popular with the motorsports media. Here, he talks with reporters before the start of the 1996 Coca-Cola 600, a race he dominated and won.

Though he has expressed displeasure with NASCAR's aerodynamics rules at Talladega and Daytona, Jarrett has developed into one of the most adept draftsmen in the Winston Cup series. Here, he leads the field during the 2000 DieHard 500.

Though Dale Jarrett's success in Winston Cup racing is unquestioned, he still has a way to go before catching up with his dad. In eight seasons, Ned Jarrett won 50 races and two championships. Dale has about half as many of each, with 28 career wins through the 2001 season and a single championship.

Jarrett pops the cork on another victory at Daytona. His 2000 Daytona 500 win earned a No Bull Million dollar bonus, the second such prize of his career.

Jarrett hoists the Winston Cup champion's trophy at Homestead-Miami Speedway. He clinched his 1999 title with a race still remaining on the schedule, winning by 201 points over Bobby Labonte.

Jarrett's sponsorship deal with UPS, announced in November of 2000, put him in the same high-dollar league as Jeff Gordon and Mark Martin.

Index

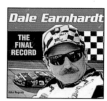

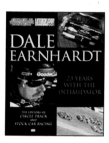

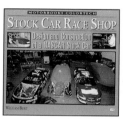

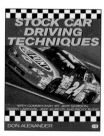
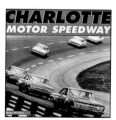